MW01289406

Spinning on a Barstool

A True Tale of a Waitress

Glenda Toews

Spinning on a Barstool
Copyright © 2023 by Glenda Toews

For copyright permission or to contact the author please visit her website; glendatoews.com

The language used in Daryl's dialogue reflects the actual vocabulary he used in conversation. The author understands that the term "Indian" when applied to an Indigenous Canadian is offensive and inappropriate. It is used in this narrative to accurately convey the words spoken by Daryl.

Tellwell Talent
www.tellwell.ca

ISBN
978-0-2288-9120-8 (Hardcover)
978-0-2288-9119-2 (Paperback)
978-0-2288-9121-5 (eBook)

Enjoy my
Story!
Glenda -

Cheers.

For Danielle

For Taylor

For being dreamers with me

My philosophy is: Life is hard, but God is good. Try not to confuse the two.

—Anne F. Beiler

Preface

Inspired by Jordan Peterson to "do the difficult thing," I did.

I realize now that doing the difficult thing is actually really difficult. I don't know exactly what I thought it would be.

Living can be so very hard.

While stepping purposefully into difficult, the pandemic rolled in. It brought new challenges, it brought new rules, it brought in Daryl.

Daryl brought in amazing stories. Daryl brought in wisdom. Daryl brought in hope. Daryl brought in big dreams. Daryl pushed me to think limitlessly. Daryl brought in friendship. Daryl brought in difficulty.

This book is about that.

Woven between our story are the stories of real-life, ordinary people. I pour them pints … they pour out their lives. Some of them funny, many of them not.

Living is hard for everyone.

What strikes me about their stories is their ability to endure. It's impressive. I'm left wondering how they do it and am inspired to do it myself. If they can, so can I.

In this book, God lives. Not in a churchy, preachy kind of way. Not in that happy, joyful, wonderful, perfect kind of way. God lives within the "Oh shit" and "Fuck offs." And he responds to the whispers of the human soul when all it can breathe is, "Oh God, help." Perhaps this book is a little about that too.

Acknowledgments

Haney, thanks for being the kind of person who is good with going along with all my insane ideas. Without your encouragement, we wouldn't be living in this amazing piece of the country to build a story off.

Danielle for being a woman who desires to help the world, and for listening to me vent without telling me how I should vent.

Taylor for being eternally optimistic. What a gift and a breath of fresh air!

Ann for being my life-long cheerleader.

John and Trish. John because you have that super heart that believes that good happens, and because you use your hands to make good happen. Trish for being his beacon and my friend, sharing your wisdom not judgement, and damn, girl, you move big seacans with little Kabotas—still so impressed with that.

Tina for walking that whole walk with me. Thanks for your ear. And for taking all the tables when my feet hurt.

My Proofreaders, Dave and Stephanie (you know why!) Mom for your early eyes and Vivien for you final eyes!

To Kerry my editor for your advice and your magical grammar wand!

Matt Hawkins of Hawkins Media www. matthewahawkins.com for helping me with all that stuff I'm not so good at!

To my customers at Corky's who share little bits of their lives with me.

Jordan Peterson for kicking my mind in the ass.

God, creator of this big old world, and his son, Jesus, whose words echo when I want to hit people, and for your forgiveness when I scream at you. Thank you for your steady keel and for letting me live in such a beautiful place.

And Daryl. Meeting you pushed me from being a writer to becoming an author. Thank you.

Introduction

I met the owner of SoFi Stadium. Not the one who owns the Rams, but the one who is quietly seeking to build another version of SoFi in San Diego, back home, back to the fans. The owner of the Chargers. He's not the owner seen on TV; he's the money behind the team. He's the one who was able to purchase controlling shares due to internal Spanos family problems. The one whose fiancée, Tina, messaged me from the sidelines:

"I can't believe I'm in this life, Glenda! Who just jumps on a jet and flies down like this? Daryl and I are on the field near the cheerleaders. I'm trembling with excitement! I'm so happy he told me to take my heels off on the plane – the field is so soft! The head cheerleader just looked at me and told me I was stunning! I can't believe I'm here!"

"Doe-eyed Tina" is how Daryl describes her. Tall, long legs – "giraffe legs," he giggled, recalling how she looked on the jet ski when he took her out on the boat on their last trip to the Cayman Islands. Five-foot-seven, perfectly proportioned, a gentle mane of blonde hair framing her face that was, as the cheerleader stated, "stunning." Absolutely perfect from top to bottom. A graduate of the university in LA, wicked with numbers, brilliantly funny, Holstein Fund Management Group's number one woman and General Manager Account Service.

Brilliant but broken, as Daryl has found out and has struggled with this past year. When you're in a relationship with someone who suffered horrific abuse as a child, it's difficult in ways you can't imagine.

The sight of a barn and the smell of a farm has this beautiful blonde curled up in a fetal position for days, unable to venture out, crying to get back to the city. Too many memories: her father, her uncle, repeated visits to "the farm." Sometimes Emily, her sister, went, and sometimes just Tina. The abuse was so bad at ten years old that she was in hospital having her insides repaired. Repaired but forever damaged. Tina can never have children. The authorities did nothing. Small, backward town in Ohio, no escape for the women there. Numbers were her salvation. When the abuse was happening, she would go into her head and add numbers, strings of them; they became her lifeline.

From the age of fourteen she would hide money. Her father would find it and she would be beaten, so she'd find new spots, endure new beatings and more trips to the farm.

At eighteen years old she was able to flee to California, to school. Emily helped her get there, and together they immersed themselves in their studies. Together they had strings of unhealthy relationships, survived more sexual abuse from men they thought loved them, and took more beatings when they didn't say the right thing, didn't wear the right thing, or looked at a friend a wrong way. Emily escaped into drugs, Tina into her numbers.

Tina's girlfriend from university went north to Seattle and started working at Holsteins, whose offices were in the fifty-five-storey building hailed by the *New York Times* as one of the three best when it opened its doors in 1988: 1201 Third Avenue. The girlfriend recommended Tina to Danny, the owner. A perfect fit, really: Tina's mind for numbers, combined with her broken past, flourished under the wings of Danny and his wife, Tanya. For ten years she worked with them, managing accounts as they nurtured her spirit.

Danny is an American who graduated in business from McGill in Montreal. It was there he met his wife, Tanya, a waitress working at a local restaurant. They fell in love and married sixteen years ago and have two children—a boy and a girl fourteen and twelve years old.

Christmas 2020 they spent in Hawaii with Tanya's family. This wasn't what Danny was expecting; he thought he was having a nice vacation with his wife and kids on the island alone. They were there already. Work detained him. When he eventually flew in from Seattle, it was, "Surprise, honey, my whole family is here!"

He endured the holiday by cracking off sarcastic messages to his buddy Daryl via text.

Daryl, sitting in a pub called Corky's in the corn-growing capital of Chilliwack on the west coast of Canada, sipped his pint, laughed at the incoming messages from his long-time friend, and together they commiserated.

Daryl had in-law problems of his own: they just wouldn't leave the "fucking house." Thus Daryl's days at the pub grew longer, and our conversations grew deeper.

My name is Glenda.

I was his server.

That Day

It was sunny—not July sunny, it didn't entomb you in a casket of heat demanding you sweat as you sit. No, it was September sunny. Sun that entered the day on the edge of a brisk night. Sun that warmed your skin and smelled fresh and clean and right and good.

Joe found me on the patio at the pub emptying ashtrays and straightening up tables. He was carrying a white tube filled with my future.

"That's it?" I asked

"This is it," he responded and smiled. "You might need more copies; if you do, just ask. There are five in here."

"I'll open it when I go home. I don't want any of them getting damaged."

Joe handed the tube to me like the third passes the baton to the anchor. It weighed gold.

Our house design.

"I've never been in here before," Joe said, his eyes absorbing the surroundings.

"Ha, I'm here all the time." I grinned. "Can I pour you a drink? Would you like something to eat?" I asked.

"No thank you, Glenda, I have to get back. Call me if you need anything."

"You bet I will, Joe," I replied. "Thanks again for the house; it's amazing."

"You're welcome, Glenda."

He turned from the patio and headed to the front door.

I tucked the tube under my arm, wiped the last table, and headed back into the pub.

Leaving the bright, sunny patio and entering the dim interior of Corky's took my eyes a moment to adjust. I did a quick scan, checking for new tables and empty drinks, customers in distress because their money isn't being accepted by the lotto machines or their bank card didn't work in the ATM. Fifty things could go wrong in the five minutes I was outside. All looked calm. A new customer was walking past the Bone.

The Bone is a long, tall table stretching ten feet across, separating the bar from floor tables. Beat up barstools banked side by side. A rank of soldiers all eager to enter the day, expecting the usual, anticipating the unusual, prepared to take their licks while standing firm in battle. Worn, deep green leatherette and faded wood carry the scars of human encounters.

Each soldier bears the weight of life, holding solid under fans cheering for their teams, giving courage to couples who've met online now meeting face to face, being the place to rest after a long day at work, upholding souls encased in sorrow or in shock from sudden, unexpected bad news. They hear the whisper of secrets, the laughter of friends, and stories spun, threads of experience woven into blankets of time, tales of those that got away, the promotions, the lovers, the fish. These soldiers rise gallantly under the foolish fist, steady the gladiator roar, and stand silently amused as they watch men pick up women, women pick up men, and men pick up men who look like women.

The Commando has seen those in commando.

The recruit, the guerrilla, the mercenary have held back their younger selves while the veteran holding the veterans look on, look over, look past, look back.

The Bone, where the barstools sustain the soul.

He looked homeless.

The man by the bone.

A little lost, a little unsure, a little shuffle to his walk.

There's a look the homeless carry with them, invisible but weighty. They don't come into the pub very often; they prefer to buy their bottle and sit in the corner in the parking lot.

"Good morning, Glenda." They wave when they see me exit my Santa Fe at the start of my day.

They smile. Most of them are missing at least one tooth. All of them need a good bath. When they come close, they have the distinct homeless smell. Thrift store mixed with urine? All walk slowly like it hurts—their feet, their minds, their bodies, their lives?

"I'm still beating back those demons," Albert sighed on a warm day five years ago when he was alone. I admire that. He takes ownership for where he's at.

Together they are a band of brothers and sisters enjoying the comradery of each other in much the same way my customers in the pub do. If you shined them up and stuck them at a table in Tim Horton's, you wouldn't look twice. But in the corner of a parking lot, this band of brothers and sisters appears intimidating.

At first I feared them, then I pitied them, now I let them be.

Time and experience have moved my mind. They like it in the corner. Why should I demand they live a life like mine?

"Find some shade today, guys; it could get warm," I holler back, waving as I do.

"We will, Glenda. Have a good day."

I picked up a couple of empty pint glasses with my free hand on my way to the Bone.

"Can I sit anywhere?" the newcomer asked.

"Absolutely, I'll see you through the crowd," I replied.

He smiled at that. A handful of people were dotted throughout the pub, clearly no crowd. I was mildly shocked that he had all of his teeth.

"What can I pour you?" I asked. He was busy looking around for the perfect table for himself.

"Just a lager, whatever you've got on tap will be fine. Is it okay if I sit here?" he said, pointing to the Bone.

"Sure, I'll bring your beer right over." As we passed each other, I felt slightly ashamed of myself for assuming he was homeless. He was clean, he smelled like fresh soap, he wore simple but clean clothing with no holes, and his face wasn't etched in "street."

I tucked the tube with my house plans safely behind the bar and poured his pint.

He took a cell phone from his pocket and laid it on the table before he peeled his light blue jacket off. He hung it on the back of the barstool then ran his left hand through his hair. It was long; it needed a cut—light blond, white? It was hard to tell in the light. He climbed up on the barstool and gave his knee a rub and looked around again, this time absorbing the atmosphere.

Hmm, I thought, *sore knee, the reason for his shuffled walk.*

I put a coaster and his pint before him.

"Thank you," he cooed

"You're welcome," I smiled. "My name is Glenda; if you need anything, just holler."

"I will, thank you," he smiled back. "I'm Daryl."

Before That Day

"What are you doing today, Glenda?" Jamie asked. "I have a couple of hits of acid we can drop them and head to the city and people watch."

I shoved myself into the back seat of his beat-up Datsun B110; his buddy was shotgun.

A warm summer day in 1983. He popped in Def Leppard's *Pyromania* cassette, we popped our hits, and into Vancouver we went, peeking as we arrived on Granville Street.

Quietly the three of us inspected the Vogue's sign: the dots that made up the letters, the letters that made the words, the words on the building inviting you to come in to play.

The Vogue was one building, and the building was one whisper from the Grand Lady of streets: "Let me entertain you," calls Granville. "If not my buildings, then the people walking in front of them. The suits and the sinners and the lame beggars in the corners."

The eye inspects trails of light as the mind absorbs how every little bit fits together: a pixelated puzzle, the anatomy of an atom in the emotionless ether for a five-dollar entrance fee. Hours of wandering the world from one single spot, and there the three of us sat until dusk, until our voyage was complete.

We found the car and drove back to Abbotsford, the trip done but our minds still alert, too alert for rest. We did what all the teenagers did—we drove up and down the strip, South Fraser way, then turned into Sevenoaks shopping mall.

From the back seat I could see them in the dark—a group of people, ten, fifteen maybe. It wasn't that they were a large group of people in an empty parking lot that caught my attention; it was that they were a large group of glowing people.

Did you know you're glowing? I thought to myself, but realizing how nutty that sounded, I didn't speak up.

Each one had a white glow emanating from their body, and as they walked, it walked with them. Was it the street lights? I wondered. *No, that would come from above; this is coming from the bodies and radiating outward.*

Jamie pulled up the Datsun next to them and rolled down the window.

"Hey, did you know you're all glowing?" he said out loud. I sighed in relief because he saw it too!

His buddy in the passenger seat leaned in and said, "Ya, you're all totally glowing!" He saw it too!

Given the freedom of voice my travelling companions displayed, I piped up from my spot in the back, "Ya, you're all glowing!"

A girl from the group leaned her head in the window. "I'm not surprised; we're all Christians, and we've just come from a prayer meeting."

This was something new for me to consider, and I did, for months and months and months. I considered it with all the little bits and pieces of the other things I considered as my mind developed. And then I considered it more.

This world is awfully big, but that sky is bigger. It's amazing that I'm not flying off the globe; it's amazing that little tiny me is in this great bigness, I thought when I was ten.

Why am I here? My body is still, but my thinking still moves; it's like they're different from each other, I thought at eleven.

Who is God? What is God? I thought at twelve.

If there is a God, I'd like to know that. Hey, you up there, wherever you are, if you exist, can you show me? I thought at thirteen.

Why did I have that weird dream? What was that scary voice demanding I never play with the Ouija board again? I don't know what it was, but I think I'd better listen to it, I thought at fourteen.

Why do Christians glow? I thought at fifteen.

By the time I was sixteen years old, I took the bits and pieces of the things I didn't know and combined them with the bits of things I thought I did know and asked myself more questions.

If Jesus Christ truly walked the earth and wasn't some sort of Zeus myth, what does that mean?

If our history books agree that Jesus actually walked the earth, then that's a good indication he's not like Zeus. So, Glenda, what does that mean?

Glenda, that means either you believe what Jesus claims of himself, or you don't, so what is it? Do you believe it or don't you?

You believe it, don't you, Glenda? Guess you have no other choice; you're going to have to get down on those knees of yours and become a Christian.

Well shit.

When I got over that fact, I did it.

But I wasn't going to tell anyone.

Are you kidding me? I'd get eaten alive by my friends, laughed at, mocked, and ridiculed by my family—oh no, I was just keeping that little bit of what I'd done all to myself.

Only I ran into a little problem.

I woke up the next morning in a state of joy. And peace. It was like all the little things that were at war in my soul that didn't even know they were at war were all gone—*poof*—just like that.

"What is this?" I asked. "I don't know what this is, but it's awesome."

I went to our bookshelf and found a Bible my parents got when they became Canadian citizens. I opened it to someplace in the New Testament and started reading about this Jesus whom I'd met last night. Weirdly, I could understand what I was reading. Weirdly, I couldn't anytime I'd tried to read that book before. Just weird, all of it was just weird.

Weirder still was that this feeling of supreme peace and utter, magnificent joy lasted for a week, then two, then three, then four. It was about the fourth week when I decided that everyone should know about this amazing peace and that all people should have access to God, and if it's through this Jesus, like what happened to me, then everyone needs to know how easy it is and how awesome the results. I wanted my friends and family to experience the same peace and joy I'd found, so I spoke up and told them, fully expecting that they would want it.

Only …

They laughed and mocked and ridiculed.

Sometimes they still do; sometimes I join them.

The wonderful feelings I experienced when I became a Christian ebbed as Jesus and I figured out our footing in this world. Sometimes we get along, often we don't, but even when we don't, I absolutely trust that if I follow the instructions he laid out for me, my life will go better for me and for those around me. This is why I was praying as I was walking old, grumpy Jersey.

I unclicked her from the leash and watched her run. She did, stopping occasionally to shove her nose to the ground or look my way to ensure I was within sight. Such a grumpy old girl in the house, but outside? Outside she relived her youth. I smiled.

"Thank you for her, Lord God," I prayed, interrupted by airbrakes. *Waaaaaaa.*

"Thank you for Haney—" A horn blared. I jumped. "Thank you for my children and my—" A Harley rumbled, then roared. The neighbour let out her chihuahua and it started barking, and barking, and barking, and barking.

Shit.

"Lord, I hate this noise. I really hate this noise! You ask me to tell you the desires of my heart, but you know them. They've been in my heart for my entire life. Speak them? Then I will. Oh God, you know I'm thankful for our house, but I want to live in nature. My inner being yearns for nature, but you know that, right? So here's the thing. I want to live up on a mountain, surrounded by trees. I want some water, a river or a creek maybe. I want to look at a mountain. I don't know how you can do that, me on a mountain looking at a mountain, but that's what I'd like. I don't want traffic; I don't want to see people. I just want to breathe … oh, and I'd like that with the mortgage I have now, or better yet"—I grinned—"with no mortgage at all!"

I felt guilty because I have these first world desires when some desire bread for the day, but I also felt good that I can just be me when I pray.

Jersey turned to make sure I was following. "Good girl, old gal, good girl," I said to her. She nodded in approval and scampered off.

I tucked the prayer away as I walked and then did with it like I've done with most prayers I've prayed. I forgot what I prayed for.

***

"Du bekommst nichts! You get nothing!" my grandmother muttered under her breath just loud enough for my father to hear. "Both of you! Your brother in America, you in vat? Alberta! Vat is dis Alberta anyway?" She flicked her left hand at him. Translated to English, she flipped him the bird.

This is how me, my brother, Michael, and all of our cousins became the sole beneficiaries in her will. Granny was just pissed off.

Granny owned a lot.

After the war, she squatted on properties in Stuttgart. If the owners came back, she would return their properties to them, but those who didn't return, she claimed them for herself. As it turns out, she ended up owning a whole city block in the downtown business district of Stuttgart.

My grandmother and grandfather divorced, which was quite uncommon back then. My grandfather was a musician, an artist, a quiet man. My grandmother was very good at business.

My father was fine with being passed over. He had a successful auto body business in Calgary, Alberta. I grew up in an upper-middle-class home. We were very comfortable. My father's business did quite well.

I was very involved with downhill skiing and hockey and was approached by equipment companies to be sponsored by them. This actually paid me quite a bit of money. My skiing career ended with a horrific wipe out, so I then concentrated on hockey. I was a goaltender and even played on the Penguins draft team, but my knee couldn't take it. The ski accident really ended that all for me.

I was about nineteen years old when my grandmother died. We were going to sell the properties in Stuttgart when my cousin Steffanie, who lives in Germany, counselled us that this wasn't the wisest thing to do. In Germany you didn't sell property, you leased it to others. My cousins and my brother wanted to sell, but I thought long and hard about what she had said, and I ended up buying them out with my sponsorship money. It was the best decision I ever made. I was about nineteen collecting the equivalent of $100,000 a month in rent.

I'm very lucky to have Steffanie. She runs everything for me over there; she's in charge of our Europe division.

A year after I bought out my brother and cousins, they sued me.

Michael and I don't get on so well—I mean really, who likes to get sued by your brother? I ended up paying them all off some more, but it left bad blood in our family.

Reading

Softly closing the book, I let my hand rest a moment on the cover. It was chewy. Jordan Peterson had a way with words, or perhaps his words had a way with my mind. At any rate, I was left there sitting in my leather easy chair looking through the french doors that separated our living room from the back garden, abundantly covered in all things growing green. I was thinking about "doing the difficult thing."

At fifty-one my life was comfortable and easy. Haney and I had been married for thirteen years. We both had average children and held average jobs. We lived in an average house in an average city. We drove average cars, ate average food, and kept ourselves entertained with average things.

Difficult things are what I avoided. If I found myself in a difficult thing, I would quickly look for a way out of it. To step into a difficult thing on purpose even seemed contrary to my perfectly-controlled, average world. Yet those words "do the difficult thing" were charming me out of average. After all, average is a wee bit boring.

As I was reading Jordan Peterson, Daryl was reading the room in a pub in Chilliwack.

With an eye for new business and a strong desire to make money, Daryl was willing to go and meet with anybody who looked like they had a promising idea. Today he was sipping a pint and listening to a long-winded, uninviting prospect in Characters pub. The prospect pitched. Daryl declined. The meeting ended early, leaving Daryl with time to kill before the chopper would take him back to his jet. He moved himself to the bar, turned his head, and started a conversation with a woman named Denise. One conversation led to another, another led to a date, the date turned into a relationship.

Denise knew Daryl was in investments, but as the relationship grew deeper, he knew he had to reveal more of his life if they were going to be honest with each other.

Flying into Abbotsford on his plane, he gave her a call and asked if she could pick him up at the airport. Daryl was already off the jet when Denise arrived.

"I have something to show you," he said and walked her to the plane.

"Why are we here?" she asked

"Well, it's mine," he said. He was amused with her reaction.

"Fuck off," escaped her lips.

Denise stepped on the plane and into the life of the exceedingly wealthy. Retiring from her job as a cook in a kitchen of a Fraser Valley prison, she and Daryl married. For two years they flew back and forth from the Cayman Islands to Chilliwack. When the pandemic hit, they got stuck in Chilliwack.

Who I Really Am

It kept hitting solid stones. The ground turned mud in the rain, but the shovel kept finding that stone it couldn't move through.

Whoosh, clack, whoosh, clack. Then *clack, clack, clack* as he tried to loosen the stone free with the tip of the steel.

He wasn't in a hurry. Mud had jumped up and splattered dark little flecks across his nose, which he wiped with the back of his hand and then wiped his hand on the leg of his blue jeans. He was crying, his face smeared in mud and snot.

After two deep breaths and a groan, he turned to me. "How deep should I go?" Haney's voice dropped and then cracked. Pain etched his heavy brow. The weight of his grief hunched him over and he leaned heavy on the shovel waiting for my reply.

"Deeper. I don't want anything digging her up," I whispered.

I pulled the blanket across Jersey, pretending it was keeping her warm. A wave of sobs trembled uncontrollably, leaving my face smeared in mud and snot.

We buried old grumpy where she loved it best.

***

It's such a small, weird world when you contemplate how lives meet up together. I wouldn't be here if my dad hadn't left Germany, if he hadn't gone to that dance that

one night in Alberta where he met my mom. If not for that, I wouldn't exist.

My mom was a terrible cook, and my dad cooked everything well done. Must have been something about that era—kill all of everything by cooking it to death.

My mom loved my brother best.

***

Healing the sorrow of a broken heart sometimes requires a puppy, and that's who was licking Haney's ice cream cone.

"Ewww, you're licking it? You just let Petey lick it? That's so gross!"

Haney smiled and took another lick.

"You're so weird." I scrunched up my face. He grinned.

It was Canada Day 2019. While the world celebrated the birth of our nation, Haney and I took Petey for a drive through the Fraser Valley looking at all kinds of properties.

This wasn't a new thing. On and off through our marriage, I would scan our Multiple Listing Real Estate Services. Hundreds of houses have passed by my eyes, each asking me, "Do you want me? Can you afford me? Maybe you want me, a vacation cottage in the woods? What about me, a renovator house? Perhaps you'd like to build me?"

"Look at the expensive listings. Wow, most of them you wouldn't like, though this one is cute, woodsy, nice pool, nice barn, nice greenhouse. Too bad it's $4,000,000 and far too big, but nice! Oh, there's one that's interesting. It needs to be torn down. Nope, not that ambitious, too lazy. Ahhh here's one, a little one up a mountain. Let's go have a look!"

Haney popped the last bite of his ice cream into Petey's mouth and then the three of us drove up the mountain to have a look. It wasn't as it appeared in photos; the cute little house had close neighbours. We slid out of the car disappointed.

The afternoon was early and the surroundings were gorgeous, so we decided to go for a walk. At the bottom of the hill, we found ourselves standing in front of a property that was overgrown with grass and running over with rubbish.

"I've seen this house before. I'm sure it was in a *Realtor* listing that said the house needed to be removed." I was pulling up photos in my memory. "Yes, I'm quite sure this was the one. I'm going in."

"No, you're not!" Haney said.

"I am!" I replied rebelliously.

Through the weeds up past the house, tripping first over one tire, then over another, I muttered, "Who does this?"

Moving toward the sound of water, I spotted a creek. *It's beautiful. It's babbling. It's breathtaking!*

To the right, a rotting log picnic table whispered, "I was beautiful once. Happy humans sipped wine and ate cheese on me; turn around, you'll see why." I complied.

A horseshoe ring of Douglas fir and cedar trees stood stately, surrounding the mess of man. Dead ahead was a mountain peak in Swiss Alp fashion calling out, "Bob Ross! Bob Ross! I'm here for you!"

Not a house could be seen.

I sighed. "Wow, this place is amazing!"

***

The Calgary evening was calling winter. A fresh dusting of snow made everything look bright, clean, and hopeful, and the evening was waiting for me and Theresa to enter into it.

I had finished playing hockey, and I wanted to shower. Theresa didn't want to wait. She had driven herself to the rink, so we decided to meet up for a burger later. I gave her a quick kiss and turned into the locker room as she left through the front doors.

Theresa, I have never had another love like that love, never in my life have I met someone so compatible with me, and funny. Oh God, she was funny. She knew me in and out and still loved me. She was a year younger than me. She was my high school sweetheart.

The first time I picked her up I was driving my '66 Nova SS, the one I spent the summer fixing up and that ended with its motor's bits and pieces trailing behind me down Main Street, like an arrow or a finger pointing, silently snickering: "He went that-a-way." At the end of the trail was me, my car, a cop, and the ticket he was writing.

"I'm giving you a warning, son. You have enough money lying on the ground back there to hurt you more than I ever could."

I had my slicks on the Nova the first time I picked up Theresa from her house. From the window, her old man watched me drive in and get stuck. It had rained just enough that I couldn't get traction to turn around. My initial meeting with her father had me asking if he wouldn't mind coming out to give us a push off the driveway.

Sometimes I think of how my life would be today if Theresa waited for me to shower after that hockey game. If I'd insisted that she leave her car at the rink and we drove for burgers together. But she wanted to go. It was a simple decision.

A car slipped on the fresh snow through the intersection.

She was T-boned.

She died.

***

I brought the *Realtor* listing up on my computer, read thoroughly and carefully, then sent a quick message off to the listing agent. His response was a curt. "Contact regional district; they have a file on the property."

It was the long weekend, so I couldn't contact them. Instead, I typed the property address in Google's search engine. Up popped the file, and online public record. I spent the rest of the weekend reading, as the file was just that big.

***

I took bigger risks after Theresa died. We were planning to get married, to have a life together, and in a moment, in a blink, that was taken from me. I just stopped caring.

I went to business school and did well. I didn't have to study much ... just went to class enough to get by and to pass my exams.

It was during this time that my friend RJ left Calgary and came to Vancouver. He started Cafe Cucamongas. Another location in North Vancouver was found and he contacted me to come start this restaurant with him. It was the very first Cactus Club.

It didn't do well in the beginning. I remember my credit cards loaded to the max and not knowing if we could make another month. Then we got this crazy idea. You know the Cactus Club cow? The one that looked like the *Far Side* cow? Geeze, how we didn't get sued for using the likeness of that cow for Cactus Club I don't know. Anyway, we had a big cow on the roof of our restaurant and we took it off. We stuck it in the back seat of RJ's convertible and drove up and down the streets of downtown Vancouver. The cow got the job done. It caught attention, and people followed us. We led them right back to the restaurant. We packed the place that night. That was the turning point; we'd started something.

RJ was the face; I was the money in the background. I went back and forth from Vancouver to Calgary to finish my schooling. It was exhausting, but I was determined to finish.

I butted heads with a couple of professors in school, but there was one who was a great mentor and taught me how to set up holding companies under other companies, layers under layers, branching the companies in sections, brick and mortar, entertainment, oil and gas, that kind of thing.

***

Off to the regional district Haney and I went, just one week after reading the file online. The deceased owner of the property had ongoing issues with the regional district, and I wanted to know exactly what they were.

The Planning Development Department notified us that there was a notice on title primarily because the previous owner was not in compliance. The current buildings were put on the property without proper permits. The property needed a valid geotech assessment and a biology assessment was needed because of the creek in the back.

Geotech?

Riparian?

I was a waitress in a pub; these were new words for me.

What were the costs involved? Where does one find someone to do geotech? Could one fix up the house so it could pass a building inspection? If not, how do you get rid of it? What's the cost to do that? There was a very steep slope on the west side of the property. What if the geotech found that slope not stable? We wouldn't want the property then, but we'd be out the cost of the assessment. Hmmmmm.

And Jordan Peterson whispered in my ear, "Do the difficult thing."

***

Banff Springs Hotel was where the wedding was held. Three hundred guests joined me and Jane. We were twenty-three years old and doing pretty well financially. We paid for our own wedding, with the exception of the booze.

"Your father will be very unhappy not to contribute something," my mother said. "Unhappy and offended. It doesn't matter that you can afford it; let him do it." So I let him.

I paid the stipend to the church and had the only priest I could imagine marrying us—the one who knew with a nod and a wink that the only reason I ever sat my body in the pew was because of Betty Sue. Oh God, she was beautiful.

The Anglican Church. Its history was woven into the fabric of our family. The bones that held our bodies

upright. Ancient tradition, sacred tradition. Tradition that often found itself sitting on our orange covered-wagon tapestry, three-seater sofa that sat in our shag-carpeted living room. Tradition was sipping tea and nibbling on cookies while wearing lipstick in shades of plum purple and freesia pink, staining floral napkins used to wipe away crumbs, tea drips, gossip. My mother's Bible study group.

She was that kind of religious. Joel Ostein religious, sending him money, my money, expecting God to answer her prayers with dollars. God, he makes me mad!

I told my dad once I was going to start a church and take people's money tax-free.

My father's faith was deeper, established within the wickedness of war.

It wasn't easy being a German after World War II.

The Anglican church.

The one where your stained-glass window is from Glenda, the hunter scene "Jager" from the sixteenth century. My dad and I pulled it along with several others from an old Anglican church that was sitting in ruined condition on one of our properties in Stuttgart. I took the baptismal as well. Steffanie asked me what I was going to do with it.

"A punch bowl, of course." I grinned.

Her body shivered involuntarily, glancing up as she stepped away from me to avoid the lightning strike.

We spent our honeymoon in California. San Francisco.

One afternoon when Jane was out shopping, I wandered into a car dealership. Posh. I was doing well but not "this" kind of well. I wandered around Ferraris and Porsches in my flip flops and shorts. The salesman approached me, and I thought I was getting the boot.

Instead, he said, "They are beautiful, aren't they?" I nodded in agreement. "Do you want to take one for a spin?" he asked.

Clearly I didn't look like I could afford anything in this place. No Rolex graced my wrists, no suave English accent outed upper crust, no alligator emblem logoed my polo shirts.

"I can't afford this."

"I know," he replied as he handed me the keys.

Ten years later, when I was doing really well, "posh" well, I went back. That salesman was still there. I bought ten cars—a couple for myself, and the others for my top team members. I like to do things like that. After we had written up the paperwork, I told him that I'd been there ten years prior and he'd let me take a Ferrari out when he knew I couldn't afford it. I asked him why.

He smiled and said, "Son, you just never know. A few years ago, this guy stumbled through those doors, long locks tangled beneath his beat-up straw cowboy hat. He smelled like day three of a bender; he looked like day three of a bender. Bloodshot, bleary eyes, stain-covered t-shirt, grubby jeans. Someone needed to throw him in a shower and put him to bed.

"'I'll take that one, and that one, and that one.' He swayed.

"'Sure, let's write them up,' I replied.

"In my office, he swayed a little more before his butt made contact with the chair.

"'How do you want to pay for this, sir?' I asked.

"'Oh, hmmmmm, good question,' he said, looking up to his right, then to his left. He sighed and then stood up, slightly swaying still. He put his right hand into the front pocket of his tight jeans, struggling for a moment or two. He grinned devilishly as he pulled his hand out, holding a bite-size bit of paper with a phone number scrawled on it. He simultaneously flopped back into the chair as he tossed the number in my direction. 'Call this' he said.

"I picked up the phone and dialed. A kid answered.

"'Excuse me, I hate to bother you, but I have a gentleman in my office who told me to call this number. He says he wants to buy some cars.'

"'Just a minute,' the kid said, and you could hear the phone drop against something.

"A moment later, a deep voice said, 'Hello?'

"'Hello,' I said, and I repeated what I'd told the kid.

"'Does he happen to have a straw cowboy hat on?'

"'Yes,' I confirmed.

"'Does he look a little like David Lee Roth?'

"'Hmmm. Yes, he could.'

"'Well, damn, we've been looking for him for four days!' the voice said. 'Give us your address, and we'll send someone by to pick him up. And to bring payment for the cars he wants.'

"You just never know."

***

Chances. We spent a month contemplating chances.

If we're too scared to take a chance, then we don't open ourselves up to opportunities, and we allow fear to dictate the moments of our lives.

Coming to grips with this is unsettling.

Coming to grips with this is scary.

Coming to grips with this is exciting.

With all relevant information about the property requirements in front of me, in order to proceed we needed to take a chance.

We needed to pay for a geotech, which could be upwards of $7,000.

Haney was my cheerleader.

With a plate of spaghetti in one hand and the remote control in the other, he extolled between bites, "Put on your big boy balls, Glenda!"

"The property has so many issues, so many hurdles to overcome. If it doesn't pass the geotech, we're out that money, but at least we'd know if it's worth it to gamble on this. The property is beautiful. I just don't know. And now I found archaeological issues. Up the road from this property they found grave mounds, ancient Stolo native grave mounds. I have to contact the government to see if there are any concerns on this property."

Haney flicked the channel and chewed. "Put on your big boy balls, Glenda!"

His mantra

Be brave Glenda

Be like Nike, "Just do it."

Take a chance.

Move out of your comfort zone.

Whatever you choose, I'm there with you.

Put on your big boy balls.

It's always fantastic to have someone so utterly and completely on your side. But those who offer their undying support don't really know the pressure it creates on the human soul.

If I choose wrong, I affect you as well as me.

If I choose wrong, you work more years as well as me.

If I choose wrong, it touches you too.

I can choose for me, I'm responsible for me, I can live with my own choices for me.

But I don't know that I can live with making a wrong choice for you.

The squeeze of the pressure of this kind of decision left me gasping a little for air. It was my dream, not Haney's, to move away from town. *Am I being selfish? What if my selfishness ends badly? My experience with selfishness is that it pretty much always ends badly. But if one never takes a chance, one doesn't get to experience amazing things.*

"Put on your big boy balls, Glenda"

"Choose the difficult thing, Glenda"

And then it happened.

Three weeks later I bolted upright in bed.

2:00 a.m.

Jolted wide awake, a clap of thunder shaking me from slumber, though the sky was calm. The streetlight and the neighbour's LED porch light fought valiantly against each other for space in our bedroom, lighting up a sound in my mind. A voice? A thought?

"It's what you prayed for Glenda, isn't it?"

Hello? What? I thought.

"It's what you prayed for, isn't it?" the thought repeated itself. Then a gentle ripple of a giggle, almost tangible, whimsical, light-hearted, said, "Did you think I'd just hand that over without a little bit of work?" The thought nudged me in the same way a best friend playfully nudges when you're not quite getting something.

What did I pray?

When did I pray?

My mind settled back into a memory, instantly before me, like a TV screen replaying the moment.

I was walking Jersey.

On the path.

What did I pray?

"I want to live surrounded by trees, in nature."

"I want to live on a mountain looking at a mountain. Good luck with that, snicker."

"I don't want to see neighbours."

"I want to be near water, a river, maybe a little creek."

Holy shit, it's absolutely every little thing I'd prayed for.

I was stunned.

I was stunned I had forgotten what I'd prayed for.

I was stunned that the memory came flooding back almost instantaneously.

I was stunned at the voice.

I was stunned at the accuracy of the property to the prayer.

A wave of peace generated by a whimsical giggle in the middle of the night reminded me that no matter what I chose, and no matter how it ended, God is here.

We made an offer by the end of the week.

***

Valentine's Day. A blanket of snow shut down the streets of Vancouver. Commuters stayed home, sipping their hot chocolate, their Earl Grey tea, their Pinot Gris and Merlot. Some turned the TVs off and opted to watch the stillness of the snow through their windows, tucked inside their sweaters, tucked under their blankets. Others turned on their computers and their kettles as they listened to the scratchy sounds of the internet connecting them to the rest of the world.

Weee ohhh weeeeeeee chhhhhhhhh.

I was at The Granville Room

One long bar. Wood tables stretched out on the right, end to end with a gap wide enough to allow the working class to squeeze in and out.

The bar on the left balances the feel of the tables, drawing your eye inward, downward, elongating the

length of the room. If all interior walls fell down, your eye would run from the front door straight to the back.

The back door. If one was obnoxious, that back door was your exit. It was unfortunate that you slipped and broke your ribs and your hand at the same time. "I don't know how that happened, officer; he must have tripped or something."

A spot under the TV, against the brick wall, beside a cluster of pictures that had meaning to some and meant nothing to others, the perfect spot to observe Aramis courting White Linen.

The click of the bartender's opener against beer bottles. A pint of ale in front of an old guy humming Billy Joel's "Piano Man." Bottles of twelve-year single malt standing like aged soldiers next to vanilla and espresso vodkas brought in especially for the twenty-something city girls. "Cappuccino martini please, hold the chocolate rim, but don't forget the cherry." Lined up, top-shelf alcohol sitting on mantles of wood sweeping the back of the bar three rows high.

And the smell of stale cigarettes from the '60s, like aged French oak bourbon, subtle in flavor, silkier in texture, a gentle aroma of an era gone by, a reminder of the history within the cask. The Granville Room. I owned it.

I got on top of the bar that Valentine's Day and yelled, "No fancy ass martinis! You get your choice of beer or wine, and from the kitchen you get burgers, no steaks!" The crowd, shocked initially, cheered and clapped at what they couldn't have.

An hour before they had my one waitress in tears; no cook showed up to work. It was me flipping burgers. That's what an owner does—you get in there and get it done, whatever needs to get done. My teary eyed waitress was near a breakdown, on the verge of grabbing her coat and purse and running into the snow to escape the throngs of demanding lovers set to celebrate their love with chocolate martinis and cinnamon schnapps, only nothing was open in downtown Vancouver that night. Nothing but us. Those brave enough to venture out on foot found themselves here, getting yelled at by me and loving it. Once I set them straight the mood shifted; their impatience and agitation at the one waitress who defied the snow and made it to work ebbed away to sympathy. By the end of the evening, it was hard to part ways. Such a night, never a night such as that night.

The Granville Room.

The bar in Nickelback's Rockstar.

The bar where even bodyguard bribes of Schwarzenegger couldn't get you in—well, couldn't get you in on the first try, but make a hefty donation and promise to tip my staff well and I'll consider it.

The bar where I saved Chad Kroger from getting his ass kicked. Geeze he was a hothead that one, couldn't take criticism.

We were sitting at the bar and the speakers started thumping "Burn It to the Ground." Some jerk in the room screamed, "Nickelback sucks!" And off went Chad; he liked a good fight!

We were in business together. We were the financing behind Silverside.

Years after Jane and I had split up and I was dating Lynn, Chad and I were out for dinner at Carderos. I got a call from Lynn. After the conversation finished, I hung up and said, "Ahhh, it's how she reminds me who I really am."

Every time I hear that line in that song I smile because I know exactly the moment where it came from.

And that jet, that big black jet, that was mine. I let them use it for the shoot.

As their fame grew, they needed us less and less, so we finally made a deal for them to buy back my portion. I don't do what I do only for the money. I love being that leg up. It's funny, we parted ways and didn't see too much of each other after that, though there was one time when I was just newly dating a model I had met … Geeze, what was her name? Oh well, she didn't know the depth of what I owned. I don't generally provide that information to dates, but she knew enough. Anyway, I was picking her up at the airport and was sitting in the lounge at Vancouver International waiting for her. After her flight arrived, she found me there. She was full of excitement. She had flown first class; her seat was beside Chad Kroger.

They had a long, full conversion the entire trip.

Hmm, I thought, *we should probably leave quickly*. I was directing her and her luggage toward the exit, right through the VIP lounge. Headed straight for me, smiling, was Chad.

"I knew it was you!" he exclaimed. "She was telling me all about her boyfriend, and I thought, *Damn, that sounds an awful lot like Daryl*. I knew it was you!" Big teeth grinning, he smacked me on the back. "It's been a long time."

My girlfriend looked at Chad, then back at me.

Needless to say, I had a bunch of explaining to do on the ride home.

Doug

I stepped right into it. Rolled up the cuffs of my pants and let the water steep right into my hiking boots. I was following Sean the Biologist up the creek, a step creek, three feet at its widest point, the water line cutting a path through mossy rocks, natures' tell-tale sign of how high the creek rose within the last year.

A hundred feet away, Emily the Geologist was inspecting trees on the slope. I had met Emily a couple of weeks before, at her suggestion.

"Why don't I just come up to the property, Glenda, and for $500 I can tell you immediately if it's worth it to do a full geotech report."

"Fantastic!" I exclaimed. If the property was unbuildable, I could know this for much less money than the $7,000. I was all over that.

We walked the property. I followed Emily up the slope, and she pointed out "pistol butt" trees, trees with their bases malformed, like a hunchbacked human, but at the bottom, not the top. "Why do they do that?" I asked,

Emily pointed toward the slope with her clipboard. "They do that when the ground on the slope moves. When they're pistol butted slightly, the ground is moving slightly; if they're deeply butted, then the ground is moving more intensely. These ones are okay, only slightly pistol butted and not many of them, just the occasional one spotted within the other trees on the slope. I wouldn't cut any of them down, or if I had to, just leave eight feet so that the roots in the ground are left to do their thing, which is hold the ground in place."

Emily continued. "I see a lot of good building spots on the property, Glenda. Did you want to go ahead and order the full geotech report?"

"Absolutely." I smiled and gave a little happy dance.

We had two months to get the experts out, analyze the property, and report their findings. Two months in a contract that at the end would see us as owners of a bit of heaven or not.

The property required a cash purchase, as it was unmortgageable. With a notice on title due to noncompliance with building codes, we'd be responsible to bring the property back to notice-free. We could pull equity from our home to purchase the property until the house sold, and once our house sold, we would rent while we built. We were in a good position if the property passed the scrutiny of our geologist.

This was why I was standing in the middle of the creek in my hiking boots on the sunny August day. I was eager to learn what a geologist and biologist did, eager to learn more about this property I'd fallen in love with.

"You'll need a site survey," Emily said, "just to get the setbacks from the creek. And I'm curious where your property line on the east is. My GPS placed it a good twenty feet farther east than the property maps you have. That gives you even more building options. Then off she went up the slope.

After I finished my riparian education by professor Sean, we joined Emily. She was standing at the bottom of a cleared portion on the slope, looking concerned and shaking her head, puzzled.

"I don't know why I didn't notice this before."

Her furrowed brow freaked me out a little.

"This is bad dirt," she said.

"Bad dirt? What's bad dirt?" I replied.

"In the event of an earthquake, this stream of dirt folds like a surfer wave. It's not good, Glenda. I don't know why I didn't notice it before."

The three of us stood silently contemplating the implications.

"I'm so sorry," she said. "I'll model it, and the model will tell us what it really is, but on the surface it just doesn't look good. But again, I can't draw any conclusions until it's modeled. I wish I had better news."

Whenever information is unexpected and not welcome, the heart responds with a heave. My heart was heaving.

"It's better to know now, Emily. This is why you're here, to find this information out for me so that we know. It's better to know before we purchase the property than afterward. I'll wait for your model and take it from there." Outwardly I was understanding, but inwardly I was in a gyre.

Victor Hugo picked up his pen and wrote the word "lugubrious." As he spoke, a whisper woven in cognac respired in a deep French accent breathed, "Now you shall feel it, Glenda."

The drive home was heavy.

I thought about my prayer. I thought about the voice in the night. I cried.

"Why, God? Why bring me to this? Why like this? What's the purpose of this?"

As my heart heaved and the tears rolled and the whys escaped my being,

a gentle breeze of a whisper touched my being.

"It's not a no," it said.

And strangely, the heaving ebbed ever so slightly into hope.

***

Jane was pregnant with Robbie. The morning was crisp. I can't even remember where we were going, but we were going there.

Christine buckled in behind Jane, Nelson buckled in behind me, and the baby in her car seat between them both.

You don't actually think about how sounds affect you. I didn't think taking my kids to see the fireworks could be so traumatic.

The brilliant splinter into colour. Prisms exploding into prisms exploding into crystals dripping in the night sky. Beauty mirrored against terror, the look on Christine and Nelson's faces startling, shocking.

"It sounds like the accident," Christine whimpered. Her little hand clung to mine tightly, unconsciously tightening further with every crack of firework. Wisps of blonde hair had escaped her ponytail. A piece was stuck to her cheek, glued there in sugar—pink cotton candy sugar.

The rage returned.

He came out of nowhere.

The what ifs follow me everywhere.

What if we'd left five minutes later?

What if he hadn't been drunk?

What if we'd left two minutes sooner?

What if he'd never been born?

What if I'd stopped for gas first?

What if he'd run out of it?

What if I hadn't looked in the rear-view mirror at that exact moment.

What if, what if, what if ...

Her little head lolled from one side to the other on impact.

Lolled? Whipped?

Quick death or slow death is still death.

I saw it in my rear-view mirror. I still see it in my rear view mirror, every time I look back.

Baby Stephanie, our baby Stephanie, died.

He kept getting off, court delay after delay. He'd hide on the reserve, fucking Indian, hiding behind his status like it gave him an excuse.

"Mr. Schmidtt, we're going to delay this hearing one more time" came the voice from the court.

I seethed.

When we reconvened in spring, the Indian didn't show. Nobody could find him.

That's what happens when the court delays shit.

People disappear.

Some run off to the reserve.

Some run off to Mexico.

Some run into Doug.

***

One week lapsed into the next as we waited for Emily to complete her model. Limbo, a pause in life, unconsciously holding your breath.

I don't know if it was the potential loss of the money it cost for the reports or the potential loss of a dream property that hung heavy over me. Maybe a bit of both. When my mind got lost in it, right beside it was the thought, *It's not a no, Glenda.* And I'd breathe again, completely unaware that I had stopped.

A couple of weeks later, a messaged appeared in my inbox: "I haven't quite finished my model, Glenda, and not to get your hopes up, but it's looking good. Regards, Emily M.Sc., P.Geo."

"What does that mean exactly, 'not to get your hopes up, but'? A bit of hope but not too much?" I said to Haney when he got home from work.

"It's going to be all good," he said. "I can just feel it."

He felt right. A couple of weeks later, the modeling was complete. The bad soil was on the surface caused by water runoff from the top of the slope; it wouldn't turn into a liquid wave in the event of an earthquake.

"Build thirty feet away from the slope and put up a retaining wall to hold back rolling rocks and debris that could tumble down and you have yourself a beautiful piece of property to build on," the report stated in a nutshell.

It wasn't a no!

We contacted our realtor.

The last i was dotted.

We closed on the property.

***

A strict diet and a strict routine at the gym, sometimes in Vegas, maybe Monte Carlo, the Baltics, Belize, or Calgary. It didn't matter where; it produced the same results—330 pounds of muscle. He is big; he always was big.

Black t-shirts did little to hide what he'd spent years creating—roped veins wrapped around rippled muscle, a thick neck on shoulders of steel. At six-foot-five, his

presence was menacing, but it was his eyes that shot fear into the core of your soul. Completely colourless stroma, every bit of light entering scattered back into the atmosphere; in a dark room they were blue, in the sunshine they were ice blue, and if he was sent to do business with you, they were cold, colourless crystals. Dead eyes, they would have described them, if they could have gotten the words out of their mouths, but the moment they realized Doug's eyes were dead, they were dead themselves.

A beach, a gun, and a bottle of tequila—not a good mix for anyone, not a good mix for me and Doug.

I can't remember what brought him down to the island this trip.

We had spent the afternoon sitting under patio umbrellas, drinking bottles of beer as we watched the servers deliver fruity drinks with umbrellas to chubby, pink-skinned people smelling of coconut sunscreen.

The surfboard sign, a whimsical hand-painted beacon, said "Welcome to Coconut Joe's." A little monkey hanging from a coconut branch etched in chalk. Another sign listed the daily specials; today it was the "All American Breakfast" of bacon, eggs, hash browns, and toast. Ready to tantalize the All American Tourist, sent special delivery via the cruise lines.

I was paying tax to the Germans as my funds left Germany, and I paid tax to the Canadians as the funds entered Canada. My tax man suggested a better way to avoid this double tax. Run it through the Cayman Islands. Set up new finance structures through the Isle of Man. I went down to explore the options. In order to make these things possible, I would need a Cayman Island address, a Cayman Island business.

At the southern tip of Seven Mile Beach, hidden in the shadow of the Casa Caribe on West Bay Road, was a little bar and grill. Caribbean BBQ, crawfish boils, curry goat on coconut rice, Coconut Joe's. The owner was facing financial difficulty. I needed a business. A deal was done. I bought it, and he ran it. Win-win.

We spent the afternoon catching up, Doug and I, reminiscing about our first meeting in elementary school. His daughter was doing well, living with his mother in Calgary. I was surprised when he married. I wasn't surprised when it didn't work out. I never asked how his ex-wife was or where she was. I always asked about his daughter. He sneaks back to Canada now and again to visit. I never ask how.

I lent him my car once. He brought it back and disappeared for a while. I never asked why. He was transporting a bunch of cash in a briefcase once for me. He never made it; the money never made it. He showed up at my door two years later with the briefcase. I never asked where he was. He saw me seething with anger at the drunk Indian who killed my daughter. I never asked what happened to him. Don't ask; asking makes you responsible for what you know.

Doug came with me to Calgary the time we had to chat with Jane's new boyfriend. Some bigwig oil and gas dude in snake oil fashion slithered his way into her heart deep down into her pocketbook. She called me for extra money. I didn't mind giving it, but I was confused that she needed it. Our divorce was exceedingly amicable. She still owned part of the company. The company was doing very well. After further conversation, I found out she had lent him a couple of million, financing his company with promises of bigger and better tomorrows. Only it left her pretty broke in the today. She had wanted to do something for herself. She wanted to prove to herself that she had the ability to do business on her own, but she got sucked in, and she was at the point where the mud around her ankles just wouldn't let go. Doug and I went up to his third-floor office building, walked right past reception, and into his glass-walled office. It didn't take much. A short explanation of who we were, why we were there, and what would happen by the end of the day if that money wasn't returned to Jane. One chair through a wall of glass. One big ass Doug holding one little oil and gas dude by his throat made it pretty clear we meant business. I don't know how he did it, but by day's end the money was there. Jane has remained single ever since.

I saw him soften only once.

It was the week before Christmas, and I had sent him to LA to collect on the deed the plastic surgeon had signed over. Casinos don't do that anymore, but back then we still did. This particular surgeon was losing badly, and instead of walking away, he bet his home. He lost. Doug was there to collect. The only problem was that a kid answered the door, and another kid ran up beside the first. Inside he could see two more watching TV. *Rudolph the Red Nosed Reindeer*, the Burl Ives version. A Christmas tree dotted with hand-cut snowflakes sat in the corner, silver tinsel draped over branches, a piece here, a handful there. A plastic Santa stood guard next to the fireplace. A string of blinky lights hung from a curtain rod. The smell of vanilla mixed with cinnamon, something homemade was cooking. The mother came to the door.

"I'm looking for your husband," Doug said.

She looked up and replied, "I haven't seen him in a month." Tears welled up.

Doug excused himself for a moment, went back to the car, and phoned me.

"It's a week before Christmas," Doug whispered into the phone. "I'm not kicking them out. If you want the house, you can come do it yourself."

Every part of me was all about money: how to make it, how to make more of it, how to use it to make more of it. It was at this moment that changed.

I was sitting on a barstool in the Lobby Bar at the MGM Grand, drinking a draught when I got the call from Doug. I flagged the bartender and ordered a double single malt neat. I rolled the Scotch around on my tongue as the thoughts rolled around in my mind.

I phoned him back

"Sign the deed over to the wife," I said, "and tell her to file for a divorce."

It was a pivotal moment

Kids came before cash.

Now six years later, here we were, discussing the future and remembering the past. Another round of Buds downed and another and another until the bar closed. We thought it was a great idea to take a bottle of tequila to the beach. Doug thought it was a great idea to pull out his gun. We took turns shooting shit on the beach between shots of tequila. We shot at anything that moved, waving the gun in the air and shooting again. My phone rang and slurrily I said, "Hello."

"Daryl, look behind you," the voice said

I turned around and saw a row of cop cars, red lights flashing. My phone pressed to my ear with one hand, the pistol waving in the other.

"Put the gun down, Daryl," the police chief said through the phone.

"Sure." I threw the gun on the ground. "But why not just come down and ask me to do that yourself? Why stay up there?"

"Because you have a fucking gun in your hand and you're shooting things with it," the chief said

"Ohhh," I realized.

The next morning, I found myself at the police station making a hefty donation to their next policeman's ball and promising never to drink tequila ever again.

Vegas

The leaves were turning. Vibrant oranges and vivid reds fluttering gently, caught on a bit of the breeze breathing up the Chilliwack River Valley. Their colours sharply contrasted against the evergreens. A hundred shades of green live in the forest.

The clarity of the sky accentuated the edges of two mountains: on the left, Slesse, on the right, Church. Both dusted with snow, both had Bob Ross's "Happy Little Trees" peeking out here and there.

The day we got the key.

Only there was no key.

And the only thing we moved was our arses, up the mountain, in my old Santa Fe, a cooler full of beer, a couple of chairs, and Petey the beagle.

We arrived on the property and really didn't know what to do first. We were scattered, feeling a little like trespassers. Poking our noses here and there and wondering if anyone was going to come and tell us to get off the land. We grounded ourselves with a campfire, a view of a mountain in front and the little creek behind. We sat, cracked a beer, and cheers'd.

Two beers down and we ventured into the basement of the mobile home. A deep, musty odour assaulted us as we entered. We investigated and cringed. The back of the basement was beneath a deck.

And it wasn't a basement. I don't know what it was.

It was a place in Stephan King's mind. It was a place where Pennywise and Jame Gumb smoked cigars and played chess.

Water was dripping in from the deck above, landing on boulders, a cellar of rocks.

Two-by-four posts propped up by a rock here and there held up the deck. A metal post in the centre of the celler held up a beam that was cracked partway through.

"It rubs the lotion on the skin."

"Checkmate," says Pennywise, grinning devilishly

We went back to the beer.

***

Gambino. The name alone plunges one deep into a bottle of Chianti sitting on a table at Rao's. Mob bosses twirl spaghetti on their spoon, and Alessandro Safina serenades the scene with Luna.

If one looked out the window, they could imagine a big black caddie pull up and three men with Thompson 1928s jumping out. The door to Rao's opens and they open their Tommy Guns on the boss.

The scene is in black and white to avoid the horror of blood splashed on the bar.

Plates of spaghetti fly in the air as Safina crescendos.

The end of the song ends the scene. The men in black disappear as fast as they came.

In their wake, they leave shattered bodies, shattered crystal, shattered bottles of wine dripping their grape into puddles of blood so red it's difficult to determine which is which.

Gambino.

Where Little Italy meets Vegas.

Gambino.

Sitting at my table on the patio at the Warf.

I walked in and asked the bartender to please escort the people sitting at my table to another table, as I had a meeting. The bartender looked at me, shaking his head from side to side, silently saying "nope."

Verbally he said, "They're waiting for you, boss."

Michael Gambino and his "friend."

"Your name came up," he said as I introduced myself and asked the nature of the visit.

"Came up?" I responded

"Yup," he said. "We're looking for someone to work with us in Vegas."

"Vegas?" I replied

"Yup," he responded

We talked for a couple of hours. As he was leaving, he turned and said, "Think about it, Daryl."

So I did

For a while.

Do I want to go to Vegas? Do I want to work with a Gambino? Would they let me run Vegas legitimately?

I ordered a Scotch, added a couple of drops of water to my dram, tipped it back, and thought about it.

***

We had some work to do.

I ordered the site survey through a local company.

We met with a house designer, Joe.

We contacted the Fire Department.

Do you want to burn down a house?

"What are you thinking for your house?" said Joe, sipping his tea.

Sara Bella's is a broody coffee shop. Dark ceilings, dark walls, wood everywhere. Rich roasted coffee, the scent completes the swaddle.

I'd like a t-shaped house. Guest bedroom up front, mudroom, master bedroom at the back, then in the front; the kitchen, dining and living area all in one room, and please a vaulted ceiling in the shape of an A. We have a beautiful mountain to the south, would love the living room windows to that view.

***

"We would love to burn down your house," said the fire chief. "It must be mortgage-free and asbestos-free."

The first one was already taken care of. And the asbestos testing was ordered for the following week.

"We can be at the property in November to start the site survey. Does this work for you?" said Al from the survey company.

And so we began.

***

I was standing in front of the elevator door, two dancers swaying against each other waiting alongside.

Dancers—one thing Vegas had an abundance of.

Six hundred a week if you were just starting out; fourteen a week if you were Broadway production good, but so much more if you didn't mind peeling the clothing off. These two were the latter.

"What floor?" the one dressed in red asked. A bottle of something bubbly waved with her right hand, her flushed face indicating that wasn't the first bottle of the evening. She hiccupped and giggled, leaning into her friend. The friend had Double Ds. A gift from an

ex-lover? To herself? From her mother? It was Vegas. Everyone with a history ended up here.

I smiled, the doors opened, and we stepped inside.

"What number shall I press?" I asked the ladies as the doors closed.

"Thirty. What floor are you?" said Double D as she scanned.

The Scan.

Originally I called it the Vancouver Scan.

Sitting at the bar sipping a beer at Joey Bentalls, waiting for Josef, a Macleod Dixion lawyer to arrive, a meeting to bring me up to speed on the acquisition of the old post office building we were purchasing. A woman and her friend walked in and sat to the left of me. I turned to the one closest to me and said hello.

She responded with the Scan.

Her eyes started at the top of my head, scanned slowly down to my feet, then up again. Without acknowledging my existence, she turned back to her friend, ignoring my hello, ignoring my existence.

"Well then," I said, and went back to sipping my beer.

A short time later, Josef arrived.

"When did you get in?" he said "I see Pattison moved his boat for yours again." He grinned, shaking his head. "How you get him to do that for you, I'll never know."

Josef was dressed in a blue Emporio Armani. I was in shorts and flip flops.

I could feel Miss Vancouver Scan turning her ear toward our conversation, which was full of dates, delays, and dollar amounts.

"Josef," I asked, "is the woman behind me looking at us?"

"Yes," he responded.

I wheeled around toward her and said, "Too bad you didn't know all that information an hour ago." I smiled at her and then turned my attention back to Josef, inviting him to Coal Harbour for drinks on the boat.

"Oh, I'm one past thirty," I said, surviving the Vegas Scan.

"There isn't one past thirty," Double D insisted. "We're at the top; there are only thirty floors at the MGM Grand. Everyone knows that."

I smiled a little, pulled out my card, and swiped it through the slot next to the elevator buttons. Up we went. The car smoothly arrived and the doors opened right into my apartment on the thirty-first floor of the MGM Grand.

"I assure you," I stated, "this is the thirty-first floor."

I always get a bit of a kick from the response of people; these two's eyes went wide and some private dances were offered and declined.

I stepped out of the car after pressing number thirty, leaving the ladies to absorb the existence of floor thirty-one as the elevator took them back down to their "top floor."

***

"Racks of clothing! Glenda, you have no idea! This place is amazing! It has a second floor and its own pool. I'm lounging by the pool on the very top floor of the MGM Grand!"

I could hear Tina's squeals of delight coming through the email. Daryl flew to Seattle, picked her up, then darted off to Vegas for some quick business.

"He just picked me up from the office. I wanted to go home and change, but he said not to bother, Lyndsay was taking care of things. And she did, Glenda. When I got here, she rolled in a rack

of clothing. I just picked what I wanted and—poof—off we went. I can't wait for you to come. I can't wait for you to see this place! Who knew an apartment could exist such as this, and here I am!

"I had a tour of security, the rooms of screens, the 'eyes' then the eyes watching the eyes, then the eye in the sky watching the eyes watching the eyes. You wouldn't believe the levels of security here!" she gushed. "Daryl had to go to a meeting, so he left me with his team and suggested they show me around. I had no idea there was this level of security!

"Then we went for dinner, and Daryl and I were sitting at a table and some guy came up and said, 'Excuse me, you're going to have to move; you're at my table.' I just cringed, but Daryl didn't even flinch. He looked up at the jerk and said, 'I think you're mistaken; this is my table, and we are staying.' He hasn't one stick of fear in him. Me, I'm just cringing inside the whole time, but he just reaches out and grabs my hand and holds it. The jerk turned red in the face and started spouting, 'You don't know who you're talking to!' Daryl quite calmly said, 'I don't think you understand who you're talking to.' And before I could blink, there were some very large men escorting the jerk away. I don't even know where I am anymore, Glenda. This is just amazing!

"Today we went to Wet Republic; they're doing some renovations and they wanted to show Daryl the progress. Oh Glenda, the women there are all just gorgeous. He could have his pick of any one of them, and he's chosen me! I don't know what I've ever done to deserve this; I don't deserve this. Just for the afternoon, to make things special, he packed a picnic lunch and helicoptered us up to Mount Charleston. The hikers didn't look too impressed, disturbing their peace flying in, then poof, out of the helicopter comes cases of beer and bottles of Champagne, and he's just handing drinks out to people! He just does that,

Glenda! He's so generous with everyone around him. I've never met anyone like him in my entire life!"

***

It was dark.

When you're surrounded by the glow of suburbia, darkness doesn't exist, but you don't know it doesn't exist until you're walking up O'byrne on an overcast November evening. The sound of the river, ominous not because it's rushing but because you can't see it.

The invisible roar, warning the listener "STAY TO YOUR LEFT OR YOU WILL SURELY DIE!" Shadows of evergreen branches reaching out in blackness, a dark warning on a dark night by dark trees on a dark street, whispering, "That way please, come no further this way, go that way please."

That way we went, heeding the warning. We reached the switchback, and the scene in front of us looked like a movie shoot. Fire trucks with lights flashing, smoke rising up from the house, directors pointing, the next scene is set, and the actors walking around in fluorescent fire gear, with beeping bottles of oxygen strapped on their back, the smallest one steadying herself on the ladder. Fire practice.

The fire chief invited us up to the property to watch the practice.

Tonight was ladder drills.

The energy was focused yet exciting.

Sixteen? Thirty people? I couldn't count. If they weren't standing in a circle getting direction from the directors, they were doing a job. Lifting this, holding that. And they were tiny. Just little bits of human beings doing bits of big things.

The senior volunteer firefighters stood beside us, describing the drills. We were in awe; we had no idea the exertion required to complete the smallest task, exertion and attention to detail. It's always about the smallest detail. Lives are at stake.

We didn't realize the impact of us donating the property for their use had. After observing, we were certainly thankful we did.

***

It was my decision to go to Vegas to legitimize the Gambino interest there that changed my life.

Two hundred and thirty-two Casinos we own world wide now

My favourite?

Monte Carlo.

An acquisition made available by ... let's just say Doug finding a dirty little secret that nobody wanted exposed. It bought us controlling interest.

I have the house next door to the Prince of Monaco's house. One day I want to put on blue, fluffy little slippers and walk next door to borrow a cup of sugar, just to see what happens.

We will go there, Glenda, the month before the wedding. I have to do business anyway. You and Tina and Danny and Tanya, you can wander through it all. I'll give you cards, and you can just swipe for whatever you want to buy. It will all be billed back to the Casino de Monte-Carlo. I'll have to go up to the Baltics after that to check on those casinos there, but we'll enjoy at least a week in Monte Carlo. I can't wait to share that with you all. You'll need the card.

A couple of years ago, we were at one of our restaurants overlooking the water. Usually I just pay cash. Most people don't know who I am, and I like to keep it that way. This day I was drinking bottles of Heineken. I got the bill, eight euros each. I was both pleased and appalled. Happy to have this kind of money brought in, sorry to have to pay that amount for one bottle of Heineken!

When we're in Germany, we'll visit Casino Baden Baden. Steffanie informs me we've just acquired this one. The roulette ball has travelled 150 years here. The grand steps will take your feet to visit the same rooms that enchanted Dostoyevsky—when he took the time to look up, that is.

But for now, I'll concentrate my interest in the Canadian casinos. COVID has allowed me to purchase these at a fraction of the cost. Great Canadian, Gateway, purchased through Maverick, through Apollo, the layer under layer so one doesn't look like it's owned by another. The governments frown on monopolies here, so we just purchase under a different head under a different branch. The government has done me a great favour by shutting down all of the casinos over COVID. I picked them up for such a good price. Now I need to get my people in here; we'll start running them like we run them in Vegas.

We'll add on to the Chilliwack casino, and we'll renovate Parq. Abbotsford city council are a bunch of backward Bible thumpers. Do you know that one councillor there suggested I make a donation to his church!

I told them if they wouldn't let me relocate the casino to the Abbotsford Events Centre, I'm going to move it out of the Abbotsford area. I'll relocate into the Fraser Valley Regional District and they'll lose all of that income. Our people have spoken with the regional district and they're completely interested in working with us. We're looking at the property, the golf course near the freeway, The Fraser Glenn. We'll move it there, build a big casino, and Abbotsford can go fuck themselves.

Burn It!

"I just need your signature." The email read.

Sign and begin the design.

It was the beginning of December.

The fire department was scheduled for their final practice on December 8. The neighbours were informed and invited. Volunteer firefighters from three different areas of our community were invited to participate, outhouses were delivered, spectator sections set up.

"Joe," I replied, "I just want to contact the surveyors to see if their site survey is complete and to make sure this design will fit with all of the setbacks. I only want to design one house."

The second email I sent that morning read, "Good morning, Albert. We are in the process of signing on the dotted line to begin the design of our house. I thought it would be wise to have the completed site survey before we begin. What is our ETA?" Sincerely, Glenda.

And off to work I went.

I arrived at the pub, turned on the bank of light switches that took the pub from vampire dark to moody gloom, and checked my phone for messages.

An email from Albert flashed. "Good morning, Glenda. The survey is complete; we need a meeting."

"Excellent," I typed my reply. "I'm available tomorrow morning. Just tell me I have a place to put my house and I'm a happy camper!" I hit the send button. Turning to our remote control, I hit "ON" and watched ten TVs and a big screen jump to life. I unlocked the pub.

The daily regulars so regular you see them more than your own family wander in. Big Doug and little Doug take their seats at the bar, leaving the corner open for Mark, who's busy locking up his black HellCat.

Mark stands five-foot-eight and is one hundred pounds soaking wet. Bruises appear, disappear, and reappear on the back of his hands, indicating he's not well. His silver hair, closely shorn, highlights the shape of his skull.

"You should have seen me yesterday, Glenda. My HellCat turned heads! I was on the freeway, and as I cruised past people, I'd look in my rear view and could see their heads turning." Mark sipped his wine and reminisced to us.

"They weren't looking at your fucken car," little Doug said. "Their heads were turned because they've never seen a skeleton driving a Hellcat before."

The bar snorted in laughter.

I poured a pint for John and one for Lee.

"How's the house coming, Glenda?" asked Dave.

"Just met with the architect, Dave; it's progressing." I smiled

"Hey Skeletor," I hollered to Mark, "you ready for another wine?"

"At your leisure." He smirked. We both knew it's not at my leisure; it must be there before his first one is finished or he starts twitching.

I took a peek at my phone between pours and noticed a message from the surveyor. I clicked on it

"That's what I want to talk to you about," read Albert 's email.

That's what I want to talk to you about?

I delivered another pint to big Doug and returned to my phone.

"You can't leave me hanging like that, Albert," I replied.

My guys from the insurance company walked in. I poured their pints as a group from the HSBC came in. A couple of groups of two, a group of three, and my realtor and her friends showed up. I was officially busy.

I picked up my phone, and a message was flashing.

"Here is a site map. I would have preferred to do this in person. I'm sorry, Glenda," said Albert's email.

I opened the PDF.

"Glenda, I need another pint," said big Doug.

"Yup, yup." I put down my phone, quickly poured the pint, and ran back to my phone to inspect the map.

I was busy.

I was so busy.

But I didn't need time to process what the map said. I put my phone down.

I ran drinks to tables, took food orders, delivered food orders, forgot food orders, forgot drink orders, apologized, and forgot more. The bar's beers were running dry, and they were becoming impatient with me. Mark was twitching because I forgot his wine. I took a deep breath to keep myself from panicking.

"Sorry," I said to a glaring Mark because he had to wait for his wine. "I just got this, so I'm completely off my game." I flashed a picture of the map to him.

"Shit, Glenda."

"Shit, Glenda," said big Doug.

"Shit, Glenda," said little Doug.

"Shit, Glenda," said Mark.

"Shit, Glenda," said the map. "You have one foot to put your house on."

***

Bald-headed, blue-aproned brew master holding a pint. The Shaftesbury Tap handle. It was our goal to have this tap handle in all drinking establishments in all of Vancouver.

I had gone around undercutting our keg costs just to get those tap handles installed. If the major company was $80 a keg, I dropped our cream ale to $75. It wasn't long before this caught the attention of their suits. Mr. Head of the Suits called.

"You can keep doing that, Daryl, but I guarantee you're dancing with the devil. We will give our product away just to keep you out. So I suggest you rethink your marketing strategy. Do you really want to go bankrupt before your third year is finished?" Mr. Suit postulated over the phone; a cigar cough followed the question mark.

Big business putting little business back in its spot. We stopped undercutting. We still did exceedingly well. In the late '80s, the beer climate was lager. We pushed our cream ale and Vancouver responded. We sold Shaftesbury to Sleeman in 1999. I guess they figured it's better to buy out the competition.

Paul contacted me a while back. We've been considering opening another brewery, one that would supply all of the casinos with their draft. We'll see how our negotiations with the bigger names go. If we can't get the price we're looking for, it's something I will consider.

Shaftesbury and *Poker Stars* were two of my investments that turned out bigger than I could have imagined. Isai was a computer programmer who had developed the software for *Poker Stars*. He was looking for funding to get it up and going, so we did that. We didn't have a clue it would get so big. The hockey strike happened, and *ESPN* contacted us and asked if we wanted to televise poker. Who would think people would want to watch poker, but here we are today. *Poker Stars* entered unchartered territory, and I found myself being handcuffed by the US Treasury Department. I was escorted to Washington. Obama was charismatic but firm. We agreed to pay something like 730 million in American taxes, even though we were running through the Isle of Man. It seems like a lot of money, but not when you consider what we were pulling in a day. The securities commission asked how we were going to arrange payment, and I said, "Will a cheque do?" I called and had a cashier's check done up. You should have seen his face; he stumbled a little over his words after that.

We sold *Poker Stars* in 2014 to Amaya, then we bought it back for a fraction of the cost because they didn't know what they were doing. Obama and I have since become friends. He and Michelle will be sitting with us at the head table at the wedding, Glenda. I can't wait to see him banter with Jack.

Poker Stars, Full Tilt, and we're starting another one in Australia. COVID shut down our buildings, but our online profits have gone through the roof!

***

Roast beef dinner. How else could I break this news to Haney but over food?

I brought an order from the pub, placed the brown take-out box on his lap, and burst into tears.

"Well, worst case scenario, we have a great camping spot," he said, licking gravy from his lips.

"That wasn't the plan!" The new reality pressed against my mind, and I started sobbing again. "I want a house in the mountains, not a camping spot! The mobile home is halfway on Crown land. The septic mound is halfway on Crown land. All of the maps in the regional district reports, with every report we had done for all of the concerns of the property, there wasn't one time at any moment that anyone brought up concerns of the property lines!" And the tears rolled and Haney calmed, and the night was long.

The next morning, I sent off three emails.

"Emily, here is the map from the surveyor. I don't know what to do."

To our engineer, Collin: "Here is the site map from the surveyor. I don't know what we are going to do."

And to Gail in the planning department at the regional district: "Why was every map the regional district had on this property not this map?"

"How is that even possible?" said Emily. "Even my GPS had the lines placed farther east than the regional district map."

"Well, that's a conundrum," replied Collin.

"I don't know," Gail's voice came across the email.

Within the shock, minds were turning. Collin came to the pub with his pencil and said, "If we can get Emily to move back the retaining wall to the slope, Glenda, you'll have a lot of room to build. I'll talk to her to see if that's something we can make happen."

After their meeting, Emily over the phone said, "I had the retaining wall thirty feet away from the slope because you had a lot of room and it would save you the expense of drilling the slope for stability. If we drill the slope and check its stability, and if it's stable, we can move the retaining wall right back to the slope. A drill would cost around $1,800. Is this something you want to do, Glenda?"

"Yes, Emily, of course. I really don't have another choice, do I? Let's hope it's stable."

The drill was ordered for the following week. Results would come in January.

***

Jambalaya, New Orleans style, rich in paprika and cayenne and who knows what other spices that woman used for the finest meal I've ever eaten. She cooked in her house, that big Black woman they called Babette. You had to walk across a wooden bridge deep inside the bayou to get there. Fifteen tables. You can't get a reservation. If you're there, she feeds you. If the tables are filled, you're out of luck. I was lucky. John led the way. Only locals know about places like Babette's— authentic Cajun food, you don't ask what's in it, maybe alligator, maybe chicken. Don't ask unless you want to know.

I'd like to go back there one day.

I don't want to go back to Colombia.

In Colombia I was sitting on bales of something in the back of a Jeep, me and two of my team. We were picked off the side of the road. Left stranded by failed mechanics of another Jeep in the middle of two hundred acres we were visiting. That's what we do; we look for places to build casinos and hotels.

The longest project like this took over twenty years. Belize. There was no infrastructure. Before we could build hotels and casinos, we had to make sure the village had fresh water and good sewage systems and that the people weren't starving. You can't have tourists driving through these kinds of areas to get to their destination; it must all get cleaned up. We clean it up and then we employ the locals. Win win. Belize I'm most proud of because of the number of humans we helped and continue to help, but to be honest, I didn't do it to help the people. I did it because I wanted to make more money by putting my casino and hotels there.

In Columbia we were now facing a couple of problems. Problem one: we are in Columbia in the middle of nowhere with a broken-down vehicle. Problem two: accepting a ride from strangers in Columbia, in the middle of nowhere. Which problem is less of a problem? We chose the latter. Which is why I found myself sitting on a bale of something in the back of a Jeep driving up a muddy road flanked on one side by a cliff and on the other by green trees of some kind—so green it's like you have to redefine the word.

"We need to make a stop," said Hurculano, the name I attached to the oversized Columbian in the passenger seat. Hurculano's partner pulled up to a stop in front of double iron gates.

"You can't come in."

I didn't argue.

The two of them disappeared behind the gates, leaving the three of us contemplating what we were sitting on but not brave enough to investigate. In under ten minutes they returned with a man who was clearly in charge.

"Who are you and why are you here?" the ominous voice said.

I explained, and I guess I explained well, or perhaps he had heard of us and what we did. This I don't really know, but a grin broke across his dark, brooding face. He patted me on the back and said not to worry. "My boys will get you where you need to go. I just need them to drop off those bales you're sitting on first."

Off we jumped.

Hurculano and partner drove the Jeep through the gates, returning empty a few minutes later. We jumped back in and, as promised, Hurculano dropped us where we needed to go.

That was the only time I felt fear in my life.

We didn't buy the Colombian property.

Dealing with dirty politicians is one thing, but dealing with the Cartel is another.

***

"You!" Albert waved his finger at me from across the boardroom table at the survey office. "You dragged the news out of me in an email. I just normally don't do that."

He smiled. I smiled. Haney smiled. Mary-anne and Trey, our realtors, smiled. Apprehensive smiles. Getting the feel of the land smiles. Let's make the most of this situation and smile, smiles.

"Things like this just don't happen often," he continued. "In BC, it's illegal to sell a piece of property that doesn't have an adequate building site on it. There is recourse for you in that you're able to sue on that ground. Everyone who had a hand in this from the regional district to the realtors to the geotech company would all be involved in the lawsuit."

"I don't want to sue anybody," I said. "We"—I looked at Haney—"we don't want to sue anyone; we just want to build a house. We've ordered a drilling of the slope to check the stability, and if it's stable, we'll have a building site. So there's no point in talking about suing anybody or entity until we get the results of that. Besides, I like my realtors." I continued looking at both Mary-anne and Trey, who were intently listening. "Everyone was just trying to help. Everyone was just doing their job. This is just a really shitty situation that we've been handed, so we have to handle it the best way we can."

The relief sighed out of everyone in the room.

"You're handling this amazingly well," Albert voiced as a look of softness flickered across his face. "I didn't know how you'd be. I expected you to come in here screaming and yelling at me."

"It's not your fault, Albert," I stated. "You're just the bearer of bad news. Don't get me wrong, though. If you could have seen me yesterday, I was not this calm. I was bawling my eyes out!"

Haney's head bobbed up and down in adamant agreement with that statement.

"But," I continued, "we realize this is situational, and we can't control the situation. The only thing we can control in the situation is ourselves, so we will do that. The more important thing in this is our relationships with the people involved. The people didn't do this on purpose. Nobody was out to screw us; everyone has just been trying to help, so we keep that first in our vision."

These thoughts I was speaking had developed the evening before. To keep us sane? To keep us from blame? To keep us from rage? To keep us focused? To remind us what was most important. Yes, that. Souls before stuff.

"The house is scheduled to be burned down in two days," I said. "What do we do now with the house half on Crown land? The fire department has been gearing up for this burn. The house has to come down; it's not safe."

"I'd send an email to the fire chief and let him know what we've discovered and let the conversation move from there," Albert suggested.

"Okay, and I guess for everything else we just have to wait for the results of the drilling."

I turned to Mary-anne and Trey. "Let's not show our house for the rest of the month until we know if we can build."

"Oh God, Glenda!" Mary-anne exclaimed. "We'll stop all activity to sell your house until this is done! And when we do sell your house, we'll take the cost of the drilling off our commission."

"Mary-anne, thanks so much!" I replied. "That's exceedingly thoughtful of you, and I'll take it!"

Smoulder

Five flat stockings lay under bits of torn paper and ringleted ribbon.

The mantle, two hours before, picture perfect, mini lights carefully woven within boughs of green, voluptuous red ribbon bows draping the corners, all now askew. Santa left the treasures; the children left the mess.

"What?" came an unappreciated exclamation from Nelson, who had just opened a video game. "That's a stupid one."

"I know," commiserated Christine. "I got some stupid gifts too."

Robbie was sucking on a candy cane, looking unimpressed with the whole Christmas thing.

Jane had spared no expense. She had spent hours decorating the house, picking out the perfect gifts for our three, and here they sat in a pile of crumpled paper, complaining. Jane was in the kitchen making something that smelled of cinnamon as she pushed back her own tears of disappointment.

I was seething.

"Pick out your worst gift," I said.

"Huh?" Three pairs of eyes stared up at me from the floor.

"Pick out one gift from the pile of gifts you have in front of you that you hate the most and bring it to me right now," I demanded.

It took less than a minute.

"Go get a roll of wrapping paper, and each of you wrap the gift you picked," I instructed.

They complied, and within a few minutes the three of them had completed the task.

"Get your boots and coats on, bring your gift, and get in the car."

"But Daaaaddd," they whined. "It's Christmas morning!"

"Get in the car," I said.

Three miserable children followed me to the garage and resentfully buckled themselves in the back seat.

A few minutes later, we found ourselves in front of Bethany House, a shelter for women and children.

"Stay here," I commanded while exiting the car.

Inside I was greeted by reception. I explained that I had three ungrateful children with three gifts that I was sure someone there could use. Could my children please come in to give them away?"

"Of course!"

Back out I went to the car, opened the back door, and ushered the three into Bethany House.

They went from being miserable to being confused as to why they were there. The lady at reception had found three children of the same ages as mine, and I instructed my children, "Give the kids the gifts you wrapped."

My children looked up at me in a muddled state.

"Go ahead," I encouraged.

They stepped forward with their gifts and handed them over.

The children who had received the gifts' eyes shone, and glees of delight escaped their being as they unwrapped the treasures.

"Momma, look what I got!" cried one little boy.

"Oh Mommy, look at this! Just look at this," cried another.

The third child just hugged the gift to their chest, smiling.

When we were back in the car, I said, "Those gifts you picked, the worst ones you got, were the very best ones they got. How did that make you feel?"

The three of them were very quiet.

Nelson looked at his feet. Robbie looked up out the window, avoiding my gaze.

"It felt like I should give them all of my gifts," whispered Christine.

Nelson and Robbie nodded in agreement.

That Christmas was a good Christmas.

That Christmas was the day my children understood the difference between getting and giving.

That Christmas was the birthday of philanthropic hearts in my kids.

Every Christmas since that Christmas, they've been active in buying gifts for the kids at the shelter and have even moved on to make sure there is something nice for the mothers under the tree too. I'm extremely proud of them.

***

It was breathing. Hot reaching behind heat, parturition of hell. *One step*, I thought, *just one step and my entire being would be consumed, flames licking their lips as they savoured my skin greedily, gleefully. It would hurt. For how long?* Less time,

I imagined, than being burned at the stake. That would take time to build up. This? This was already deep in the bowel of Leviathan. Fire in the throng of digestion, and I was two feet from its throat.

Fire fighters were milling around; a few were sprawled on the grass in front of the building … well, in front of what was once a building. Soot stuck to sweat, leaving streaks across a forehead, across a cheek bone. Attempts to wipe the face clean failed. They were spent. I was a little surprised they didn't tell me to keep my distance from the dragon. Maybe they understood. Maybe they'd been there themselves. Maybe it's a natural reaction when coming face to face with fire, real fire, not the friendly fire you roast weenies on, not the happy hearth-roasting-chestnuts at Christmas, but this …

"Let her contemplate it," I could imagine they said.

"She will do well to contemplate it," another responds.

And so I did.

The day started early, and we sat in the spectator section underneath the evergreens on the east side of the property with friends and family and the firefighters' friends and family. "Come see what Daddy does. Come see what I'm doing when I can't be there to tuck you in at night. Come see what happens when our beepers drag us from your birthday party. Come and see what your little girl is doing. Watch me drag a body from a burning house. Papa, can you see me through the smoke, Papa?" Safe over there, you can watch us over here. This one's fun; there's no terror attached to this one. Pull out the popcorn and get ready for the show.

It didn't go up all at once. Too much to learn, too many volunteers needing to try different things. Start the fire, let them put it out. Start it again, save the body from the smoke, put it out, and start it again. Hours of practice before they let the mammoth eat his meal.

"Thank you for letting us do this." He grinned from ear to ear, not more than seventeen years old. "I felt the heat creep up my arms under my coat. I've never felt anything like that before. I know what to expect. I know how to deal with the feeling; I know not to panic if it should happen again. Thank you for donating your house to us!"

We the spectators were there for the show

While we sipped our beer and ate our sandwiches, we forgot this wasn't actually for our entertainment.

The situation is different according to perspective.

When all that could be learned was taught, they lit it one last time. Safe from the sidelines, we watched vinyl siding change stages, melting into black billows of smoke as it vanished. *Poof!* Gone.

Plumes of smoke rose.

Flames reached up after it, as if to say, "Don't you dare leave without me."

And the firefighters manned the hoses, soaking down the slope of evergreens on the west side.

Contain the beast.

Let it feast.

But if you let it out, it will devour all.

"Watch the west side, people!"

It burned big and hot, and as the flames abated, so too did the spectators. The big show was done. Those of us who were left were the ones contemplating the power of fire.

***

"It means the building is currently sitting half on our land and half on Crown land." I said to the fire chief over the phone shortly after we'd left Surveyor's office!

"What do you want to do, Glenda?" he asked.

"Burn it down," I said

And now, two days later, I was looking down into the fiery belly of the beast.

***

Legs. Legs perched in heels. Red open-toed. Pink pumps. The classic black stiletto. Jewellery on the end of the foot made to stretch the leg longer, leaner, oiled and bronzed purposefully to reflect light. Bar light, stage light, the Orange No. 5 neon light glowing from behind the bar dances on the skin, teasing the eye. Look up. It can't be helped—it's like a magnet. The legs lead, like a map to the curves of the buttocks, soft but firm, topped with a tattoo tramp stamp. Flowers? A symbol? Date of birth? All you want to do is run your fingers across the ink, savouring the skin, wishing you could taste it. Up to the breast, over the breast to the neck, up the neck and stopping at the frosted pink lipstick to breathe, the desire to devour suppressed.

One long silver earring drapes down, weaving itself through her blonde mane. A rhinestone necklace drips against her chest, between her breast and heels.

This is what she wears. This is all she wears as she dances for you.

The dark-haired one in the red toe heels runs her own finger down her own thigh while looking you in the eye, a playful grin, a little wink, inviting you to want her. The red head wraps one leg around a pole, the emerald green heel flashes, catching your eye. "Look this way," it beckons. "Look at me; you want me."

The blonde wearing the rhinestone necklace looks past you, eyes glazed. It startles you. A little shiver moves your soul. Just for a moment you think about the human being behind the eyes. The brunette notices your shift and bends before you; red lips part into a white smile. She licks her red gloss and beckons your eye, "Look at me; I'm the entertainment. I'm your dream. Look at me; we'll have fun tonight. Tonight's going to be a good night; tonight's going to be a good, good night."

And the music thumps.

As the girls dance.

I catch Nelson's eye, and he's grinning stupidly.

Lit up.

I grin back.

Our bodies unconsciously moving to the thump of the beat.

We're caught up in the crowd.

Hands up, one pounding the air, the other wrapped around a long neck with a lime shoved in it.

Looking at each other, smiling. Air clinking bottles.

Singing like we're rock stars.

Nelson's nineteenth birthday.

Twelve hours later I was stepping over Nelson's body, sprawled out on the floor in the Chairman's Suite at the Fairmont Pacific.

"Well? Did you get any?" I asked my son.

"If I did, I don't remember," he murmured, peering up at me with one partially-opened eye. "Why am I on the floor?" he asked as his hands moved up to rip the glow necklaces off his body.

The driver reported that Nelson and his friends flipped back and forth from the Roxy to Orange Number

5 all night long before finally bringing the party back to the suite. Doug and I had been there for hours already, leaving the "kids" to have their fun.

That was a hell of a party, though. Some chick was setting up lines on the coffee table, and Nelson said, "You'd better get that shit outta here. Dad's not going to like it."

The chick, dressed in cheap leather boots with dripping makeup, laughed sardonically. Just as she was putting her head down for a snort, the table got dark. It was a shadow. Doug's shadow. He leaned over and blew that shit right off the table like it was a birthday candle. The chick was pissed and started in on him. "Who the fuck do you think you are? Don't you know who owns that stuff?"

Doug picked her up, took her outside, and hung her over the patio rail.

"You're going to take that shit and your shit friends right out of here, do you understand?" he said evenly, with no emotion. After he set her back down, she complied hastily.

I love a good party but was never into drugs. They just fuck you up.

***

"It's too hot to do anything with it yet," I messaged Asbestos Monty.

We had met Asbestos Monty a couple of months before when he did the asbestos testing on the building. One conversation led to the next, and we were talking about demolishing the building and/or burning it down and the clean up after.

"My company does that," he said. "We can handle it all very professionally for you, Glenda. You won't have to worry about a thing."

So we hired his company to clean up after the fire.

All of the ash would be put in a bin, and I would arrange and pay by the weight for this. Before the fire, the bin company informed me that nothing hot could go in the bins, so it would be best to wait a week, let the embers cool, then load. I informed Asbestos Monty in an email.

"You tell the bin company not to worry, Glenda. This is all being handled professionally; you don't need to worry. I'll have an excavator there the day before the fire to knock down the shed in the back. During the fire, the excavator will push the shed into the fire and we'll leave the excavator there to remove the cement, steel, and ash. We have a plan."

Every plan is great until it doesn't go according to plan.

The fire was on Sunday,

Monday it was still glowing hot. Knowing Asbestos Monty's excavator was there waiting to clean the embers, I contacted the fire chief and asked if the fire department would mind going and hosing it down a little more. He sent a truck that night.

Then it rained, and it didn't stop raining. *Well, this is good*, I thought. *Let's get those ashes cold so we can take them away!* Only the rain didn't cool the ash; it was still glowing on Tuesday. In an effort to cool the embers, I again asked the fire chief if his team could go once more to the site and hose it down. "Absolutely," he responded.

Rain was coming down in buckets on Wednesday. Asbestos Monty messaged me and told me they were up at the property, good to go.

"Fantastic!" came my reply. Off to work I went.

71

Later that afternoon, my phone rang. "Hi, Glenda. It's just too wet; we won't be able to complete today. You're not in a rush, though; maybe in a month or so we'll come back and finish up. Everything is getting stuck."

"Ahh, that would be a problem," I said as my mind sorted out his words. "You are right, we don't even know if we can build. We're still waiting on the drill results, so let's go ahead and postpone the clean-up until then."

After I hung up, I called the bin company to inform them of our decision.

"Glenda, he would have just kept loading those bins if we let him," came the voice from the other end.

"Excuse me?" I replied. "Please explain."

"Our guy got there to take away the first bin. It was overweight, but he took it anyway, sloppy wet ash. When he got to the landfill he got stuck. We had to hire a big tow to pull him out. We refused to send another bin up. Monty demanded that we had to. We refused. He would have just kept loading those bins, and you'd be paying for water weight, so we just refused to take any more bins up there."

"Hmmmmm. Ahhhhh … thank you for saving me thousands and thousands of dollars," I said.

"No problem," the voice replied. "It's too wet, and you were just paying for water."

Funny how one side of a story can sound so reasonable until you hear a different side. Funny how you think you're helping a situation by ordering more water to be put on embers, not realizing that you're creating another problem. Funny how days of rain can change a plan. Funny how the one who professed to handle things professionally would have had no problem ringing up my bill in order to meet his timeline. Funny how the professional disregarded our direction to wait a week to clean up the embers. Funny how a week later I received a bill from him demanding payment in full. Funny how I wrote him back and said the rate quoted was for a job that was complete, and this job wasn't complete.

After a few emails back and forth, we agreed that I would pay less. We agreed to part ways, and we agreed that I would find someone else to clean up the fire.

My only problem …

I'm a server in a pub.

I have a property filled with cement and steel and ash.

And I haven't a clue what to do about it.

And Jordan Peterson's voice is whispering in my ear, "Do the difficult thing."

And I'm yelling back, "Hello!!! Do you not see me doing it? Look what it's got me—a property that I don't know if I can build on, and a pile of ash and steel and cement to get rid of. And I don't know what I'm doing. I'm a fricken waitress in a pub! Time to call in the big guns, old Jords. You're great at giving advice, but your follow-through sucks. I'm going to the head honcho!"

And I did what I always do when I don't know what to do …

"Oh Lord God …"

"I Needed You to Buy It"

"Your wallet is in the blue pants. I have your satchel. Your first meeting is at 11:00 a.m., and damn it, eat your oatmeal. I don't care if you wash it down with a fucken screwdriver, just eat it. Hands off the bacon; here's some fruit. It's your anniversary in a month. What do you want me to buy for Jane? Are you joining me for the meeting in Texas or am I doing it alone?"

I sipped my OJ and nibbled on a strawberry. "Do Texas yourself. I'm flying back to the house after this. Christine has a dance recital."

"Ah, okay, I'll rearrange. What time do you want the plane ready?"

"The meeting should be done by 11:00 a.m., so right after."

"Your jacket." She holds it up as I'm walking out the door. "I don't know how you'd survive without me," she said, shaking her head.

"Lyndsay, I wouldn't survive without you," I replied.

Fresh out of Harvard.

My team found her and invited her to be interviewed by me. She was, still is, extremely beautiful. "What if I were to hit on you?" I asked her.

"If you get a sex change, you might have a shot. I don't swing your way." She smiled. I knew we'd get along just fine.

Not even thirty years old, bright and confident. She wanted to practise law; after all, that's why she went to law school. I invited her to visit our offices in the Caymans, stay for a weekend, look around get a feel of who we are.

"I've got the jet waiting. Bring a friend if you feel more comfortable."

That was twenty years ago.

Man can get along without a wife, but take his assistant away and it's a bloody war.

Anyway, we had the Bellagio, MGM, and New York, New York. I was in my element. Making money. I absorbed myself into everything casino. Jane stayed in Calgary with the kids, and I would fly in and out. Christine's dance recitals, Nelson's hockey games. Even though I was back as much as possible, Jane did the brunt of the parenting. She was good at it.

I walked through the door one day and said, "So what's up for this weekend?" Jane looked at me as she was towing a small suitcase behind her and said, "I don't know about you guys, but I'm having a girls' weekend. You entertain the kids; see you later."

Three pairs of eyes looked expectantly up at me.

"Let's go," I said.

The next day I was standing in a lineup with Robbie tugging my hand when my cell phone rang.

"Hello?" I said.

"It's a Small World" piped in from an invisible speaker, entwining its tune with the giggles of delight and crying, tired tantrums erupting from children everywhere.

"What is all that noise?" Jane said from the other end. "Where are you?"

"Well, you told me to entertain the kids, so I'm doing that. We're in Disneyland."

"Daryl! I told you to entertain them!" Jane hollered.

"I am! They're having a great time!" I smiled into the phone just as Christine and Nelson ran up to join me and Robbie in the line. "We gotta go, Jane; it's our turn to go up Magic Mountain."

***

"You can build right on the lot line," read the email from Gail at the regional district. "We can reduce the 1.5-metre setback and apply for a variance that will allow that."

"Well, it's something," I said after I read the email out to Haney. "It gives us five extra feet with the one foot we already have, so we can have a 6 X 120 foot house. I wonder if Pinterest has any ideas for this." I smiled sarcastically and hung another ornament on the Christmas tree. We had taken our house off the market as we waited on results of the drilling.

Limbo is a strange state to be in.

Limbo is a strange state for me to be in. I suppose I've always been moving forward to something, planning the next thing, reaching around the next corner. It's a natural progression I think, or maybe an expected one, starting off from the time we were children when we couldn't wait to be an adult and, after arriving, having children of our own, anticipating the moments of their next milestone.

This limbo was new for me. It wasn't comfortable.

The days had a dark cloud hovering over them.

The Christmas season was less magical, the lights less twinkly, the food tasteless. It was difficult not to get sucked into a season of sorrow, to assume the worst, to plan ahead.

I would remind myself that it's material stuff, not our health. How much more dreadful would it be if our limbo was brought on by a cancer diagnosis? That ... that is something to be devastated over. This? This is a blip of unexpected circumstance, but at least we had each other, and we had our health.

It was thoughts like this that kept me grateful.

Though I forced myself to be positive, the wait was excruciating

And so very long.

***

The years of going back and forth took its toll on our marriage. One day I got into town and Jane was sitting in the kitchen drinking a glass of wine. She looked at me and said, "What are we doing, Daryl?"

"I don't know. You're the one who plans the weekends. You tell me what we're doing."

"Not that. I mean what are we really doing? You're living your life, and I'm living mine, but we aren't really together. Maybe we really should just think about ending it."

I was shocked, but not really shocked. I was actually too busy thinking about how to make money, and that's where my energy was going. She was right. We really had grown apart.

"I've never cheated on you, you know," I said as I grabbed a wine glass from the cupboard. Picking up the wine, I poured myself a generous portion as she held her almost-empty one toward me for a refill.

"Ha," she laughed. "Your mistress is money; you don't have time for anything else." We clinked our glasses and took a sip.

She was right.

Rihanna was in Vegas demanding we do this and this and that for her, and all I thought was, *I don't care how beautiful you are, or how well you can sing, or how much of a princess you want to act like, as long as you make me money, I'm happy to have you here.* But that's it. I'm sure there were a lot of times I missed trying to be seduced by beautiful people because I didn't see that. I saw a dollar sign, not a face.

The divorce was very amicable. There was one hiccup when Jane's girlfriend counselled Jane on how she was entitled to half and should demand to be bought out of Crystal Castle for half its worth.

"I can do that if you want, Jane," I replied, "but maybe instead of listening to your fucking girlfriend, who knows nothing, you might want to call up our lawyers and have them explain to you what that looks like."

Jane did that and then declined on demanding to be bought out. She made a wise decision. Crystal Castle is now over a trillion dollar company, with her name on half of everything.

Just last week she called me and we reminisced over the phone

"How did this even happen?" she said. "It's like a snowball—it just grows and grows and grows."

"I don't even know how it happened, Jane," I replied in equal astonishment. "I just kept buying things I thought sounded like they'd make money, and they did."

Jane takes care of the philanthropy department. I think her latest endeavour is saving the elephants in

Africa or something like that. I don't know. I let her worry about that; I just make the money, so she can give it away. I trust her with my life.

I bought a house down the street from our family home. The kids would run back and forth when I was in town. It worked quite well.

In the Cayman, Jane designed the big house, but she prefers to use the small house beside it. She and the kids go down there quite a lot still.

***

"It's not a no."

The words once again whispered themselves into the depth of my soul.

Hmmmm, I thought, *do I dare believe them? Do I hope in them? And what happens if they're just the wish of my mind and not that of an encouraging Creator?*

The mind has the ability to manipulate. In hunger, in desire, the mind will murmur and mutter. Yet there have been those times in the depth of my angst when something has whispered the exact thing I've needed to hear to keep me moving on.

I'd been at this crossroad before; anyone who has any faith in a power stronger than themselves will be met at this crossroad. *Whose voice do I trust, the one whispering hope in my ear, or the other one seeping in skepticism and cynicism coming from who knows where?*

"You don't know the plans I have for you," played in my mind.

"Maybe I just don't really want to know the plans you have for me," I said back.

I closed my eyes.

"Oh God, I'm so tired. Could you not have warned me?"

"If I'd warned you, Glenda, what would you have done?"

"I would have investigated. I would have paid for the site survey before we bought the property. We did all the other tests, for sure if I had had just one person say 'It's a good idea to get the site survey' I would have done it."

"And then what, Glenda? You would have gotten the survey, and then what?"

"And then I would have known where the lot lines were."

"And then what, Glenda?"

"And I wouldn't have bought the property," I replied. Silence followed.

And then, like a crack of light pushing the dark storm clouds aside, the voice whispered, "But I needed you to buy that property."

"Excuse me, what?"

I was startled

"You wouldn't have bought the property, and I needed you to buy that property."

"Why?"

Silence

It was the strangest conversation. I left my eyes closed as I contemplated it.

Where did that thought bounce from? If from myself, how on earth would I just think something so weird like that right out of the blue? If from God ... well, then what? Do I worry about the situation we're in? Okay, let me think about that for a minute. Set aside the thought that it was your own mind. What if it was God telling you he has a purpose you know nothing about but was weirdly entwined with you buying this property? What about that? How exactly do you feel about the whole thing then, Glenda?"

After reflecting on that as a possible reality, I responded, "I wouldn't worry about the lot lines and the results, and I wouldn't worry about where we would live, or what the future would look like. I wouldn't even worry about why God needed us to purchase the property. I wouldn't worry about why he needed it. I would let it go and let it do what it intended."

Maybe that in itself has nothing to do with Haney and I; maybe we're the catalyst for something we will never in our lifetime see. Maybe it's something that will be in our children's lives or their children's lives, and maybe it has nothing to do with any of us but for someone else at a different time. Who the heck knows? But in this blip of time, our buying this property was needed.

Is the purpose important? No.

Will it make everything okay? Not necessarily; in fact, it could be exceedingly shitty for us.

Is it strange that you desire to live on a mountain looking at a mountain, and God needs you to do exactly what you desire? Well, yes, that's weird. Impossible? No, God is strangely amazing like that. It's not at all impossible that he lays desires in us that benefit other bits and pieces within the deep cogs of his creation.

Okay, how do you feel about everything now? Hmmmm, strangely rather good. It's all good. I kind of like being a piece of a puzzle, even if I don't know exactly what kind of piece it is.

It's like a good book, Glenda. You don't know the ending, so just enjoy the story where it is. Be excited to turn each page to see what happens next. Don't dread it—look forward to it.

With that, I flipped the last page and closed the chapter of "Why me?"

I put the book down and I smiled.

Time for coffee!

Gotham

Tucked below towers of glass, flanked by the Hudson's Bay building on the left and the old St. Regis Hotel on the right, sits Max Downing's Art Deco. Eighty-nine years she's been watching over Seymour Street like a Tamara de Lempicka portrait with a quellazaire in hand.

Today her simple signage taps you on the shoulder: "Didn't you always wonder about me?" it breathes in a hushed tone.

The black and glass double door beckons: "Didn't you want to enter? Surely you want to enter, darling; you simply must enter."

They open wide, invitation extended, and as your foot crosses the threshold,

Gotham welcomes you.

On a tan, tufted leather banquette at the far end of the lounge I sat. My girlfriend on the right, her girlfriend on the left, overlooking well-dressed visitors perched on barstools beside tall tops, tipping back Tanqueray and tonic. Holt Renfrew and Harry Rosen nonchalantly sip pinot as they listen to the pianist at the black grand. Breitlings and Cartiers flash. Kelly dog cuffs and double tours place their Hermes clutches on the white linen table tops. All of it whispers, "Let me impress you."

The serving staff smile as they watch Gucci and Hugo Boss surreptitiously drink in the atmosphere. They enjoy this; it's particularly entertaining to watch this.

The moment when eyes expose inner awe. When those who so desire to impress are caught being impressed themselves.

Gotham does that to them.

In the corner, across from us, sitting on leather wingbacks, a male in a black three-piece with the jacket hanging from the chair, label out, is trying too hard to impress his date. The beautiful brunette sips her Merlot as she politely listens to his stories, a hint of boredom evident by her wandering eye. He doesn't notice.

It's a Friday night, the room is humming, we are enjoying the ambiance, our wine, our steaks, our conversation. I excuse myself and head to the men's room. Label Out is there just finishing up as I walk in. He performs the male scan.

"This place isn't for people like you," he concludes out loud after he completes the scan.

"Excuse me?" I respond

"This place isn't for people like you," he repeats as he washes his hands. "This place is too high end for people like you."

His arrogance was dripping.

I was seething.

He opened the door and left.

I stayed a moment longer. I was boiling, searing at his smugness, and I needed to compose myself because I wanted to let loose.

Julie, our server, was at the table when I returned.

"Julie, what is she drinking over there?" I asked, nodding my head toward Label Out's table.

"They're sharing a bottle of Roth," Julie responded.

"What's your priciest bottle of red, Julie?" I asked

"The Chateau Mouton Rothschild Cabernet Blend Pauillac 2005, just over three thousand a bottle, Daryl," she responded.

"Please send a bottle over to that table, but please do me a favour, Julie."

"What's the favour, Daryl?"

"Deliver only one glass with it, for the lady."

"As you wish." Julie smiled.

Five minutes later, Julie was tableside with the bottle. The brunette was noticeably impressed, Label Out slightly confused. As Julie poured the wine into the woman's glass, she heard Label Out say, "I wanted this date to be very special, so I ordered the very best bottle for you."

Not missing a beat, Julie responded, "This bottle was purchased for you by that gentleman at that table." She nodded her head in my direction as she continued to pour.

Briefly befuddled, the brunette's countenance changed from delight to disgust.

After a moment she arose, tucked her clutch under her arm, picked up her glass of wine and the bottle of Chateau Mouton, and walked to our table.

"Would you mind if I joined you? I have a great bottle of wine that needs good company."

It was such a great moment.

One would think Label Out would leave, but he didn't. He sat there all alone in the corner, eating his food and looking both pissed and sullen.

We decided to head to a club afterward, so I had car service bring the car around. Standing on the sidewalk as our car pulled up was Label Out—waiting for his, I supposed. Anyway, just before I slipped into the back seat, I said, "You never know who you're talking to; you don't know who 'people like me' actually are."

Bleating Lambs

Damp, dreary, and dark was the day in January when I opened my laptop and saw a message in my inbox from Emily.

I held my breath. *This is it*, I thought to myself as I hesitated to open it. *Am I ready for the answer?*

"No!"

But I need it.

So I breathed deeply and clicked open.

"The slope is stable!" I could hear the joy in the words. "We can move the retaining wall back, Glenda." Emily continued, "You have space to build on."

As relief washed over me, I could feel the grip of tension release its claws off my limbs. I didn't even realize it was there until it let loose.

"WE CAN BUILD!" I cried out to Haney. "THE SLOPE IS STABLE! WE CAN BUILD!"

And it didn't matter that it was the darkest, dreariest day in Chilliwack. In our house, it was lit up with joy!

We can build. We can breathe. We can end this limbo and move forward.

It's not a no.

***

"Good Scotch." Some people connect over hobbies, others over common experiences. Vincent and I connected over good Scotch. That was until he quit

drinking, but by that time we had already become such great friends.

He loves golf and is always inviting me out. I'm not good at it, but I enjoy the company, so I drive the golf cart and drink beer.

His parents were the ones to pull him from his bed after his wife, Sheryl, left him. If it weren't for his parents, who knows where he'd be today? But they waded through the whiskey bottles, pulled him off the mattress, and plunked him in rehab.

He adored Sheryl, so he did the work to get sober; he does the work to stay sober. They're still together today because he is sober. They are amazing together. I'm happy to call him my friend.

I met him at his work once. We were doing business together, purchasing a golf course. I needed his signature on some paperwork, so I went to see him. He was pacing back and forth and back like the duck on a Duck Hunt game.

"Can I do it? Can I do it? Can I do it?" I heard him mutter.

"Yes, you can do it," I said as I approached him. He turned his head toward me and smiled when he realized who the voice belonged to.

"Daryl, you came!" he exclaimed.

"I can't stay for long. I need you to sign these papers, then I have another meeting I need to get to," I replied.

"Just for a bit, stay just for a bit; it will be great to have you here," he proclaimed.

"Sign them." I held the papers in front of him.

"It's time," a voice came from the dark.

He grabbed the pen I offered him and signed his name. "I gotta go. Man, I sure hope I can pull this off," he whispered as he put on his white top hat. "See you in the front row, Daryl!" he said just as the guitar started: *bum bum ba dum, bum bum ba dum.*

And then his voice parted the thunder. "School's Out" lit the crowd.

I stood in the front row for two more songs and watched my friend perform.

He did it. It was his biggest fear: "Can I be Alice Cooper sober?"

***

"The regional district has given us permission to build right on the lot line, on the east side," I informed Joe in an email.

"Glenda, you won't get any window glazing if you build right on the lot line," he said.

"What?" I replied, confused.

"It's not within building code to have any glazing if you're on the lot line."

I sighed at the dilemma

"So I can't have the mountain view because of the lot line change, and now I can't have the forest view because of the lot line building code? What if we push the house back the 1.5 metres? Can we have windows then?"

"Yes, you can have 7 per cent," he said.

Absorbing the information slowly, he sent an image to help. "If your house is sixty feet deep, you can have two windows."

"So basically, no windows," I concluded.

"Not against the east side."

"I have about forty feet from the lot line to the toe of the slope. I need to have a six-foot-high retaining wall at the toe, and Emily suggested that we build six feet away from the six-foot wall so that if anything rolls down the slope and crashes into the wall, the wall is far enough away from the house. So that leaves me with a thirty-four-foot frontage. Now if I take off the 1.5 metre, that's five feet, and then I can have a house front that is twenty-nine feet. Yes, we can build it very long, twenty-nine feet by sixty. But really, no windows on that foot east side?" I shook my head. "This is really ridiculous."

No mountain view, no forest view. Well, shit.

I sent an email to regional district's Gail: "Good morning, Gail. My house designer just informed me that I won't be able to have any windows on the east side of the property due to the lot line. Is this correct?"

Two days later, her response flashed in my inbox: "Good news, Glenda, the building inspector manager states that because the east side of your property is unbuildable Crown land, you have no limits to the glazing on the east side."

I breathed a sigh of relief and did a little happy dance.

"Joe," I typed into the email, "we have permission from the regional district to have no glazing limits on the east side."

"Do you have that in writing?" came his reply.

"I have it in an email," I respond.

"Let's hope that's good enough," he concluded.

"I'm having a problem envisioning any other house," I continued.

And it was true. I had one house in mind when we bought the property, but the property lines dictated that I couldn't have that design. My mind was stuck in the groove, like a needle on vinyl, not jumping over but bumping back and singing the same two words over and over and over.

"Would you mind driving up to the property? Would you mind seeing beyond what I'm stuck in and help us come up with something?"

***

Silence of the Lambs.

The book's words flickered through my mind as I sat at the Lily Lounge's bar sipping a pint. He was there, sitting quietly by himself, cradling something golden on the rocks. A hundred mirrors on the wall picked up a piece of him. There was no hiding in this room.

He caught my glance and in his distinct British accent said a simple, "Hello."

"Hello," I replied. "It was my favourite book." I smiled and picked up my beer for a sip.

He nodded. "The character was amazing. I had a good time with it. Are you a guest here at the Bellagio?" he asked, swirling his glass.

"I wish," I said. "Alas, I'm a working stiff." I smiled. "What did you enjoy most as that character?" I asked

"Ahhh," he reminisced, "breaking for lunch, keeping my character. Jodie was standing in line waiting for food, and I snuck up beside her and—"

And he did it, the Hannibal Lecter slurp, that intake of breath with the teeth. It's just as creepy sitting at the bar as it was in the movie.

"She didn't like it at all." He grinned after he finished. "She told me that moment was worse than any part we filmed."

Just then Sean, the operations manager of poker, interrupted. "Your meeting is in five minutes, Daryl."

"Just a working stiff?" Anthony Hopkins said with a smirk and a nod.

"Yes, sir." I smiled back. "It was an honour to meet you, Mr. Hopkins."

***

"You have a mosquito on your cheek," I said to Joe as he reached up to whisk it away.

Looking beyond the ashes and debris of the fire, we both were contemplating the different views in front of us. The east side, a deep forest view, the south a rolling mountain view, the west a forest slope view, the north a forest view.

"I mean, everywhere we turn the view is much better than in town. It's just those peaked mountains over there that I wanted, that now I can't have," I said as I pointed southwest. "My next favourite is this east view. But I just can't think of any kind of house that will go there. The house doesn't have to be that big, but we want to invest in windows. We bought the property because we wanted to be in the forest. I want to look at it. And I still need to find someone to clean this up," I said, pointing at the pile of ash.

Joe quietly absorbed, and after a half hour or so he said, "Give me a little time, Glenda. I'm quite certain I can come up with something for you." He jumped into his truck and left just as the rain started.

I glanced at the mound of ash left over from the fire as I opened the door to my Santa Fe while whispering, "Oh Lord, help me get that mess cleaned up."

A Pot of Happy

The three of them were in the back seat, sullen. I had just picked them up. We were headed to the jet, the jet was headed to the Cayman. Christmas in the Cayman and they were in the back seat sulking.

I expected happy chatter. They loved Christmas, and they loved the Caymans. It didn't make sense.

Halfway to the Calgary airport, I pulled over.

"What gives? It's Christmas time, so why are you all so miserable?"

"Mommy's going to be alone for Christmas," Christine whispered. A tear squeezed free, and she brushed it away with the back of her hand.

It was the second year of our divorce, and we were doing the "taking Christmas turns," as done by millions of divorced parents. Last year I kept myself busy at the MGM when Jane had them; this year was my turn.

"What do you mean Mommy is going to be alone for Christmas? Won't she spend it with Grandma and Grandpa?"

Nelson shook his head side to side. "They're going to England this Christmas."

Shit, I thought to myself. *What kind of Christmas are my kids going to have if they're worried about their mom?*

I turned the car around.

"Where are we going?" Christine asked

"I have exactly thirty minutes to go get your mom before the jet is due for take off."

Three children cheered.

I pulled up in the driveway, jumped out of the car, and opened the front door. Jane was nowhere to be seen. I ran upstairs and found her face down on the bed, sobbing uncontrollably.

"Get up and pack a bag," I said. She turned toward my voice, stunned.

"What ... what the?"

"I'm not having our children being miserable over Christmas, so pack a bag and grab your passport. You're coming with us to the Caymans for Christmas."

I've never seen a woman pack so fast in all my life.

That was the last time we ever tried to do Christmas apart. Every year we just did it together. People thought we were nuts; they could never understand how we could still be friends, and we couldn't understand why they thought we had to hate each other.

***

"Rye and Coke?" I asked as John and Trish slipped into booth 6.

Trish stands five-foot-four and is size nothing. John is taller and is size jollier than Trish. Both are wearing their fluorescent orange work wear.

A nod of agreement from each and off I went to make their drinks.

It was 11:00 a.m., but in their world it was the end of the work day. They were relaxing with a drink, sharing some nachos before going home.

Today they were looking over real estate pictures, and this caught my attention. The day was unseasonably slow.

Mark was content in the corner with his carafe, and both Dougs were out on a job.

"What are you looking to buy?" I asked them as I put their drinks in front of them.

"Something with a space for all of our equipment would be nice," John said.

"Out of town," Trish added.

"Way out of town," John agreed.

I smiled. I understood.

"The property we're looking at would be perfect for you, but hands off." I grinned. "It's up in the mountain surrounded by trees, and no view of any person anywhere."

The conversation was held before I knew what a pistol butt tree was or how a site survey could change my world.

"What do you two do for work anyway?" I asked.

The couple had been coming into Corky's for a couple of years a couple of times a month. They were unassuming, save the early rye drinking and the above average tips they would leave. They kept to themselves, talked quietly to themselves, never complained. They were actually perfect customers.

"We seal cracks in asphalt," John replied.

"And in the winter, we plow snow," Trish added. Their fluorescent attire matched their profession.

"So what are you going to buy?" I pressed.

"We're just looking; we're always looking," Trish said.

"Me too. I always have my face in the real estate here. I'll keep my eyes open for you too." I smiled. "Hopefully I'm done looking for myself, but if we get this place, man oh man, there's a lot of cleaning up to do. The previous owner was a pack rat; there's junk under grass, piles of tires, old car parts. It's going to take forever to clean it up, but it will be so worth the energy." I grinned.

"Well, Glenda," John said, "if you get the place, let us know. We have one of those big garbage bins. We can come and put it up on your property and you can fill it up."

"Just no drywall," Trish added.

"That would be amazing," I replied, "and something I might just take you up on. I'll rent it from you."

"Before you bring our bill, can you just add that old guy's tab to ours?" John pointed to old Ike, who was sitting alone mouthing an old argument to himself. He did that sometimes, got lost in his mind in the past. Occasionally he would shout, forgetting he was living in the today.

"But don't tell him we bought it," John whispered covertly.

"Done." I smiled.

***

We needed gas, so I pulled into a little gas station in some backward redneck town in Texas. Lynn and I were taking a road trip in the Lamborghini. We would have been better off in a rusted 4x4, I tell you. I was inside paying for the gas, and one of those four wheels, decked out with roll bars and a gun rack, pulled up beside my car. Lynn was sitting quietly in the passenger seat, minding her own business. Two dusty cowboy wanna-bes jumped from their ride and started in on Lynn. "Latino, you have no business here, go back from where you came from," they hissed as they ran their fingers along the curves of my car.

You don't realize how racist some people are until they drive up to you. God, I hate that.

I closed the door to the gas station behind me. The dingle of the bell caught the rednecks' attention, and they whipped their eyes in my direction.

"Get the fuck away from my car," I said as a matter of fact.

The one in blue plaid and with big teeth sneered at me. "Who the fuck are you? Gringo with the Latino?" He snickered.

Lynn was looking more than a little uncomfortable; her eyes darted from him, to me, and back again. She remained silent.

"It doesn't matter who the fuck I am. It matters that I know your fucking boss, so you best get your eyes off my girlfriend and your fingers off my ride or you'll have trouble hunting you down in an hour."

Number two's eyes flickered when I mentioned their boss, and I sensed a moment of apprehension. It's the same with all those assholes—big mouths to match their big hats, but push back a little and they're like terrified little weasels. These two were exactly that. They jumped back in their dusty 4x4 and took off.

We decided to detour out of Texas. Lynn didn't need any more of that shit.

You'd think racism would be over in this day and age, but it's not. For the most part, we have no problems, but sometimes … ugh.

Lynn was beautiful. Dark, long hair, Latin hips, and that Colombian confidence Colombian women have. Like Gloria on *Modern Family*. Just like that. It was amazing; she spoke just like that.

Do you remember the Bavaria Beer commercials? She was the model, the one in the red bathing suit. Simply stunning. She was doing a shoot for something in the Caymans and was at the Warf. God, that place was amazing for beautiful women. I don't even know how I got that first date. I must have said something she liked. And a temper—that woman had a temper. I remember one day we were on the boat. We were disagreeing about something, I can't even remember what, but she let loose with a string of Latin I didn't understand but assumed she was telling the crew I was a son of a donkey and needed to die. Then she jumped right off the boat and started swimming.

The captain looked at me, and I looked back at him. What should we do? Let her swim to shore? Could she make it? Try and retrieve her? I had the captain cut the motors, and I watched her swim for a while. She didn't get far. When she was treading water for a rest, I said, "Here's a life preserver. I suggest you grab it, because there's a shark over there." I pointed twenty feet past her head.

The look on her face was amazing. She grabbed the preserver and we pulled her up. The crew tossed out a rope ladder, and she climbed back into the boat.

She was too tired to care that I'd lied about the shark.

We dated for three years and would still be together, but she wanted children, and I was quite adamant that I was done. She broke it off with me, married a nice guy, and got her children. They live in North Vancouver now. I bumped into her a couple of months ago, at Joey's on Burrard of all places. She's started a clothing line, bathing suits. She's looking well.

***

"I think it's time to put the house back on the market," Haney said at the end of January. "I don't like paying the interest-only payment on the property. I want to just sell the house and pay it off."

"I get your point," I replied, "but I don't have such a problem with that. The mortgage on our house is at the point where everything we're paying is going straight to the principle. It's like we were fifteen years ago, with the interest we're paying on the property, only we own some property and we own the house."

These are the conversations husbands and wives have. Differing opinions, neither bad, just different comfort levels.

I contacted Mary-anne and Trey, our realtors, and asked about the climate.

"Let's wait until the first week in March," Mary-anne suggested, "then open with gusto for the spring selling season."

"When it sells, are you able to help us find a place to rent that allows our old cat and dog?" I asked.

"Trey does a lot of property management. I'm sure he won't have any trouble finding a place for you while you build," Mary-anne assured.

***

I got in late. I didn't have time to change. I don't dress the part. I wear what I like, and I like shorts and flip flops. My staff gives me grief, but I don't care. But I understand their point in Monte Carlo. In Monte Carlo I try to wear something other than my shorts and flip flops, but it was late, and I really didn't even think about changing.

I took the elevator up to the high stakes poker room, and just as I got off, I was jumped by a couple of gorillas in black suits. One of them was on the radio, and the

other had a tight grip on my wrist, which he had planted in a lock behind my back.

To the one on the radio I said, "Could you just tell security to tell Ronaldo you have Daryl in an arm lock."

"We're so sorry, Mr. Schmidtt," they apologized when Ronaldo arrived. "We had no idea."

I didn't mind. They did their job well.

I did get a kick out of the look on their faces when Ronaldo informed them I was their boss. Priceless.

***

"He did what?" John asked in surprise as I told him my story of Asbestos Monty.

Trish sipped on her rye and Coke, listening intently.

"He really wanted me to pay him in full for a job he didn't complete," I reiterated.

"I hate shady people," John said.

"Right!" I agreed. "That's why I just can't do business with him anymore. I don't trust him. So now we have a big mess of ash and cement to clean up. Know anybody?" I smiled.

"Why don't we just do it ourselves?" suggested John. "We can bring the Kabota up, and the garbage bin. We can rent a hammer and hammer the cement into bits, and put the ash in the bin and haul it away."

"I can pay you! I'd rather give you the money than that shady Asbestos Monty!"

"Hey, Glenda, can I get a beer over here?" hollered Doug from the bar.

"Duty calls." I smiled and left the table.

That's interesting, I thought, *look at that, help to clean up the mess. Look at how God answers prayers with people in your path.*

***

She was just a little bit of nothing, runt of the litter. I can't even say she was the last one picked for the team. She was the only one to pick, her siblings gone long before I came to the farm.

"You need to go to the farm and pick up the puppy," Jane said over the phone.

"We're getting a puppy?" I replied. "Look, Jane, I'm just getting on the plane now. Can we talk about the puppy when I get there? I'll be landing at about 5:00 p.m. What time is Nelson's game? Can you pick me up directly from the airport? We can just go straight to the game; we'll talk about the puppy in the car."

I had spent the last two days sorting out a problem in Belize. It was the early days, and we were at the start of building the infrastructure to support the casinos. Tourists didn't like driving through poverty, so we were working with the officials to clean it up, but the officials were still learning how we did business. We had to weed out the ones who worked by bribe. It was a very slow process. I left Lyndsay to finish up so I could be back in Calgary for the weekend.

The plane landed and Jane was at the airport holding a parka, jeans and boots and shaking her head.

"Fuck that's cold," I said, shivering

It was a balmy -24 and I was in shorts and flip flops.

She was always good at thinking ahead. She knew exactly what I'd be wearing and what I was walking into.

"The puppy is already paid for," she said as she directed the car onto the Deerfoot Trail. "After the game, I'm headed out for the weekend with my friends. I need you to go get her; they're expecting you tomorrow."

And that was how I was forced to meet Winnie.

I could feel her shudder every few minutes as she tried to bury herself deeper into my lap for the drive home, this little ball of fur with black eyes. A golden lab. Picked for her ability to be a great family pet. "Good with children" read the tag, if a tag existed.

I let her sleep in my bed.

Winnie seemed surprised that she would have to share our bed with Jane. That was the look on her little puppy face, anyway, the day Jane arrived back home.

The kids thought Winnie was their dog, but the truth was, she was mine. She would travel with me. I even had a passport for her.

I dug my hands deeply into the fur of her neck and nuzzled her with my face. I pulled back and inspected the gray fur around her black eyes. My heart was heaving inside of my chest. Jane told me to take her for a last walk, and she would take Winnie to the vet so that Winnie's last time with me would be good. She couldn't walk far. Everything was failing on her. Fourteen years we travelled together, and this last day had me—nose to her nose, breathing her in deeply, wordlessly saying goodbye.

There are times when I'm near a dog and at that smell, I'm transported back to that moment.

Sometimes I think I might like another dog, then I remember that day and I change my mind.

***

"Angle the tip toward the edge," John yelled up at me, as if I had full command of the Kubota, as if I had done this before, as if smashing concrete with this thing called a hammer was as familiar to me as changing a keg.

And there he was, that Jordan Peterson whispering again: "Don't be afraid to do the difficult things. Try things you've never tried; be okay with being uncomfortable."

And so I was sitting on a Kabota hammering cement, all of which was new to me, all of which was intimidating. Bit by bit I was pounding cement footings out of the ground.

Haney and I both took our turns. He liked it better than I did, so I went back up to the fire and sat with John and Trish. We bonded over beer, occasionally yelling over to Haney that he'd missed a spot.

It was our new fun thing to do, sit by the fire by the creek drinking beer. I bought a portable canopy especially for this, so we could sit out in the rain, by the fire, drinking beer.

And it was a good thing I did.

It was pouring.

Torrents of rain poured on us.

It took a few weekends.

We found interesting things. Treasures, Trish called them, bits of things collected by humans buried under ash, bits of things done by humans that seemed weird, like part of the concrete footings was strengthened not by rebar but by iron chains, metal bars, and a car axle. A car axle stuck deep into a concrete wall. We were amazed.

We hammered and chiseled the iron away from the cement and we loaded that cement into the garbage bin, some by machine, a lot by hand.

We became intimate with that fire pit of ash.

We found a new friendship in John and Trish.

And God snickers. "Ha, Glenda, you asked to have that cleaned up. Did you think I'd just hand that to you without a little bit of work? So you did the little bit of work. Was that so hard? No, not at all so hard. And what did you get? You got a cleaned mess *and* you got new friends, cause that's how I roll!"

***

She was working. I never went to watch her work. I often went in just to sit at the bar. Her name was Denise, and she was a stripper. I dated a few strippers; I didn't care what they did for a living. We were headed to Calgary to spend some time with the kids. Denise got in touch with Blondies and set up a couple of weeks of shows. When she told me, I laughed.

"Why are you laughing?"

"You'll see," I smiled.

Denise wasn't a two-bit stripper; her show was pretty spectacular. Blondies was smart to hire her. We arrived at the venue in the early afternoon so Denise could unload her gear, then we headed to my house. I was going to have dinner with the kids. Denise was going to dance her first show.

I decided it would be wise to have the car waiting outside of Blondies for about 9:00 p.m. Denise's show was scheduled for that time, and right on cue, at about 9:10 p.m., there she was, storming out the door pushing some gear in front of her, and pulling a suitcase behind her. She saw me standing at the car holding the back door open for her.

"What the hell is that?" she screamed at me. "Who the fuck thinks it's okay to throw coins at you when you're on stage?"

"Alberta," I replied. "You strip in Blondies and they throw loonies and toonies at you. Welcome to Alberta." I laughed.

With that, she ended her stripping career in Canada. We also ended our relationship

The next evening, Denise and I took Christine and her boyfriend out for dinner. Christine was chattering away about her grad that had taken place in June. Denise was reminiscing about her own grad with Christine. As I sipped my beer, I asked, "When did you graduate, Denise?"

"Oh, two years ago." She smiled.

Weeeellll!

It just never felt right between us after that dinner.

I knew she was younger, but I didn't know she was that young.

Christine and I have a new rule. I can only date women who are at least ten years older than her. That was just a little too weird.

***

"The property is clean," I wrote in my email to the regional district. "Ready for Inspection."

We needed the inspection so we could clear the notice on the title. This was an invisible huge step in the whole process.

Clear the notice on title.

Get the development permit.

Get the building permit.

Get building.

A week later we received the news: we passed inspection.

Only those who wait for inspections know the feeling when they are passed without complication. I'd found a pot of happy. If someone asked how it felt when you signed the papers to get the notice off title, that would be my response. A little bit of work, a little bit of frustration for a tremendous feeling of accomplishment, and the feeling of being happy.

I live in a world of expected instant satisfaction :D

Whispers of "You must be happy to be satisfied" have youth seeking to be happy. The interesting thing is that it's backwards. Being satisfied makes you happy. And satisfaction comes after completing something that has been difficult to do.

Sometimes I think we have an epidemic of depression in our Western youth partly because they seek happiness, and when they can't find it and don't feel it, it leads to confusion and despair.

Superman didn't become Superman because he wore a cape and tights. Nope, he's Superman because he conquered shit.

Put your head down and do something you don't want to do; at the end of that rainbow, you'll find a pot of happy.

Damn Fine Wine

Softly and so very gently, I ran my finger over her leather. I closed my eyes and breathed deeply.

She was sleek.

She was black.

She was exquisite.

Some moments you just know you will want to remember forever. Some moments are worth lingering over. Some moments, like a Cohiba and Cognac, you just want to savour. I was there doing that. There was absolutely no rush.

I had been anticipating that moment for two years, and while I kept myself busy with other things, she was often on my mind.

I desired from the first moment I saw her.

All men desired her.

She did that.

The desire for her couldn't be met instantaneously; this was part of her allure.

Now that she was in front of me, under my fingertips, I was exhaling the wait, inhaling the exordium.

Her name is Chiron.

Crafted by Bugatti.

The finest in my collection.

***

"Why the hell is everyone buying toilet paper?"

Haney and I said the same thing at the same time.

"You should have seen the aisle, Glenda—no toilet paper, no tissue paper, no paper towels. People were lined up with their shopping carts brimming, but not just one cart, two and three!" Haney shook his head, amazed at what he'd just witnessed at the grocery store.

It was the beginning of March, we had just re-listed our house, and I was at home getting it ready for viewings.

"The toilet paper thing just doesn't make sense," I reasoned. "I mean, worst case scenario, take old tshirts, rip them up, wipe and wash; it's hardly something to panic about."

There was a knock at the door.

"We're here to see the house," said the suit on the verandah.

"Excuse me?" I said. The realtor had a young couple peeking out from behind him, looking slightly uncomfortable. "Sorry, we weren't expecting you, but come on in."

I opened the door widley. "Please ignore us and do your thing. If you have any questions, feel free to ask."

For ten days it was like this. People showing up randomly, appointments made and canceled at the last minute, more appointments, so many viewings, and then … it stopped.

And all the world went silent.

***

They were touring the Casino de Monte Carlo. I mean, what high school student doesn't want to see the James Bond casino while in Monaco? Robbie tried to tuck himself under his ball cap, he tried to hide himself under his backpack, he kept to himself, stood behind

his peers in the line in the lobby, staring intently at the toes of his Vans. None of it worked.

It was his grad year Senior trip and they were touring Europe. Raising your children middle class means they get to do all the things middle class. The European Senior class trip was one of them, only he didn't realize they'd actually be touring this casino. He figured he could fake it, that he could just blend in with the group. He would have succeeded too if Ronaldo hadn't happened to be right in the lobby speaking with the concierge at the very moment Robbie's group entered.

Robbie walked right in front of him. Ronaldo clapped him on the back as he exclaimed, "Robbie! I haven't seen you in such a long time! Are you here with your dad? I didn't hear he was coming." He glanced around as if to expect me within eye distance of my son.

Robbie shook his head no, and his buddies in front of him turned around to witness the interaction.

"I'm here with my high school," he said quietly, trying desperately to find a rock to crawl under.

"Well," Ronaldo proclaimed, "it was good to see you. Tell your dad I say hello, but I'll be calling him soon anyway. I have a few things I need to go over with him."

Robbie nodded his head, happy to have this unexpected meeting be done.

He had a bunch of people with a bunch of questions on the bus. Robbie's a quiet kid who doesn't enjoy the spotlight. He left those who wondered about it to wonder about it, and briefly gave an overview to his close buddies, who already were in the know of some fun facts of the Schmidtt family.

***

We were serving green beer and practising our shamrocks in the foam of the Guinness we poured as the bass thumped the Irish Rovers' "Must Have Been a party." People wearing oversized green shamrock hats, "Kiss me I'm Irish" pins, and "Pinch Me and I'll Punch You" t-shirts were slowly strolling in. We see them once a year.

The regulars followed, scowling at the strangers sitting in their seats. They sip their green beer as they get over the offense.

All could be caught tapping their toe to the tune.

St. Patrick's Day at Corky's.

Normally busy.

Normally exciting.

Normally fun.

There was a different feel in the air this day.

There was no St. Patrick's Day crowd. There were St. Patrick's Day couples.

The crowd was at home.

The crowd was cowering.

Media of all kind blasting terrifying news: "COVID is in Canada."

By 8:00 p.m. we closed the pub down. Two days later, the government officially forced us to close our doors.

The pub, now empty, sat with a cooler full of kegs for a party that didn't happen. We froze the food we could, throwing out the rest that would rot. Our hearts heavy with anticipation of the unknown.

Tony, the owner, handed me my last pay cheque, along with my record of employment

> "Three weeks, Glenda, I think three weeks. We shut down for three weeks like China and it will all go away," Tony said, more to himself than to me. Tony's Chinese;

he follows their news. I'm hoping he knows something more than I do.

***

"Why would you even ask us to pay you anything? You're rich! Why wouldn't you just give us your old house?" my brother Michael's wife said when I sold them our house in Calgary.

I have a problem with people like this, people who think I owe them something because I have money and they don't. I gave them a great deal on the house and carried the mortgage interest free. It's just never enough. Everyone thinks they're entitled to more, even though they don't work for it. Michael is like his wife, and he's a cop, which makes things worse. Cops just think there's something special about them. It just makes my skin crawl. Michael was Momma's boy; she loved him best. We don't get along.

***

COVID hovered. King's "The Stand" tapped at the back of my mind. *Tap, tap, tap.* I drove to the property, leaving the ominous air of town. I checked the rear view expecting to see Trash Can Man saunter down the sidewalk with a jerry can in hand, following me. "Bumpty, bumpty, bump, Glenda, bumpty, bumpty, bump."

Streets were deserted. Every traffic light was green. "Sorry We're Closed" signs dangled on shop doors.

Petey slept in the back seat. "Well, if the world goes nuts, Petey, we'll camp on the property. Lots of freshwater and fish up there." Petey looked up and yawned. No fear in him.

"You don't know how to fish, Glenda," whispered Trash Can Man.

Fuck. I shivered.

"I can bloody well learn," I whispered back

It was all unnerving.

Haney had taken me to the sports store on the weekend. I wanted an archery set, and he was buying it for my birthday. He wanted me to pick, only there were no archery sets, and the men at the counter wiping sweat off their brows could only answer "sold out" to every inquiry of "I need ammunition."

"Why are people buying ammunition?" I asked.

"To protect their stuff," they said.

Mr. King leaned in, cupped his hand to my ear, and whispered, "She looks like the type that might freak out. It's something in the eyes, Frannie. It says if you shoot my sacred cows, I'll shoot yours."

Fiction is a hell of a lot more comfortable living in a book.

***

He tied his tie on the high collared shirt, stretched his neck first to the left, then to the right. "Parfait," he mumbled in perfect French, underpinned to his thick German accent.

"Quand vous êtes prêt, monsieur. When you are ready, sir," the butler said, lowering his head in respect and waving his right arm toward the door. "The carriage is waiting."

Baron James de Rothschild nodded his head in understanding, slipping his arm through his coat. It was the middle of August, a little warm still for a coat, but this was business, and business required a certain form.

The month before, he and Betty had travelled through Bordeaux, a bit of a vacation in their very busy lives. The Baron, fond of red wine, was eager to see the vineyards in Pauillac. He was mixing a bit of personal pleasure with business. In the process of purchasing the estate of Ignace-Joseph Vanlerberghe, this vineyard was included. He was fond of the notion of owning it.

Today he was signing the final papers. Next month he would go to Château Lafite to run his fingers over the grapes, over the vines. A little bit of him touching that which would create the wine and would touch the lips of others.

He didn't know that he would live only to see this one harvest.

Baron James de Rothschild died in November.

The vine held between the fingers of Rothschild as he inspected the grape of his only harvest yielded another harvest in 1869. Bottles of Château Lafite 1869 lived in wine cellars throughout Europe. Some were consumed, others were hidden away, saved for a special occasion, some plundered in war and hidden.

One bottle survived all.

Purchased from a Southby's auction for 1.8 million.

I was on my boat, sitting at a table on deck, the bottle in front of me. I was looking at it, contemplating all of the years it travelled to be here: 150 years in front of me. It was a monumental thought. Grapes from 150 years ago, in this bottle.

"Are you going to open it, Daryl?" asked the captain.

I stared at it.

It stared at me.

"Yup," I replied.

And I opened it.

And I drank it.

And it was the best damn wine I'd ever had in my life.

Trailer Trash

By the third week of the COVID shutdown, we were adjusting. King stopped whispering in my ear, and the *Red Dawn* sequel was put on hold. Toilet paper sat on supermarket shelves again, and realtors resumed showings in our house.

Every day I drove to the property, puttered, and prayed.

Every weekend Haney and I picked up a little of this, raked a little of that, drank a little of this, ate a little of that. Today we were burning a little of this and a little of that.

"We should buy a fifth wheel like Ann and Donny have and just live in that while we build," Haney suggested as he blew on his jalapeno and cheese smokie.

Ann, my older sister, my paradox person. Where cynicism and finding fun things to do meet. That is the paradox, and it lives in Ann. If you're looking for something fun to do, talk to Ann; if it involves good food, that will include Donny. It's a beautiful match.

Some people have vacation homes in Hawaii, others timeshares in Mexico; these two have a couple of fifth wheels parked near a man-made lake, surrounded by other trailers that house people from other parts of the province who love to build fires and roast meat. It's a spectacular place to visit.

"I think I don't want to live in a fifth wheel with you!" I exclaimed, laughing. "You're big, and you hurt me; you don't mean to hurt me, but you do. You bang into me in this house! You're constantly stepping on my feet! You aren't dainty, you know. I can't even begin to imagine living with you in a trailer!"

Haney shrugged his shoulders and washed his smokie down with a Bud Light.

***

They were the last to arrive. The younger dressed in a cute denim mini skirt dragging her pink suitcase behind her. Her mother was also dressed in a mini skirt, topped with a tight white tank top, standing on legs tucked into purple heels, strappy heels, ones that wrap around the ankle heels. Her body was dotted with tattoos. Her face was dotted with freckles still visible under a thick layer of foundation that squeezed itself into the fine lines above her upper lip. Black eyeliner ringed her eyes. They were blue. Twenty years ago, they were probably vibrant blue; today they were worn out and ridden-hard blue.

"I'm not quite sure I feel that Tiffy will be safe on this trip," said the mother. She bent forward to adjust Tiffy's suitcase, exposing her cleavage; straightening up, she directed her black-rimmed eyes to me. She continued, "I think I'd feel better if I came along as a chaperon."

It was Christine's fourteenth birthday, and we were at the airport getting ready to board the jet for a weekend in Vegas. Tiffy, looking like she wanted to disappear inside of her pink suitcase, chose instead to anxiously hop from her left foot to her right and back again.

"I can assure you that will be completely unnecessary. The girls will be completely safe; we have a team of security arranged especially for them," I replied.

"I don't know," the mother continued. "I think you'd all feel better if I came along." She gave me a little grin, backed up with a wink.

I should have been shocked, but nothing shocks me anymore.

Ignoring her implications, I continued. "Tiffy will be fine, but if you're that uncomfortable with the idea of her joining us, she's welcome to stay behind."

Tiffy turned red and was holding back tears.

"I wouldn't want to ruin her weekend; she's been talking about this trip for a week. Are you sure the plane is safe? None of us have ever been on a private jet before. Are they safe?"

I tried very hard not to roll my eyes, but it was difficult.

"I assure you it is exceedingly safe."

"I think I'd feel better about that if I came inside to have a look," she pressed.

"That will be completely unnecessary," I continued. "Again, if you have any difficulty with this trip, you are absolutely free to take Tiffy home with you; your comfort with her wellbeing is important."

"I couldn't do that to Tiffy," she said, dejected with the knowledge that she would not be joining us on our Vegas weekend.

She gave Tiffy a hug. Tiffy, relieved, hugged her back. Pulling that pink suitcase behind her, she followed Christine down the tarmac without looking back.

***

"It's beautiful!" both exclaimed together at the exact moment.

"How are we going to afford to build that?" came the second exclamation, again at the exact moment.

Haney and I do that frequently.

Sometimes it's unnerving.

Sometimes it's just damn funny.

The computer screen was flashing our new house in front of us, and we were in awe. Joe had jumped inside our minds and pulled out this house. How he did it, I don't know.

Not very wide, the house itself was twenty feet wide with a very narrow breezeway attaching a single car garage with a guest suite on top. Shed-roof style, skillion, one slope, peaked on the east side. Sweeping back sixty feet, the entire length of the east side had windows—long, lean windows with transoms on top to fool the eye into thinking the windows were even longer. From the inside, the living room was up front, looking back to the New York style loft I had envisioned. This loft bumped half of the house into a two-storey. It was a hint of west coast architecture mixed into contemporary with a nod to mid-century. It wasn't big, under sixteen hundred square feet sitting on an unfinished walkout basement. Perfect for the two of us. Perfect for my daughters and their families when they visited from Germany. Perfect for when Haney's sons wanted to come, perfect for entertaining, but most of all, perfect for looking out at the nature all around us, which is why we fell in love with the property.

"Wow," we both sighed.

Okay, we might not be able to afford exactly this, but what a start to start from.

The task at hand was bringing this beautiful creation into something we could afford.

***

"Come with me for a drive," Mike said.

"Oh, I think it's better if we talk right here." I smiled as I responded. It's Vegas. He's a Gambino. I've seen those movies, and going for drives never ends well.

Mike smirked at my response. "I'm not going to clip ya, but you do need to explain these numbers to me."

It was still in the early days of Vegas; running things legitimately had the "family" wondering where some of their usual cuts were going.

I don't feel fear. I never have. But on this occasion, I was concerned. I wasn't sure how the family would respond. Were they patient enough to wait, or did they want to part ways?

In the end, they were a very patient family. And I became a part of it, sort of.

A daughter's wedding in New York and I was dancing with another daughter. It was a slow dance, and quite naturally my hands rested on her lower back. As we danced, my hands moved down a little; she had a beautiful ass. In a blink, Tony was tapping me on the shoulder. He pointed at Mike. Mike was scowling at me.

I turned to the lovely lady and said, "Thank you for the dance." And I walked away.

Everyone is good with a Gambino if you know your spot.

I knew my spot.

I was looking in.

I wasn't Italian. I would never be in. I was okay with that.

Sold

He laid out the plans before the city planners in Chilliwack. "Every house would be three-story, with gingerbread siding. Victorian scrolls will be the ornamental accents, and Norman Rockwell will drink sweet tea on the verandahs."

Rich ran his fingers through his hair. It was going white, and it was a little long, Richard Gere long. He needed a cut, but he was too busy.

He loved running his construction company. It was exhilarating, challenging, and exhausting. Every single day. Today was no different. It was 1990 something—one year blends into another after a while.

By the year 2001, the final phase was finished. The house on Bedford Parkway was sold. The new owner painted the door bright pink. Four years later, they sold Bedford Parkway, and the front door was painted white.

The newly married couple needed a big, affordable house for the comings and goings of their five children. Not quite the Brady Bunch, he had the three boys, but she had only two girls. Eventually they added an orange cat named Oliver, and family dogs. By 2019 all of the children were gone; some were married, others went to live in Alberta.

The front door was painted teal; the colour brightened up the tired door. A year after the front door was painted, Bedford Parkway had another sold sign on it.

It was June. We had no idea where we were going to live.

***

"Dad, I want you to meet Matt."

"Matt?"

Didn't I just hold newborn you in my trapper?

Didn't I just attend another dance recital?

Didn't I just follow you everywhere in Vegas via the eye in the sky when you were down for your girls' weekend?

When did you grow up, and how did that happen so fast?

These were the things I thought of saying. Instead, I said, "I'm at the Cathouse shooting pool, killing time till the plane is ready. Bring him in."

The Cathouse, the strip club tucked between the MCC Thrift store and Part Source Autoparts, 32nd St., NE Calgary.

I blinked once and my tiny Christine became a mother.

I blinked twice and I was watching her and Cathouse Matt get married.

She didn't want a big wedding. The baby wasn't even a year old, and she just wanted to get married. And so she did, very quietly—a little too quietly for my standard.

There was a carnival in town. I hired some of them to set up on the street outside of the small venue Christine had selected for her small reception. Nothing terribly big: a few rides, some food trucks, that kind of thing. A mini carnival, if you will. The guests were peeking out of the venue: blinking lights, carnival music, the smell of corn dogs and cotton candy caught their curiosity. And then out came Christine and her new husband.

"Dad! What have you done?"

I just smiled

"This is just so absolutely perfect."

And it was. It was perfect for her.

I had to get back to Vegas—business, you know—so I hugged and kissed my tiny dancer. I left them there to ride the rides and eat their corn dogs all night long.

***

He looked tired. The sun had crept into the lines on his face. Rugged. Weathered. A pellicle of dry dust covered him. He was in the middle of it today.

"Rough day at the office?" I asked, setting his pint of lager on the table in front of him.

"Ech, nothing more unusual than yesterday." He picked up his pint for the first draw.

"Ahhh, that's good," he said as the first swallow went down.

"Richard, I can't thank you enough for being there to answer all my questions as they arise, and being willing to do that. Not all people would. I did use the company you recommended to do the site survey. They were great; thanks for the recommendation."

"Oh hey, how did the drilling go?" he asked.

"Ah, I haven't seen you in a while! It went well. We can build; the slope is stable!" I smiled broadly.

"Ha!" His blue eyes lit up. "See, I told you these things seem to have a way of working out. I've had forty years of obstacles. It's not a matter of things not working out; it's a matter of how do we make this work. Sometimes a bit of time, others a bit of money. I don't think there has been one situation where we haven't been able to find some kind of solution. I'm not surprised you found a solution."

"Anyway, thanks again for your wisdom. This pint's on me today—actually, two. You have another one coming," I declared with a grin.

"Thanks, Glenda, you didn't have to do that. Really, I don't mind at all."

"You're right, I didn't have to, but neither do you have to answer all my questions, but you do. And I'm grateful."

"How's the sale of your house coming along?" Richard took another long draw on his beer.

"Oh, it's sold!" I exclaimed. "The subjects were removed last week. I don't know where we're moving, but at least it's sold."

"Fantastic, another obstacle off your plate," he said. "I forget, did you tell me where your house was, the one you just sold?"

"It's on the other side of town, near Promontory, on Bedford Parkway," I said.

"Ha!" He laughed and ran his hand through his white hair. "That was one of my developments."

Tiny Homes, Big Songs

It's over two hundred feet and made by Benetti. Not the largest boat we own, but every Friday afternoon all employees of Crystal Castle and their spouses and children are welcome to use it. It has loungers, a bit of a pool, and all the water toys you could want: jet skis, water skis, wakeboards, and tubes.

When I'm in the Cayman I join in. I enjoy watching them use it, but mainly it's for the team to use. I have other boats if I want to take them out. Four other boats. One is in Monte Carlo, two are in the Caribbean, and one is at Coal Harbour in Vancouver. The one in Vancouver is my favourite, probably because it was my first.

It took me up to through Haida Gwaii a while back. We dropped anchor and took the small boat to the shore of some random beach. It was like stepping back into time. Nature was untouched. I saw plants I didn't know exist, and the animal life and ocean life were teaming. It was really like stepping into another world, untouched, before humans existed. As I was thinking that, I saw a really old totem pole, and then I was amazed that man had been here, and as I was thinking that, I looked up, and there in front of me, a half dozen Indians came out from the forest. They weren't happy we were there. I had no idea this beach was theirs. It took a while, but eventually they believed we weren't a threat. Then they began to tell me about their history, and that of the totem pole.

I can't wait to take Tina up there. I think she'll really like them; they are so peaceful.

***

"When do you think you'll build?" Taylor, my youngest daughter, asked over video chat.

"Beats the hell out of me," I responded laughing.

"Where are you going in the meantime?" she asked.

"Beats the hell out of me," I answered

Zeke and Abbie were doing twirls in the background, anxiously waiting for Mama to get off the phone. It's hard to be patient when you're four years old. These two grandchildren of mine were no different. Ezekiel was four. Abbie trailed behind him—in age by two years, and also in daily events. Where Zeke is, there is Abbie, a step or two behind.

"Hey, Zeke," I called out through the phone over his mom's shoulder. He came closer as his mom handed him the phone. "Zeke, why don't you go and draw Grandma's new house? You design it the way you think it should be," I suggested.

"Mom!" I could hear Taylor's voice before I saw her face return to the screen as she reclaimed her phone from the hands of her four-year-old brother. "Zeke already had a dream and is pretty insistent that you're living in a tiny home."

"Hahaha, a tiny home? I don't think so; they're very cute but a little small for me. But if you want to design me a tiny home, I'll be happy to look at it."

We continued to chat while Zeke, in red crayon, drew my new house.

A perfectly little tiny house.

***

It was an old Tudor house, gated, with "No Parking" signs. And still the stupid people parked in front of the gate. And not only that, but the stupid people asked if they could walk through our yard to get to the beach. I'd be standing on our back patio barbecuing something, and there they were, waving their skinny little tourist arms: "Excuse me, would you mind if we just cut through your yard? Our car is parked right in front of your gate."

That was our house in Crescent Beach.

I think Jane sold it a few years ago, but boy did we love that house. Well, Jane loved the house. She'd spent hours having it remodeled, keeping the original historical aspects intact. I loved the beach. The kids loved the beach.

None of us liked the stupid people.

Who does that? Asks to walk through your yard because you're too fucking lazy to walk thirty feet around to the beach.

***

The creek was babbling—not in a slow, babble way but in a "I got a little business going on in here" kind of way.

Maybe this wasn't the best spot for the new fire ring area. It looked pretty all set up by the creek, but it was loud. And over here, I saw a snake or two.

"Move me into nature!" I proclaim. "Oh … there are snakes and bugs here!"

At first it was a little shocking. My inner instinct of snake revulsion was in high gear. For half a minute I considered collecting them all and relocating them so our land could be snake-free. We gathered five of them and put them at the bottom of a garbage can to hold them for the day. When our work day was done, we drove them down to another creek far, far away.

At the end of the day, I bravely looked inside the garbage can.

To see one snake is a little repugnant, but to see five wrapped around each other, I was expecting to recoil in horror. Only as I looked inside, a little guy raised its head and looked at me.

I could see fear in its eyes.

And then it reminded me of our dogs when they were puppies.

I became a little less disgusted.

I researched garter snakes that night and decided that they are pretty good for our environment. And I've decided to come to terms with living with them. They still creep me out a little, but I'm getting better. I saw the first one of the season a bit ago, and instead of that inner "eeewwww" I normally felt, I actually said, "Oh hey, you're out now, and you're pretty little. Don't be scared. Just do your thing, and I'll do mine."

My thing is moving my firepit away from where they like to play. And they play on the bank of the creek.

I was sitting in the new spot, testing it out. It seemed flat enough. I still got a view of the mountain and was far enough away that the creek didn't overpower conversation. "This might just do," I contemplated, and I sipped my beer.

And I let my mind wander.

And I let my mind dream.

This place does that to you. It shuts out the world and allows you to think.

Today I thought, *What would it look like if we bought an RV and put it up here and lived in it?*

"What the hell did you just think, Glenda? You thought, *What would it look like if—*"

"Ya, I know that's what I thought. Shhhhhushhh."

But it was too late. The thought was there, and I was contemplating it.

***

"How about we meet at the Drunken Tiger," Alice said. "I'll bring Sheryl. She hasn't seen you in such a long time, she'll be ecstatic!"

I was in Meza, just for the night. I took a chance and called up Alice to see if he was free. Now we were reminiscing over a plate of bulgogi fries: Alice sipping on a soda, Sheryl on a sweet tea, and me on a soju bomb. We were waiting on a plate of fire corn cheese, spicy pork belly, and corn cheese hot enough to burn your face off, Alice assured me. He understood my deep love for heat.

A bit of Americana mixed in with Korea, evident not only in the food but in the decor. Dark walls with emblems of fish and a tiger tucked between TVs and corrugated steel panels. Basic tables, basic chairs look over a basic stage. Someone was on stage. Someone was singing Neil Diamond's "Sweet Caroline," and the small crowd banged their beer bottle bottoms on the "ba ba bas."

It was a karaoke bar.

"I'm going up," Alice threatened.

Sheryl and I rolled our eyes at him

"I'm going to do it," he repeated.

"Go ahead." We laughed

Three soju bombs later, I was listening to Sheryl telling me about Mesa's School of Rock. Alice had disappeared to the men's room. Someone in the background was doing a superb job of butchering Journey's "Don't Stop Believing."

Alice was grinning when he came back to the table. "I'm going to do it." And with that, he breezed right by our table and landed on the stage.

The tin Karaoke music started, and he started singing "No More Mister Nice Guy."

He was singing his heart out, and Sheryl and I were giggling.

And he sang the second part with gusto.

And the third part with fervour.

When he was done, he was sweating. He came back to the table and took a long sip of his soda.

"Not bad," came a voice from the table beside us. "Not bad, but you sure ain't no Alice Cooper," the voice said.

Uncomfortable

It was the big picture window that sold us.

I don't know exactly the moment I decided in my mind that living in an RV would work. I think it was when I was sitting by that fire. I think it was when I entertained the thought that I started figuring out how we could make it work.

Solar power?

Rainwater collection?

Portable septic tank?

Outhouse?

I mean, other people lived that way; other people live in worse conditions. A lot of people live in RVs, so why can't we?

It would solve the finding a rental problem. It would solve finding a rental that allowed our cat and dog. We would save money in rent. So as the thought took hold and moved us forward, forward we went. Forward we went with it.

It only took a week of RV shopping before we found the one with the big picture window. We bought it.

Within a week, we had all aspects figured out, from storage to water to power to septic. And John and Trish hauled it up to the property and taught us how all things RV worked, and this night we sat on the sofa in front of the big picture window.

We had no clue what we were doing.

***

We were at the strip club. Yes, I know Robbie was only eighteen. I told him, "Keep a low profile. Don't do anything that makes you stand out; just enjoy the drinks and the night."

It was a father and son weekend. Robbie isn't as outgoing as Nelson. He's just shy, and I thought bringing him here would be fun for him. His face flushed red, neon-open-sign red, when the first dancer came out. I bought him a tequila with a beer chaser. "Robbie, it's all good. Relax," I said. Down went the shot, down went the beer, faster than John Pinette on a free fall waterslide. I ordered another. "Slow down," I instructed.

Robbie, tall but barely shaving, took a little sip from the second beer. He stood out trying not to stand out. I could only shake my head.

An old friend of mine came to our table, and Robbie excused himself. I guess the alcohol had just kicked in. He moved closer to the stage and ordered another shot.

Time got away from us, as happens when reminiscing with friends. I hadn't seen Robbie in a while, and that's exactly what I said. "I haven't seen Robbie for a while. Where the heck is he?"

Joe was laughing. "He's over there, doing the worm on the floor."

Tell your kid not to be conspicuous when he's eighteen in a nineteen-plus establishment and there he goes and does the worm.

***

It was August.

We were learning how to live in a fifth wheel.

The plans for the house were slowly coming along.

The development permit was in place.

The government allowed us to reopen the pub after the first wave of COVID had subsided.

And Jordan Peterson whispers on: *"be okay with being uncomfortable."*

We opened the door to the pub and had customers return. Happy to get out again, happy to have tapped beer again, happy to meet with their friends again. For the most part, this was the initial reaction. As the COVID restrictions were laid on the pub, forcing us to make sure our customers followed a list of Don'ts, they became less happy. They were not okay with being uncomfortable. They let you know they were not okay with being uncomfortable. They demanded you hear them as they reacted to being uncomfortable.

We had the customer COVID police, who looked over their shoulders to make sure everyone was following all the rules all the time, and if there was a tiny infraction, they were eager to bring it to your attention and demanded you deal with the offender swiftly and sternly.

We had the wanderers, who didn't comprehend that "staying seated" meant staying seated. So we were their constant reminders.

We had the cussers. They didn't mind telling us to fuck off when we reminded them of the rules. I suppose we were the closest thing to the health authority.

We walked around with a cloth and sanitizer, washing up after every table left and listening to the new customers arrive as they inspected the tables and chairs and held their fingers up in the shape of a cross when anyone sneezed.

We were dealing with staff shortages due to possible COVID exposure. Perhaps some were real, but largely these "exposures" resembled hangovers.

We were facing supply issues.

And we had visits from inspectors. All kinds of inspectors. All the time.

And while the media ranted and raved and sang accolades for our health care workers, we, the rest of the working world, were seen sitting on our barstools at the end of our shifts, trembling, beaten, worn, mumbling incoherent words into our beers, holding back our deep desire to throw copies of "Twelve Rules for Life" at these miserable creatures, if only for the sheer pleasure whacking them in the head with something.

***

"Ach." He shook his head. "How is that possible?"

The words were spoken in English but with such a thick German accent it was hard to tell.

"Dad," I replied, "I tell you it's true."

"That's just crazy, unglaublich!"

"It's true, it's true." I laughed at his astonishment.

We were in the Lobby Bar at the MGM having a pint before we continued the rest of the tour. My parents had flown in for the weekend. My dad had just watched the bartender pour four shots of Jager.

"But it's for digestion," he insisted.

I sipped my beer and smiled as I watched him come to terms with this assault.

"It's for after dinner," he continued.

"That might be so," I agreed, "but in Vegas, we charge $5 a shot because people like the way it makes them feel."

The bartender poured three more shots.

"Verruckt! Just crazy," he muttered. "Jagermeister as shots, just nuts."

***

"Are you still at the pub?" the email read.

"Yes," I responded.

"Is it okay if I drop off the plans there?" he asked.

"Absolutely, Joe!"

I closed my laptop, and a wave of excitement shuddered through me.

This is it! The house plans are ready!

***

All of the kids have trust funds. On their sixteenth birthdays, they all got to pick the car they wanted, and we bought it for them. But they had to insure it and they had to pay for the gas. The cost of insurance changed a few minds about what they really wanted.

Their trust funds would periodically pay out, on certain birthdays, as they went to college or university, and when they graduated with anything more than basket weaving. We didn't direct what we thought they should do. we wanted them to pick what they desired to do.

Christine is in oil and gas now. Nelson's company scouts places to put up cell phone towers, and Robbie went to film school and wants to be a filmmaker. He runs all over the globe checking out production sites.

I've done an extraordinary amount of things in my life, but the only thing I'm truly proud of are those three children.

Six Weeks Isn't So Long

"Morning, Daryl," I said as he walked through the door.

He had become our newest regular over the last few weeks. Whisking in for a pint, maybe two, then disappearing to wherever it was that he came from. He was always alone, always quiet, always polite, and always patient.

Today he picked a booth instead of the Bone.

"Yes, thank you," he replied as he pulled out his cell phone and took his seat simultaneously.

Tina and I had wondered about him, as we do with anyone who starts to regularly appear. Where did he come from? What's his story? We both concluded he must have been in the industry, either pubs or restaurants, as he displayed the generosity of patience when we were busy. The trait stood out like Andre Bocceli at a rodeo.

He was always busy on his phone; he never invited the company of others, nor did he seem to need our company in much the way our other regulars did. The ones who come in because they are lonely and need company. He was easy and a pleasure to serve.

"Geeze, it's chilly here," he said as I placed his pint before him. "I'm from the Caymans; I'm not used to the chill," he continued.

Ah, I thought, *an old surfer dude living on the beach. That would explain his long, light hair.* Out loud I said, "I can imagine it would take some getting used to if you normally live in the warmth."

"It's bugging my arthritis." He smiled. "I might have to have a third pint today."

"I can make that happen." I smiled back in reply and headed back behind the bar.

My phone was flashing: an email in my inbox from Gail.

A week before this moment, I was being kissed "good luck." We were in the parking lot of the regional district office, applying for our building permit. Only one of us could go to the front counter. COVID restrictions were everywhere. I took a shallow breath, unbuckled the seat belt, grabbed my purse and the tube of house plans, got my kiss, and excitedly but with trepidation jumped out of the car, giving Haney a little wave as I turned and headed into the building.

Sign in and fill out the COVID information to take the stairs to the second floor, up to the building department.

The plexiglass shields were new; the "profanity will not be tolerated" signage taped to the counter was not. I kept my distance until I was invited to the front counter. Gail was there to greet me.

"Let's have a look," she said.

I pulled the plans from the tube and unrolled them on the counter.

"Oh, what a different design," she said. Then she inspected the property line and how Joe had designed the home to avoid needing to apply for a variance.

"I'll get a building inspector."

No sooner had she said that when Bryan, an inspector, appeared in front of me, looking at the plans with a quizzical look on his face.

"The windows." He pointed to the plan.

"Yes, aren't they great?" I replied.

"I'm just going to run this back to our building inspector manager." He took the plans and disappeared from our sight.

Gail and I were talking about COVID and the effects on workplaces for only a few minutes before Bryan returned, plans in hand, face flushed.

Why does his face look like that? I thought.

At the same time, he said, "You can't have these windows."

Confused, I could feel the blood drain from my limbs, my feet get cold, and my fingertips start to tingle.

"What do you mean we can't have these windows? I was told by the regional district that we would have no limits to the glazing on the east side."

"The building inspector manager said it's against the building code. You can't have the windows."

"I don't understand. I was specifically told there were no limits. I have an email that said we have no limits—from you, Gail."

Gail turned to Bryan and said the previous building inspector manager had given the permission. "Indeed, we have a new building inspector manager."

To me Gail said, "Let me see what I have in writing, Glenda."

Tears were forming in my eyes. I felt defeated, confused, and angry.

Gail's and Bryan's faces matched each other, a mixture of embarrassment, shock, and the awkward angst in the entire situation.

As quickly as emotions boiled up, I could feel myself ready to melt down.

"We only designed this house because of the permission we got from the regional district. Had we been told we couldn't have the windows, we would have designed a different house." The tears were falling. "I have to go," I said. "I just have to go."

"Let me help you roll up the plans, Glenda," Gail said, quickly taking over where I was fumbling.

I guess this is why they have the "profanity will not be tolerated" signs, only I was in such deep shock I couldn't even form the "f" to start the word.

"Don't do anything until I see what I can find in writing," she said.

I nodded, took my tube of house plans, and left.

Haney was a little shocked over my speedy return.

"What's the worst thing that could possibly happen?" I asked as I threw our house plans in the back seat.

"We can't build?" he replied.

"Okay, second worst thing," I said. "We can still build; we just can't build this house. Apparently we can't have the windows they told us we could have."

"What?" His jaw dropped.

"That's what I said. Apparently they have a new building inspector manager, and he said we can't have them." I covered my face with both hands as I burst into tears.

That was then, this was now.

I opened the flashing email with hope.

"Good morning, Glenda. The building inspector manager suggests we take your building plans to an advisory committee for their review and advice. They normally meet once a month, but due to COVID, their meetings have not been consistent. It should take approximately six weeks. If this is a route you would like to go, please advise and we will do so."

My earlier email from the regional district granting us permission for the windows meant nothing. It couldn't compete with building code. Building code isn't site specific. So while I have vacant land that belongs to the government beside me that can never be built on because of geographical issues, we still have to build our home as if we were in the city next to a building. Our east side windows right on the property line would be detrimental to the building next door in the event of a fire. The fact that no building could be built on the property next door had no bearing.

Building code had us trapped in a rule that made no sense.

Our choices were to wait six weeks in the hope that the advisory committee would review our plans and the location and think like the old building inspector manager and allow our glazing, or redesign at our expense to the tune of about $9,000, eliminating all windows on the east side.

"Send them to the advisory committee; we will wait," I typed and went back to pouring pints. Six weeks isn't so long, is it?

Meeting the Mrs.

It was an unseasonably slow day at the end of October. The Dougs were sitting at Big Round. Big Round was just that—a big, round table. Mark, head down, reading the newspaper spread out before him sat to the right of big Doug, named big Doug to differentiate between little Doug, who was still big but smaller than the big Doug.

The Bone was taken up by the former Chilli Bowl regulars, a group that had wandered in about a year ago when the Chilli Bowl raised their beer prices, and our lone new regular, Daryl, sat in booth 13.

"Hey, Daryl," I said as I put his pint in front of him.

"Hellooo," he cooed

And he did coo, the little lilt at the end of his words. The extension of the vowel, the pitch of his voice combined sounded like a human dove.

"My wife will be joining me in a bit," he stated.

He has a wife? I thought. Out loud I said, "I didn't know you were married; you always come in alone."

"She's just had surgery on her foot and hasn't been able to get around," he replied. "We were flying back and forth from the Caymans for her doctor's appointment in Vancouver. Too many years on her feet working in the kitchen at the prison really killed them. We're quite a pair though, me with my arthritis, her with her bad feet." He took a sip of his lager and snickered. "At least this last surgery seemed to work well with timing. We had come up in March to watch her daughter graduate from culinary school. When we were here, the Caymans closed the country down due to COVID. Non-citizens couldn't get in, so I could get back in. I'm a citizen, but Denise can't because she isn't. I wouldn't be a very good husband if I left her and went back alone now, would I?"

"That would be pretty shitty." I laughed. "I say you made the better decision for your marriage."

"Agreed," he concurred. "We're still pretty newly married, a couple of years now, I think."

"Why is her daughter here?" I asked, trying to place the pieces together in my mind.

"Denise is from Chilliwack," he said. "Her father was military, and his last post was at the base here. They ended up just all settling here. That's why I'm in Chilly Chilliwack instead of back home enjoying nice temperatures and the beach in the Caymans." He gave a mock grimace. "Anyway, she had her surgery and is able to recover here and make all of her appointments without us having to fly back and forth. She could have seen my doctor in the Caymans, but she had all things lined up with the specialists here. It took years to get this far, so she wasn't about to change her treatment people when she was on the cusp of surgery she'd waited so long for. I get that. So we just flew back and forth, no big deal, till COVID anyway.

"There she is now." He looked up and over, catching her eye.

"Hello," I said to the lady who was wheeling up to the booth, her right foot perched on a knee scooter.

Denise looked like she'd spent part of her life starting her days with two cigarettes and a creamy coffee with three sugars, and ending the day sharing a joint and a fifth of whiskey with friends. Her skin was etched with life. She smiled broadly. It was warm and inviting.

"What may I pour for you?" I asked

"I'll have a double Caesar, dirty please," she replied as she tucked herself across from Daryl in the booth.

I left to make her drink, thinking they looked a little odd as a couple. Daryl's features were softer, smooth skin displaying no kind of difficulty or over indulgence. Whatever the attraction between these two, I didn't think it revolved around common lifestyles.

They seemed comfortable enough together. They had their drinks in front of them, and after some brief conversation, they both became engrossed in their phones.

"Glenda," Lee called, "whenever you're ready." His way of asking for a beer, now.

Ice Man

"Ice. Get me a bag of ice," he demanded.

"Excuse me?" I stated from my position behind the bar.

He was dirty, he was missing teeth, he was meth thin, and he was demanding I bring him ice.

"How about you go and come back again tomorrow when you have some manners, and I'll get you a bag of ice then, because you're not getting any from me today," I replied.

His face scowled. "I just want some fucking ice." His voice rose.

"You're not getting ice. Not today. Come back tomorrow when you're a nice human and I'll get you ice then. Morning, Daryl, grab a seat. I'll get your beer in a minute." Daryl had entered the building and was taking a wide berth around Iceman.

"Fucking cunt," Iceman called me loudly.

"Well now, don't bother coming back tomorrow either. I don't serve people who call me names. Goodbye, have a good day." I turned and grabbed a pint glass out of the cooler and started to pour lager into it.

Iceman was livid but he left, dragging a colourful tail of words behind him.

"That was interesting," Daryl said as I placed his pint before him.

I snickered. "Well, as soon as they're telling me to fuck off, I know the visit is almost done. It appears to be the universal exclamation point of their departure."

The Chilli Bowl regulars had had their pints and had left for the day. Daryl had the Bone to himself. "Just this one today, Glenda. I have a meeting at the bank."

"Okay, thanks for letting me know. I would have automatically poured your second."

"I might be in again after the meeting, it depends how it goes. The HSBC over here seems to have a little problem releasing some funds I wired up from the Caymans," he said.

"I hope you get it figured out; it's frustrating when delays happen," I responded.

"Bureaucracy," he said, shaking his head. "It's not even that much money, just a hundred thousand. The bank manager over there seems to have a power thing going on and is delaying its release."

"Why would they do that?" I asked.

"Interest probably. Every day it's not released, their end collects interest on it. It'll be fine," Daryl continued. "If he keeps it up, we'll just get legal to remind him that he can only hold the funds for seven days. It's day ten now; bureaucracy is exhausting."

"Oh, don't even go into bureaucracy with me. You want to hear about bureaucracy? I have a story to tell you."

And for the next ten minutes, I reiterated our experience with our property.

Daryl listened intently. When I finished my story, I expected him to say the same thing everyone else did: "Sue them." But he didn't.

"Hmmm." He stroked his chin thoughtfully. "I suppose you could litigate, but it would eat up a lot of money and time."

"EXACTLY!" I shouted, finally happy to have a kindred spirit in reading the circumstance. "That's what I have to explain to everyone when they tell me we should sue. It's expensive to sue. I'd rather use the money to build our house. Yeah, we don't get the land we thought we bought, but we still get to enjoy it, and we bought the property because it's beautiful. It didn't become less beautiful. Anyway, we should hear in two weeks or so about our house plans, so I can appreciate how your wait feels, Daryl. It's excruciating."

He smiled, gulped the last inch of his pint, picked up his phone, and said, "Well, I hope my wait is done. See you later." And off he went.

Open Up Like a Coconut

"Yes, it went well, thank you for asking," Daryl responded when he came in the next day. "It just brings back memories of how difficult it can be to manoeuvre money in Canada. We had the same kind of issues when I sold Shaftbury. It's like Canadian banks just don't know how to function in the corporate world. We have some big accounts at the HSBC downtown, and that seems to be okay, but come to Chilliwack …" He trailed off, shaking his head, only stopping to take a sip of his beer.

"Wait, Shaftesbury?" I asked "The brewery Shaftesbury?"

Daryl was talking to me in the same manner the Dougs talked about what they ate for dinner yesterday, casually and unremarkably.

"Yes, the brewery," he responded without fanfare.

"That's interesting," I replied after he had shared the story with me. "Did you by any chance have anything to do with restaurants?" I asked.

"Oh yes." he smiled and took a sip of his beer. "That's actually where I got my start, with the first Cactus Club."

"I knew it!" I exclaimed. "I have to tell Tina we were right. We thought you might have had something to do with them. You and Denise are always just super easy, in a way that you understand what's going on kind of way."

"I do for sure understand the behind the scenes." He grinned and took another sip of beer. "There were the Cactus Clubs, the Granville Room, Jezebels and Rocco's in New York, and the Warf and Coconut Joe's in the Caymans. I like Coconut Joe's the best, as it reminds me of the early days with RJ at the Cactus Club."

The day was slow, the other regulars were content. I stood and listened to Daryl unfold his restaurant stories with intrigue and interest, breaking only to pour a wine or a beer for a newcomer, eager to get back to hear the rest of his adventures in our commonality of the service industry.

It was like a little dam had burst and quiet Daryl, for whatever reason—boredom, loneliness, who knew?—chose to open a bit of the door into his life. And I, a sucker for a super story, was so eager to peek behind that door and catch a glimpse of the life in front of me, connected with a life I'd only read about.

At the end of a couple of his stories, I looked at him and said, "You're probably rich, aren't you?"

"I probably am," he replied.

"Have you always been?" I asked.

"Oh hell no." He snickered. "It didn't start that way."

Amy

She tucked the big giraffe stuffy next to the Christmas tree, smiling as she ran her fingers over the new fur. *What a fun gift for the baby*, she thought and then patted her tummy. "Hello in there; you can come out anytime now," she whispered. "I know it won't be fun to have to have your birthday at Christmas, but we are so anxious to meet you!"

Just then another contraction hit. Pretty mild still. From experience she knew that if they went to the hospital now, they'd just be sent right back home. Maybe if it was the first baby, she would have been a little more anxious, a little more eager to head to the hospital, as if being there would somehow make things happen faster, but this little was number three, and she knew the baby would come when it would come. No amount of pacing hospital hallways would help. Besides, it was Christmas Eve. *Nope*, she thought, *let's just stay home as long as possible*.

She thought about the past week. baby had been breech, and the doctor wanted to do an external rotation. They did this kind of thing in the hospital, so that just in case of an emergency, they would be right there to perform a C-section. They were doing an ultrasound and were happy to see that the baby had already flipped on its own.

"Should we do a stress test?" the nurse asked.

"No, not with a heartbeat a strong as this one," the doctor replied. "I'm not concerned at all."

She had geared herself up for this external rotation, and it was exceedingly relieving to know the baby had done it by itself. For a fleeting moment she thought to press for the stress test, but the moment vanished. And here she was a week later, in natural labour brought on by a baby being in the right spot at the right time.

She rubbed her tummy as a contraction finished and then wandered back to the dining room table to resume stuffing the boys' stockings. The phone rang.

"What do you mean the plane was delayed again?" She repeated what her mother had just told her on the other end of the line. "Will they at least make it tonight? Or will they have to wait until tomorrow? Christmas Day? That's super shitty."

Her sister and family were flying in from Alberta for the holiday. They were that headline one only wanted to read about. Today it was them. Stranded at the airport, waiting on flights that keep getting pushed back. What a terrible way to spend Christmas Eve. A twinge of remorse shuddered through her as she hung up the phone. The baby moved a foot. "Ohh, right on the bladder, you stinker." She pushed against her belly to help baby into a more comfortable position. "You're probably another little boy with a kick like that," she whispered.

I guess I really can't worry about the flight now, can I? she thought. *We're a little busy, aren't we?* She smiled. A warm surge of joy filled her.

She started humming along with the Bony M piped through the radio as she resumed filling the boys' stockings.

What a great song; it just sounds so happy, she thought. "We'll have to do some special things with you for your birthday," she whispered to her belly. "It won't be easy for you to have your birthday on Christmas, but I promise, we'll do something super special, just for you, every year.

The rest of Christmas Eve was spent preparing—the boys for Christmas to begin, she and William for this new life to arrive.

At 6:00 a.m. on Christmas Day, her dad had arrived at the house to stay with the boys. It was time to head to the hospital.

Crisp and cold, a fresh layer of snow blanketed the earth, reflecting the warm glow of Christmas lights leading them to the hospital. Bony M started singing over the radio again. A contraction hit.

"OH MY LORD!"

William looked over. "You okay?"

"Not really; just drive," she breathed out.

He did as he was told, getting her safely through the snowy streets to the hospital, parking right up front on arrival.

They walked in just as another contraction hit. Had she not been in so much pain, she would have noticed the staff a little more jovial than usual. It was Christmas morning, which brings a sense of joy even if one has to work. They were headed upstairs to Labour and Delivery when she remembered the car.

"You have to move the car," she said.

"What do you mean I have to move the car?" William asked.

"You can't leave it parked right up front."

"I can't?"

"No!" She laughed as another contraction started.

"Oh, ahh, okay, I'll figure it out after you're settled."

The nurse led them to their room and she got herself settled onto the bed. William ducked out to take care of the car as the nurses started setting up for their usual monitoring.

"Let's see how baby is doing," the nurse said as she placed the doppler transducer on the tummy. She moved it around to the side, then to the other side, then up to the top, and then farther below. Her brow furrowed a little. "Too much eggnog last night," she said. "I'm not getting this right today at all. I can't seem to get that heartbeat. I'm just going to call the OB in to see what he can do."

After another wave of contractions finished, the OB arrived in the room wearing a Santa hat. Giving a soft smile, he picked up the doppler and took up where the nurse had left off.

She gave birth to a baby girl.

She had never held anything so still.

They said she had a perfect knot in her umbilical cord.

They said she had died twelve hours before.

Silent Night.

For all her life.

They named her Amy.

***

It was November 12, eleven years later.

She jumped in her car for the trip to work, cranking the key. The radio blared to life. She turned it down to a more reasonable level, thinking it was funny that at the end of the day had the radio blaring it would be fine, but in the morning, it was obnoxiously loud.

KT was belting, "You're not the one for me."

"I agree! You're not the one for me! I haven't had enough coffee for you!"

She directed the car through the lights past Knight Road as the song finished.

"And we know you've been eagerly awaiting the first Christmas song," the DJ's voice bounced over the radio waves.

She rolled her eyes and put her hand to the dial to turn the station and then froze. Bony M.

They sang about Mary and her boychild, and
the melody brought the memory,
the memory brought the moment,
the moment brought the tears.
She arrived at work just as the song finished.
She turned off the motor and sat in the quiet.
She needed a minute.

No need for anyone to see me like this, she thought.

She pulled her fingers up at the corner of her eyes, wiping the eyeliner that had pooled with the tears into a more presentable position.

"Put on your big girl panties," she said to herself.

She took a deep breath, exhaling sorrow. Gathering herself together, she grabbed her bag and headed inside.

"Hey, Tina," Mark said as she walked past Big Round.

"Hi, Mark," Tina replied with a smile.

"Can you let Glenda know I'm ready for my other wine."

"You bet." On the outside she smiled; on the inside, she sighed.

Walking behind the bar, she tucked away her purse.

"Hey, Glenda, Mark's ready for his wine."

"Really? Oh my God, I was just there!"

She laughed.

"Oh, I have something to tell you!" I proclaimed. "We were right about that guy Daryl! He is in the business, or he was anyway, just as we thought."

"I knew it!" She smiled. "I just knew he had to have been in the industry!"

"Not just this industry," I continued. "We had a long chat the other day; he's owned all kinds of things, and Tina, it appears that he's wealthy, like pretty loaded. What are we going to do about that? We can't tell a single soul, or they'll eat him alive!"

"Oh God, no." She shook her head. "Really? Like loaded?"

"Well, with everything he's told me, ya. Oh, and we were talking about cars. He said he had a Bugatti. I don't even know what that is. Lets' google it."

Tina grabbed her phone. "Ah, sorry, I got to take this. It's Fionn."

Life is like that. Ordinary weaving itself into the extraordinary. Grief mixed with joy.

A year after she kissed Amy goodbye, on the other side of the rainbow, she gave birth to her beautiful baby boy.

They called him Fionn.

Win, Win.

"I understand. If you want in, the opportunity will be available until the end of the month; just let me know."

I overheard Daryl talking into his phone as I put his pint down in front of him.

"Good morning," he said to me, finished with his conversation and laying his phone on the table before him. "Denise will be here in a few minutes. She's at Walmart. She took me there once, and I will never go back. I don't know what she sees in that place. All I know is that every time she's there, she spends two hundred dollars." He smiled and took a sip of his beer. "Two hundred dollars on junk—on junk!" He laughed and grimaced at the same time.

"You know, when we first arrived in Chilliwack, we were looking for a place to live. Denise has a seventeen-year-old cat. Do you know the problems we had finding a place to rent because of that cat? Anyway, eventually Denise found an apartment—1,200 square feet or something like that. I walked in and said, "Nice closet, now show me the rest of it." I don't need fancy, but I do need space, so I got on the Sothebys site and found a four-thousand-square-foot log house on nineteen acres at the top of Promontory. I had my team buy that.

"Daryl, did you get any pleasure buying that house?" I asked.

"No, I just needed a house. A simple need being met."

"Do you like it?" I asked.

"Yes, actually I do. I don't like the drive up there, but the house is great. It has a pool and my hot tub, and a theatre room, and I installed eight TVs there so I can watch all the football games at the same time, and if there's a Calgary Flames game on, I can watch that too." He grinned.

"Denise got more of a kick out of moving up there than I did. Watching her adjust to what is now available to her is fun. She walked through the front door on the first day and just touched everything. It has a chef's kitchen, and she loves to bake. I love to eat it, so that's a win, win."

"I think I would have to agree with you, Daryl. Just walking up and buying a four-million-dollar home could be nice, but I don't think it would be overly fulfilling. I'm really looking forward to building our house, and I anticipate that I'll love it. I imagine a large part of that will come because of the struggles we've had to get it. To simply walk in and own something would be less satisfying."

"Exactly!" Daryl replied. "I remember my credit cards fully loaded when RJ and I were just starting the Cactus Club. I remember the stress of that, and I remember the victory in making it a success. I still shake my head at it all."

"Hey," I asked, "did you ever turn down an opportunity that you wish you hadn't?"

"Oh, quite a few, but the most significant was Starbucks. I had the opportunity to be an early investor with them, but for the life of me I just couldn't wrap my head around people being willing to spend $5 on a cup of coffee. I still kick myself for saying no to that. Every time I see their logo it laughs in my face!"

Daryl glanced down at his phone. "Looks like Denise is finished in Walmart and is on her way. Apparently we're having all of her family up at the house over Christmas."

"Is that a good thing or a bad thing?" I asked.

"It will be good. The house is big enough. Last year they all invited themselves to the Cayman for Christmas."

"They did?"

"Yup, they seem a little bit like that," he continued. "Denise's life is pretty easy now, and they have no problem including themselves in her new life. She had some tension with her stepbrother and sister she'd like to ease, so if her new life lets her do that, then I'm okay with it."

"Do you think they're using her? You?" I asked.

"Oh, point blank, I tell you they are. But if it makes their relationship better, then I have to look at that as a win, win."

"What is this 'win, win' you constantly talk about?" I pressed.

"Most of society wants to simply win, but if you step back and look for the win, win, all endeavours will be more prone to success. For instance, in the early days at the Wharf, we had a problem with theft—bartenders bringing in their own bottles and pocketing the profits. So we upped the wages of the staff by a couple of dollars, and we started a profit share program. Every week our staff were paid a portion of the profits from the sales; this had the staff selling more as well as watching over other staff, ensuring that they weren't pocketing 'their profits.' I tell you, those bottles the bartender once brought in ended when the staff saw their potential profit taken from their own pockets." Daryl smiled. "So it costs us a bit more, but look at the result."

"You are attracting a better-quality staff with the extra dollars per hour plus profit share, and you'd have less turnover rate. Servers from all over would be beating down your door to work for you, and they'd be selling more because the more they sell—"

"They sell more because they earn money on every bit they sell." Daryl finished my sentence.

"So smart!" I said.

"Win, win." Daryl smiled.

"Why doesn't every business run like this?" I asked.

"Greed. The owners want it in their pocket; they don't realize that if they give it back, it makes more. Our whole company runs like this. We always look for the win, win. Ah, there's Denise now." Daryl looked behind me as she wheeled up on her knee board.

***

"Good morning, Gail," I started the email. "It's been six weeks. Have you heard anything back from the advisory committee?"

Within an hour, my inbox flashed:

"Hi, Glenda,

I don't have any news for you, but wanted to let you know that we have not forgotten about your plans.

We anticipate hearing back from the Interpretation Committee for your property by the end of the month. I don't know what the committee will find, but we will be in touch as soon as we can.

Best,

Gail"

The end of the month?! I thought. *That's another two weeks away. That's eight weeks, not six weeks.*

I breathed deeply. The weight of the wait pressed against my soul. I pushed the frustration back, got up, and went back to work.

Even for People Like Me?

They snuck in.

Giggling nervously, occasionally looking back over their shoulders as if expecting someone they didn't really want to see.

They ducked into the booth. The darkest booth they could find. The booth with no overhead light. The booth with no view from the front door, the back door, or really any door in the building. It was perfect for them. A dark, hidden place for their dark, hidden relationship. They think they are fooling us. We pretend they are. They don't know that there were others before them doing the same thing, sitting in the very spot they're sitting now. If you're having an affair, you're sitting there. Booth 5.

Today Daryl was sitting there alone. A quiet place to do business undisturbed.

I placed his pint on the coaster in front of him.

"Just so you're aware, it closes on Friday." I heard him speak into his phone. "Certainly, yes, I understand, you did ask me to let you know. Okay, yup. If I don't hear from you by then, I'll tell them to proceed without you. All right then. Bye."

He hung up his phone, flipped it upside down on the table, then turned to me. "Thank you." He picked up his pint, taking the first draw.

"Sorry, I didn't mean to eavesdrop," I said.

"It's all good," he replied. "Just a family friend deciding if they want in on an opportunity I'm a part of."

"Opportunity?" I asked, leaving it open for him to explain, and he did.

"Yes, it's just a little investment I do with a friend of mine in Seattle, kind of for fun, but it helps him out. His name is Danny. Years ago we met when he was vacationing in the Caymans. We chatted; we had similar interests. He had an idea, and I invested. It worked out, and we still keep in touch. He's a hedge fund manager and branches out to other things when he sees a good opportunity. This one is bridge financing for a company rejuvenating a city block in Portland. They started the project before COVID, then COVID hit, and, well, you know the complications brought on by COVID! Anyway, they needed quick money to finish the project. They approached Danny's company for the financing. Once the project is complete, they then qualify for traditional financing. So Danny's company stepped in, supplying the funds at a higher interest rate over a shorter period of time. Sometimes he contacts me to invest, particularly on the bigger funds. And sometimes it's just for fun, let's see what happens kind of thing. This one I've invested a bit for my grandsons, put in a few thousand, let it roll kind of thing. They have a nice little account they don't know about. Anyway, this person,"—he nodded to his phone—"had mentioned they might like to invest, so I was connecting the two, but it kind of seems like he might be changing his mind."

"Hmmm." I contemplated what Daryl was saying. "He's a family friend, you say?"

"Yes," Daryl replied.

"Well, if he's a friend, then he knows who you are and your success. One would think he'd give you all the money he had to trust you with, considering your past history."

Daryl smiled, shook his head, and sipped his beer. "People are interesting, Glenda. They want something, but when push comes to shove, not many of them are willing to put their money where their mouth is. Most people don't like taking risks, even if it looks really beneficial to them. Just not brave enough I suppose. At the end of the day, it's nothing for me to worry about. He either wants it or he doesn't. It's up to him. I'm just here to help if he chooses to do it."

"Well," I said, "it seems to me like he should trust you if he knows you, but you're right, his choice."

"Sorry, I have to take this call," Daryl said as he picked up his phone. I nodded and went back to the bar.

Weird that his friend wouldn't invest with him, I thought. *I wonder what the friend's like.*

"Glenda, can you turn the TV to golf when you have a second?" Dave asked.

"Yup, Dave, on it," I replied.

***

"Any news on your building plans yet, Glenda?" Tina asked as she shook up a Cosmo.

"Ugg," I moaned, "nothing, just nothing. I'll be living in a fifth wheel forever! Eck, at least I have me my hound dog and a beer." I winked, stepping into the role of *Trailer Park*.

Tina laughed. "Oh, there's Daryl. Do you want him, or do you want me to take him?" she asked.

"I'll take him," I said. "His stories keep my mind out of my own misery." I laughed.

"I've only heard a couple," Tina replied. "Does he have more?"

"Oh Lord, his life is amazing, Tina. I could just listen to him all day long! He's so chill for a super-rich guy. His buddy is Alice Cooper. Did I tell you that? He just casually mentions it, like you'd bring up having drinks with Karen: it happens, we're friends, it's no big deal kind of thing. Have you told anyone about who he is?"

"Oh God, no!" Tina exclaimed. "Are you kidding? People would be crawling over him, and if he didn't buy them drinks, then we would—"

"Uggg, we would be the ones listening to them bitch." I rolled my eyes and we laughed at this fact together. "Though sometimes there's this little bitty bit of me that wants to say, 'Hey, you think your HellCat is awesome, Mark? Well, Daryl has a Bugatti!' Take that, pow, pow pow!"

"I know, right?" Tina laughed. "Silence the braggarts."

***

"Would you mind putting on the Calgary Flames game on the TV?" Daryl asked as I brought his pint.

"Sure. I guess your history is in Calgary; you're allowed to be a fan. My younger sister and her husband are huge fans. I think they have season tickets or something. They're always posting photos when they're there."

"Well, after COVID is done, we'll just fly there and you can post your own photos in the owner's box." Daryl smiled.

"Get out? You own the Flames too?" I responded.

"Almost," he replied. "Nelson and I are working on it. He came to me with the idea, and I'm guiding him along."

"That must be amazing for Nelson, to be able to step into something really big knowing he has you as a consultant." I smiled. "I would be thrilled to go to a game with you, but I'll never post a photo in the owner's box."

I laughed. "I cringe when people do that. I don't want to be one of them.

"Yup, we'll just take the jet and come right back after the game."

"Ha, okay, sure, just jump on a jet like it's a taxi."

"It is a taxi. That's what I use it for, to get me where I need to be and back again. It's really not a big deal."

"I suppose you're right. It's just something else you get used to over time, the extraordinary becoming ordinary."

"Pretty much," Daryl replied.

"You do know Tina and I don't tell people who you are? If you want to tell them, that's up to you, but be warned, they'll be all over you if they knew, so—"

"I really appreciate that, Glenda. I was kind of thinking the other day, 'Whoops, what have I done opening my mouth?'"

"Well, it's all good, we aren't saying anything. You can enjoy your peace here."

"Thank you, it does make a difference. A few years back I was in Whistler for business. I spent my off time at the Cactus Club bar up there. Well, I made the mistake of saying a little too much, and the bartender shared with the other bartender, who shared with the servers, who shared with the customers, and so on and so on and so on. I stopped going because it became uncomfortable. So I do thank you; it's nice to be able to come in here and have a pint like a normal person.

***

Temperatures were beginning to dip and November turned into December.

"On the first day of Christmas the regional district gave to me … a house?" It was the email I sent to Gail.

"Sorry, we still haven't heard anything from the Interpretation Committee, though we anticipate that they will meet fairly soon." Was the reply.

I went on a walk, and the tears squeaked out. I looked up and said, "I just want a house. I just want a house." While my heart ached to move forward, and the frustration continued to be enormous, it was hard to stay in a place of self-pity for long. The mountains were covered in snow, chimneys dotted here and there were puffing plumes of smoke, the rich smell wafted into the crisp air, a rooster crowed, the river, clearer because of the cold, ran icy rapids, snow was gathering on the evergreens that surrounded our property, and not a stick of wind to usher them off. The scene was surreal. A live Christmas card. Living bits of great moments in my life, visual memories congregating here and creating a new one.

"Thank you for letting me live up here," whispered my heart to my God.

***

Daryl was sitting on the first barstool at the Bone, nursing his beer, gently spinning his cell phone on the table top.

"Hey, whatever happened to your friend? Did he decide to invest?" I asked.

"I haven't heard back from him, so I'm assuming he's not going to," he responded.

"I still find it interesting that he wouldn't."

"Me too." Daryl laughed.

"Is this opportunity something only for your friends, or can anyone do it?" I asked.

"Oh, for sure others can do it. If I can help people out that way, I'm happy to do it," came his reply.

"Even other people like me?" I questioned.

"For sure, Glenda. If you want in, we can do that. There's about $1,300 Canadian left available to be used. I'd have to double check with Danny, but I'm quite sure that's the last number I heard."

"So is it possible for me to also invest a little bit for my daughters too then?" I asked.

"Sure," Daryl replied. "We'll just put whatever you want to invest for them in their names. I think Danny said that this turnover was three times the original investment over three months. It does close on Friday, so he'll have to have the money by then."

"How would I get him the money?" I asked.

"You can just give it to me, and I'll forward the same amount from my account I have with him."

"Does it pay out every three months then?" I questioned.

"Yes, every three months," Daryl replied.

"What if I just left the investment in for like a whole year, and had it compound? Am I able to do that?"

"Sure, that's no problem. He'll just keep it turning over for you. I do the same thing for my grandsons. It adds up quite nicely when you do that."

"So could I put in maybe like $500 for myself and maybe $100 for each of my daughters?"

"If that's what you want to do, yes, I'll let Danny know to get your name in."

"Cool. Thanks, Daryl, this will be a fun little surprise for them." I smiled at the thought of giving both Danielle and Taylor a chunk of money in a year, and a few thousand dollars for our future house would be awesome too. "I'll get you the cash tomorrow. I have a little set aside. Will you be in?"

"Absolutely," Daryl responded.

I left to tend a table that had just come in, leaving Daryl to his phone twirling and beer sipping. When I passed his table a while later, he was just getting off his phone.

"I just spoke to Danny. He said that if you leave the investment in for the year, the payout next December would be about $103,000 per $100 invested, plus my doubler."

"Your what?" I asked.

"My doubler. Anytime anyone invests through me, I double it with my money. When their investment comes through, I just get Danny to take my money back before their payout."

"Do you do that with everyone? I can't expect that you would do that with my daughters."

"Glenda, I have the money. I do it to help people out."

"So let me get this straight. I will invest $500 for me, and you will double that to $1,000, then when the payout happens, you get your $500 back?" I asked.

"Exactly."

"And my daughters you will double to $200 and then take $100 back."

"Yes, exactly, that way everyone is helped to the maximum."

"Why do you do that?" I asked.

"Well, people have to be willing to put up their own money. I don't give money away to people for the sake of giving money away. I'd rather help them help themselves. This is a way for me to help people without just giving them money. If you're not willing to invest in yourself, why should I invest in you?"

"Ahhh, that makes a lot of sense. But over $100,000? It just seems too good to be true, Daryl."

"You're right, it does, but I'm here to show you that sometimes it is true."

I tilted my head skeptically as he continued.

"The way it compounds and the future investments he's got lined up in the next nine months, he's quite certain it will be around that. The quarter after this one is set to pay ten times, and it's American and tax-free."

"How is it tax-free?" I asked, absorbing all of the information he was telling me.

"Well, he pays the taxes on it when the turnover is finished, but because you're Canadian, he gets it back. He has all the legal paperwork to give you. If the government questions you, you just send them to him, and his legal department takes care of it."

"Well, it still sounds too good to be true, but I'm a bit of a gambler, so I'll take that chance." I smiled at him.

"You'll see, Glenda, you'll see." He laughed at me.

Earl

The sun was slipping to the west, hues of pink and orange in transparent layers across the sky. The lake was quiet. They had parked their camper, a little fourteen-foot trailer on the beach. She had loosely wrapped solar lights around the awning. They were colourful; they were pineapples. He didn't like them; he wanted the white lights.

"Don't be so rigid; these are fun. Camping is for fun. Camping is for relaxing and having fun, and these lights are fun," she insisted. He relented. They were now sitting by the fire waiting for the dusk to turn to dark, for the pineapples to make their debut.

Chester, their dog, lay sleeping in the sand by their feet—spent. Running up and down the beach, jumping in and out of the water, a dream day. They heard him bark in his sleep and smiled when his paws started to run. He was such a good boy.

"Do you want a beer?" she asked.

"How about we share that bottle of white?" he replied.

"Ohh, great idea. I forgot about that!"

She popped into the trailer for a moment, returning to the fire with the bottle and two wine glasses. "Hold your glass; I'll fill it," she instructed. He did as he was told. When she had finished, she sat in her chair, filled her own glass, and put the bottle in the sand by her feet.

"Cheers," she said.

"Cheers," he replied.

They both took a sip.

They sighed.

"What a great day," they said at the same time, and laughed because they did so.

The pineapples flickered twice, then came to life.

They were fun, he decided. Just like Sharon—bright and fun and full of colourful light.

***

"Glenda, come and see this," he insisted.

"Just a minute. I'll be right there."

His laptop was open on the table before him.

"Look, look at this, it's a picture of our last camping trip."

"It looks like you had a great place to camp," I said as I looked over his shoulder.

"She was a beautiful woman. She died, you know."

"Yes, you told me."

"Our Chester died a year after her."

"Yes, you told me that too."

"It's just so hard," he said.

"I don't think it would be easy," I said. "I'll go get you another glass of beer, Earl."

Randy bought his pint at the bar, walked over, and set it on a table near Earl. He turned to the lotto machine, plugged in his Keno numbers, popped in his money, and hit the "buy" button. His ticket popped out of the slot. He returned to his table, sat down, and took his first sip.

Earl leaned over. "My wife died."

"I know, Earl, you told me."

"Did you want to see the picture of our last camping trip?"

"Of course, Earl."

All on Zero

"Oh, hang on a second. I'll run and grab the cash," I said to Daryl as he walked in the following day.

He nodded as he slipped into his barstool.

"Have you ever read Dostoyevsky's *The Gambler*?" I asked.

"Yes. I'm an avid reader."

"Good, call me granny, 'Put it all on zero for me, will ya.'" I smiled as I slid my envelope of cash into his hand.

Folding the envelope in half, he tucked it into his inner jacket pocket and laughed. "May I have an email address for you? I need to forward that to Danny's office, also the names of your daughters, with their last names. After I forward the information, you'll be contacted by a woman named Tina, so check your inbox."

"Tina?" I asked. "Like our Tina here?"

"Same name, yes. She's Danny's general manager of account services."

"Ah, okay, I will await her email. And Daryl, thank you so much for allowing me to be a part of this. You have no idea how this will affect the lives of my daughters. They have such big dreams. I'm so excited for next December. What a great Christmas gift this will be for them!"

"No problem at all. I spoke with Danny, and he said there's about $1,500 available after your investment, so if you know of anybody else who needs help, let me know. We can get them set up too."

Earl wandered by.

"Please, Earl, you need to sit down," Tina directed him. "We don't make these COVID rules, but you need to keep them for us to stay open."

Earl looked up at the Keno board then back at her and absently nodded in agreement.

"Oh my God, what are we going to do with him? He just wanders. No matter how many times I ask him to sit down, he gets back up again. I'm dying here," Tina vented as she poured a Guinness.

"I don't know if the loneliness is making him lose it or if it's something else. I do know some days are way worse than others. It's really sad that his wife died, but isn't it going on a full year now that he tells us daily?" I said, simultaneously picking up pint glasses from the glasswasher and putting them away in the cooler. Earl walked by again.

"Earl, you're going to have to sit down. The COVID rules say you have to stay seated at your table while you're here," I said.

"Yes, Glenda, I just can't sit for that long."

"I understand, Earl, but in order to be in here, you're going to have to stay seated."

Carl

He brought the cigarette package up to his mouth and drew one out with his teeth. Skillfully he rolled the smoke with his lips to the corner of his mouth. Rob reached over and lit it.

"Tomorrow we head to the ridge." His tone was low; his tone was tired.

They were both dirty; they were both damp. He couldn't remember when he was dry last; it felt like he'd been damp for all his life.

There was a crack.

They froze.

Their eyes got wide.

They held the cigarette smoke in their lungs, not daring to exhale.

VC?

They heard another crack and both heads simultaneously snapped to its direction.

A red-shanked douc was tucked in a bit of bamboo; it blinked twice, pushed out its chin, and bared a toothy grin.

They breathed out their smoke in relief, chuckling under their breath. A damn monkey.

If anything, at least this place had beautiful looking animals.

He took a last drag off his smoke and stomped the butt out. Time to move on.

Their tired eyes scanned steps before them, seeking out trip wires. The Viet Cong made some good ones. They stepped forward.

An hour had passed, and their steps became easier. Physically this terrain wasn't particularly tough, mentally it wasn't because they hadn't met any signs of booby traps.

He cracked a joke.

Rob turned to him and laughed.

At the same moment, the earth gave way and swallowed Rob up.

Rob disappeared from his sight.

He was shocked.

He moved forward.

He looked down.

Rob was laying over Punji Sticks.

One had pierced his chest.

He heard Rob gurgle.

He saw Rob blink.

He reached down to grab Rob's arm; he slipped on the mud, and his knee came down hard on another punji stick.

Rob stopped blinking.

***

"That was the worst fucking service I ever got," he said.

"You can complain about the service all you want, but don't swear at me," I answered.

"I'm not swearing at you. I'm just swearing."

Six months later he was sitting at the bar again.

"Hey, Carl, your usual?" I asked.

"Yup. Say Glenda, are we good?"

"Yup, Carl, we're good."

"Good. I'm glad we have that understanding."

I smiled, opened his bottle of Kokanee, and put it in front of him.

"You still smoking?" I asked.

He grinned. "Pick a number," he said.

"Nine," I replied.

He marked it down on his Keno slip.

"Say, when you get a chance, can you run that through for me?"

Normally we ask people to walk over to the self-serve machines, but for Carl, we ring his tickets through at the bar.

He doesn't walk so well; he has a really bad knee.

Tina Hoffmeister: General Manager Account Services

Holstein Fund Management Group
1201 - 3 Ave.
Seattle, Washington
USA
98101
March 10, 2020

Receipt #98-43387can
Reference #77359

Dear Ms. Toews,

Please accept this email confirming your recent investment via Daryl.

The following is the outline of your original deposit of funds:

Glenda $500.00

Danielle $100.00

Taylor $100.00

Original investment. $700.00

Additional investment funds:
March 11, 2020.

Ann $100.00

Haney $300.00

Danielle $200.00

Taylor $200.00

Total additional funds. $800.00

Total per Glenda $1,500.00

ALL FUNDS HAVE BEEN MATCHED ON YOUR BEHALF BY Daryl. Total funds deposited to your account $3,000.00 (Can.)
This opportunity maturity day is March 5, 2021.
The guaranteed payout of funds will be at a rate of 4 X funds. Your guaranteed payout will be no less than $12,000.00 (Can.)
You shall receive a statement of account on March 5, 2021, at which time you can direct us regarding having your funds and profits returned to you, or you may choose to reinvest some or all of your designated funds.
I trust that this information meets with your satisfaction.
Should you have any questions, please feel free to contact me at this email address.

Respectfully,
Tina Hoffmeister
General Manager Account Services.

***

I had finished reading the email and exhaled.

I choose to increase the investment for my daughters and, hey, well, fun money for my husband and for my sister Ann. Perhaps she could renovate her kitchen as she wanted, or maybe we could take that trip to Australia together that we keep talking about. What a surprise for her. I smiled as I imagined her face in a year. "Here, Ann, I knew you wouldn't invest. I know you're on the more skeptical side, but I did for you … look what happened! Enjoy!"

And for Haney? Wow, here, take a golf trip, or two or three, buy the best clubs, buy that truck you have been talking about, only maybe you can buy a brand new one!

***

Oh good, I thought as Daryl walked through the door. *He didn't abscond with the money.* I exhaled relief.

I put Daryl's beer in front of him.

"You showed up!"

He looked up confused.

"Well, Daryl, you're a guy in a bar claiming you're super rich, and I'm a waitress that gave you cash."

"Oh. Ah, I get it." He laughed.

"You could be a shyster, but I don't think you're a shyster. Do you want to know why I don't think you're a shyster?" I asked.

"Why?"

"Your stories are bloody consistent. You'd have to be brilliant to keep it all in order."

"That's what I tell my team," he responded. "You can lie, but you will eventually screw up, and I will catch you."

"Is Denise joining you?"

"She's picking me up later. She's just at the Toyota car dealership. The Land Rover we ordered was delivered today, and they're working on the insurance now."

"Oh good, you bought a vehicle snow-worthy then," I responded. "Please tell me you got her one with heated seats?"

"It's got everything, so I assume it's got heated seats. She picked it all out; it's her car. She told me the staff there had a bit of a double take when she paid for it. They asked how she was paying, and she pulled out her debit cards, picked the first one, and said, "Let's try this.""

"Daryl! You do know that's not normal. People don't pay for Land Rovers with a debit card."

"I guess not. She said they seemed a little shocked when she did."

I shook my head and laughed. "So is this her Christmas gift?"

"Oh, no, we needed something to get around on the roads here. I don't know what I'm getting her for Christmas. I'm sure something will come to mind, though."

"Did you get an email from Tina?" Daryl asked.

"Oh, yes, I did, Daryl. She sent the breakdown and mentioned that you had doubled everything! That's completely amazing; thank you so much for doing that," I replied.

"No problem. It just gives it a hand up."

"Tina seemed to be right on the ball. I can imagine her to be a chubby older gal with glasses."

Daryl looked up from his beer a bit blankly. I continued. "I suppose I imagine anyone who is great with numbers to be a little on the frumpy side, preconceived notions in my mind."

He shook his head slowly from left to right. "She is not. She is absolutely stunning."

"What?" I asked. "She's smart and beautiful?"

"Yes, she is way out of my league, besides, she works for Danny. That would have been a little awkward for our friendship. Over the years I'd contemplated asking her out, but it just never felt right. She's a little younger too, and there's the Christine rule she put in place after Denise the stripper. I think Tina's in her forties." He smiled. "Besides, she's like a family friend, taking care of accounts for Jane and the kids, and now I'm married, so it all worked out as it should."

He glanced at his phone's screen. "Ah, it looks like they're all buttoned up. Denise will be here in ten minutes. I guess I best get the bill."

Shoes

"But, Mom, they keep flopping off my feet!" she cried.

"What are you talking about? I just wore them yesterday, and they seemed fine," her mother replied.

"No, they aren't. The plastic bottom has pulled off from the toe; besides, they're dumb. I can't go to school with these things flopping around. It's so embarrassing." Tears of frustration were squeezing out of the corner of her eye.

She was fourteen, she was late for school, and these were her only shoes.

"Give them to me," her mom sighed. She took the black flat from her daughter's hand and inspected the shoe. Charlene was right—the sole of the shoe had pulled away. Hanging on only by the heel, it flopped uselessly in her hand. "Char, go get me the tape. I think there's some in the drawer by the fridge."

Heaving a deep sigh, Charlene moved toward the drawer to do as her mother had asked. "Why can't we just live like normal people live? It's not fair!"

She opened the drawer and found the roll of tape her mother wanted. Reluctantly she picked it up, knowing what was going to happen next. Her mom would wind the tape around the toe of the shoe, and she would have to wear the ugly flats with a taped-up toe to school. Char walked the tape back to her mother and her mom did exactly what she thought.

An hour later she was in gym class, running laps around the basketball court in her taped-up flats, silently wishing she could just disappear.

"Charlene, come here please," Ms. White called. Char put her head down and slowly moved toward her gym teacher.

"Where are your running shoes?" Ms. White asked.

Char stared at the floor, not speaking.

"You need to come to class prepared," Ms. White continued. "Please go and get your gym shoes."

Charlene didn't move.

"Charlene, did you hear me?" her teacher asked.

"Yes, ma'am, I did," Char replied, desperately trying to hold back tears fueled by embarrassment.

"Well?"

"These are my only shoes," Char whispered.

"What?" Ms. White asked, not certain she had heard correctly.

"I said, these are my only shoes."

"Oh," Ms. White replied. "Well, then. Charlene, why don't you go over to the counsellor's room. She has a key to the Closet. Go see if there's a pair of gym shoes there that fit you, okay?"

Charlene nodded. Relieved to have an escape from this situation, she did as she was told and headed down the hall to the counsellor's room.

"Hi, Charlene. How are you doing today?" Ms. Ranier asked the student she met in the hall.

"Oh, hey, Ms. Ranier, I was just coming to see you. Ms. White asked me to see if there might be a pair of gym shoes in the closet that would fit me."

Ms. Ranier automatically looked down at Char's feet. "Yup, those shoes have seen better days, haven't they? Come on, let's go have a look."

Together they made their way to "the Closet." Ms. Ranier pulled out a set of keys and opened the door. Flicking on the light, they entered. On the right was a shelf holding a half dozen pairs of running shoes and three pairs of winter boots.

"Try these," Ms. Ranier said, pulling a used pair of pink Nikes from the bottom shelf.

Charlene kicked off the black flat and shoved her foot into the Nike. "A little big."

"Do you think that will be okay?" Ms. Ranier asked.

"Oh, yes." Charlene smiled. "I have socks; that will help."

"Okay then, it's a done deal. I'll trade you those flats for these Nikes."

Char grinned from ear to ear. "Gladly!"

The school day passed to the next.

"Ms. Ranier, you have a phone call," the school secretary said. "Charlene's mother is on the phone."

Ms. Ranier cringed a little. *This could go good, or this could go bad.* She took a deep breath and picked up the phone to her ear.

"Alice Ranier speaking."

"Hello," came a quiet voice on the other end of the line.

"Hello," Ms. Ranier returned the greeting.

"This is Charlene's mother. I just wanted to thank you so much for the shoes you gave Char yesterday. You have no idea what that meant to her—to us, actually. We've been sharing the same shoes for a while now …"

Her voice trailed off as Ms. Ranier's mind wrapped around her words.

"You were sharing the shoes?"

"Yes, they were our only shoes."

Ms. Ranier hung up the phone and shook her head. "How does this happen? How does this happen in this day and age? How does this happen in Chilliwack?"

She mentally sighed.

Abuse.

Hunger.

Shoes.

She closed her eyes.

"Hey, Alice, Corky's after work?" Rodger asked.

"Oh God, yes! It's been a hell of a week."

***

"Hey, Rodger," I greeted.

"Hi, Glenda," he responded.

"Your usual?" I asked.

"Yes please."

"Hi, Alice. What are you having today? We have the winter ale you like on tap. Would you like a pint?" I asked.

"Oh, yes please, Glenda."

I went and poured their pints, and the teacher table grew from two to ten.

They had been coming in for a few years now. Originally I called them "The One Hit Wonders." Every Friday they came, had one pint, and left. Over the past couple of years, they have stayed for two pints. Today they all looked tired.

"What's up, guys?" I asked. "You all look tired."

"Oh Glenda, too many students suffering too many things and not enough hours in a day."

All ten teachers from the high school stared contemplatively into their pints. Collectively, they sighed.

It screamed.

Coat of Many Colours

"I'm being transferred in a month."

She picked at the aluminum side of the kitchen table; it had pulled away from the blue Arborite in the corner, where the chip was. Her momma was not happy when her new table got chipped. She had saved bits out of the grocery budget, tucked it away to buy it. It was the first piece of brand-new furniture they'd ever owned.

Her mom was gone now.

Heaven called her home.

Leaving her, her brother, her dad, and the kitchen set to continue life without her.

"Did you hear me?" her dad asked.

"Yes, Daddy. I heard."

"Eat your Corn Flakes."

"Yes, Daddy."

The words were like thunder to her eleven-year-old heart. Just yesterday she and Sarah sat on Sarah's picnic table behind Sarah's bungalow, promising forever friendship. Just yesterday they shared a ten-cent Coke they'd pulled from the dispenser in the mess. Just yesterday they sat in the "tube," an oversized acrylic tube brought in from someplace and put on the back common grass for the base kids to roll around on. The weight of leaving her home, her school, her Sarah, pressed against her.

She pushed away from the table. One of the steel chair legs scratched into the kitchen vinyl floor as she did so. If her mom was still here, she would have glued on another puffy foot pad to protect the floor, but her mom wasn't here, so a gouge in the floor it was.

She took her bowl to the sink and dumped the last bit of sugar milk down the drain. A man in the transistor radio sitting on the kitchen counter was advertising a sale at Brown Brothers Lincoln, Ford, and Mercury on Marine Drive. She sighed as she ran a stream of water into the bowl. She walked four steps into the living room. These houses were like that. Tiny two-bedroom bungalows, copy cats of each other lined up end to end like the military soldiers who lived there.

"… *and just before I say goodbye this morning, I will leave you with this last song. Sung by Dolly Parton, who will be in concert on February 20 as part of the Porter Wagoner show at the Queen Elizabeth Theatre …*" came the voice from inside the radio.

And the finger picking guitar sang through the transistor, followed by Dolly's voice singing "Coat of Many Colours."

Her memory wrapped her momma's hands around hers and they bounced and twirled to Dolly's voice, giggling as they bumped into the old brocade sofa.

"I just love that song!" her momma cried as they flopped on the sofa breathlessly when it had finished.

***

"Good morning, Daryl," I said as I flagged the table with a coaster and set his pint on top. "Did you have a great weekend?"

"It was, thank you for asking. I'm glad you're here today. Danny had messaged me earlier and said there was about a $1,000 left in the Canadian accounts if you or Tina wanted to invest a little more."

"Hmmm." I considered. "I don't need more for myself, and I don't really know anyone who would want to use it. If I chose to invest for other people, would that be possible? I know people who could benefit from the opportunity but who don't have the money themselves. If I put the money up for them, but the investment was made in their name, is that possible?"

"I don't see why not," Daryl responded, "but let me message Danny and ask to be sure."

"Did you figure out a present for Denise yet?" I asked Daryl after he'd wandered to his barstool.

"I did. We were watching *Coat of Many Colours* last night, and Denise mentioned how special that song was for her, so I phoned Dolly and asked if she wouldn't mind sending a personal video greeting for Denise. She said she'd love to and to expect it by the end of the week." He smiled and started to giggle until a lone tear slipped out of his right eye. He wiped it away, picked up his pint, and took a sip.

First List

"What are you working on over there?" Haney was sitting on the sofa across from my chair in the RV. "Your Christmas list?"

I put my hand across the paper so he couldn't see what I was writing.

"Maybe." I smiled evasively.

He turned his head back to the TV, simultaneously saying, "When you're done, please give it to me. I'm a bit behind on my Christmas shopping, and I need to get going."

"When I'm done with my Christmas list, you shall get it," I promised.

I turned back to the names on the paper in front of me.

Who, Lord, would benefit the most by this investment? Whose names go on this list? I need ten. I have $1,000 to give. Where shall it go? I prayed and jotted down names that came to mind. I tried not to over-analyze the names. I tried not to question too much if that was a name I wanted to write down. I did think, *Who would do the most with money if they got a chunk?* And the names came.

Luc
Charles & Eunice
Brenda
Trish & John
Naraleska
Ticiany
Anna

Kamie
Sara
Julie

***

From: *Tina Hoffmeister*
Sent: *December 16, 2020 3:15 PM*
To: *Glenda*
Subject: *Opportunities*

Hi Glenda,

I was just reviewing the documents and files regarding the latest transactions with my boss.

He was asking if we should extend the opportunity to increase your investment to help more people in your circle

He said he could manouevre some American opportunity to Canadian should you choose.

This is simply an offer to make things simpler for you should they need to be.

Daryl has no knowledge of this email but we are both confident he would approve.

Now I am actually leaving for the day but I will be available should you have questions.

Tina

***

I can think of a few more people I'd like to help. The funds for each person at the end of the year would be just over $100,000. Enough to give everyone a leg up, but not enough to destroy them. I know a lot of people who could use a leg up.

Second List

The smell of pot lingered. Cirrus clouds of its smoke hovered over the crowd. Heavier to the left, lighter to the right. Nobody paid much attention to it.

They had manoeuvred themselves to centre stage. She wasn't quite sure how that was possible, but there she was, in her white, sleeveless tee and khaki shorts, peering up at the stage from under her straw Molson cowboy hat she'd acquired years before at a Super Bowl party she'd hosted. Beside her was her friend.

"Do you want to go to the Rockn' River Music Fest?" she had asked her a few months before. "Rascal Flatts are playing."

"Hell ya!" her friend replied.

Rascal Flatts bailed at the last minute. No doubt there was internal scrambling with this news. Originally the girls were bummed, but then they announced the replacement. Cheers from the trailer at the Mission Raceway parking lot rose up. They got Randy Houser instead!

There they stood, red solo cups in the left hand, cheering and waving frantically with their right.

The speakers beat against their being. The cowboy crowd sang along.

The lead guitarist puffed on his pipe. Nodding his top hat in their direction, he let the first few bars of the next song rip.

Ba Ba Ba

Ba Ba Ba

Building up the crowd.

Then Houser's voice thundered, playing one hit into the next in unending energy. Houser was dripping in sweat. They were so close, they could reach out and touch him if they dared. They didn't dare.

He wiped the sweat from his face with a white towel.

He reached into his jeans pocket and pulled out guitar picks.

He tossed one into the sea of cowboy hats.

He walked up the stage, microphone in one hand, a guitar pick in the other, and he flung the second one out.

There was a brief moment of shock.

For her.

And for Houser.

Somehow, amazingly, he managed to flick that pick right down the front of her shirt.

Houser reflexively pulled his right hand back to signal "score," as if he'd just dunked a basket at the buzzer. Then he turned away in a bit of a blush.

She instinctively stuck her right hand down the front of her shirt and in sweet victory pulled out the guitar pick. Her friend watched amazed, shrieking, cheering, and splashing red solo cup beer over the both of them.

Later that night, a jam session was taking place at the trailer in the parking lot.

"Does anyone have a guitar pick?" Rob asked.

"My friend does," Cindy screamed. "Randy Houser threw it down her shirt!"

***

I was standing on a barstool weaving red and green tinseled garland above the bar while I contemplated turning on the "holiday music station."

They'll complain, I thought as I pushed the idea from my mind. My love of Christmas music doesn't extend to mainstream pubdom. We were doing Christmas at Corky's on the down low this year anyway, as COVID regulations prevented large groups and parties. As the community was gearing up for Christmas, Fraser Health was putting their own stamp on it. Mask up in public.

Tina walked in as a Christmas bulb escaped my hand, bouncing three times on the floor before coming to a stop in front of her toe.

"What's the big gift for Finn this year?" I asked as I bent down to retreive the red ball.

"I don't know yet. Dawson and Dylan's big gifts are done, but we haven't quite decided on Finn," she replied as she tucked her purse behind the bar. How are things going on your house? Any news yet?" Tina shifted the conversation.

I rolled my eyes. "Oh my goodness," I exclaimed. "This six-week wait is going on three months now! Gail has forwarded my emails to the building inspector manager, and he emailed me stating, "we have to wait for the Interpretation Committee." Hopefully in January?" I shrugged my shoulders. "Christmas in a fifth wheel, yeehaw!!" I said sardonically. "At least our surroundings are beautiful!" I exclaimed, reorienting my thoughts.

Big Doug and his wife walked in and sat at Big Round.

"Your turn." Tina smiled.

I sighed.

"Did I tell you she yelled at me for not filling her soup full enough last week? That's the second time she yelled at me for not filling her soup full enough. I don't know what's going on with her; sometimes she's nice, other times she yells. I never know which person I'm going to get!" I said, delaying my visit to their table as long as possible.

"I'm super sorry, Glenda," Tina apologized. "That's completely my fault. I was just over filling her bowl every time I served her. I guess she thinks that's the proper amount."

"Don't do that anymore!" I laughed at Tina. "It's hard on me. I don't like getting yelled at! She and I were friends, at least I thought we were friends. I don't understand why she's yelling at me over soup." I shook my head.

Just then pothead Jeff walked by. The whiffs of pungent pot tailing him were pulling me back into a memory, pulling me back to the moment when I was pulling a Randy Houser guitar pick from inside my shirt.

I sighed at what once was.

"Here I go. Wish me luck." I smiled and took their beers to their table.

"Morning, Glenda," she said.

"Morning, Cindy," I replied.

"Sorry the pint took a bit to get to you. Tina had just finished changing the keg."

"All good, Glenda, no biggy." She turned to look up at the Keno board. "Two doll hairs, Dougy, that's all that brought me." She took a sip of her draught.

A breath of relief escaped my being. It's a happy Cindy day.

***

Daryl wandered in and took his place at the Bone.

"Your usual?" I asked, flagging the table top with a coaster.

"Yes, thank you," he replied as he placed his phone beside it.

I returned with his pint and set it before him.

"I hear Danny has offered to open up more opportunity for you if you were wanting to help more people," Daryl said, picking up the pint for his first sip.

"Oh good, they told you then," I responded.

"Yes."

"I have more people I'd like to help. If the opportunity is there, it would be terrible not to use it."

"I agree. I'll let Danny know you're interested."

"Thank you, Daryl. Is it okay if I give you the list of names on Monday? I'd like to think about it a bit."

"Of course," he replied.

"Thanks again, Daryl. You have no idea how much this will help people."

"I'm glad I can help," he said as he pulled up his phone to start taking care of the business he did on it daily.

I left him and checked my own phone for message. Nothing, But I re-read the one I got from Tina that morning.

From: *Tina Hoffmeister*
Sent: *Thursday, December 17, 2020 8:22:54 AM*
To: *Glenda*
Subject: *Re: Opportunities*

Hi again,

Yes, I build fires. About five years ago, I bought an 1890 house on an ocean bluff. It has been an ongoing restoration project. But I am returning it to its old-world charm with all the modern upgrades like plumbing, electric, etc. But the fireplace will remain forever! If you're ever in the Seattle area, you'll have to come by!

Nothing like a natural wood fire on a chilly rainy night.

Time to start my drive to the office. I hope you have a day, and we really appreciate the fact that Tina and yourself are so respectful of Daryl's privacy. I know everybody always says they want to be a billionaire, but once you see how people treat the wealthy, it can be heartbreaking. Not to say all wealthy people are like Daryl and Danny (my boss); they, especially Daryl, are cut from a very different cloth.

I have no idea if people truly know his true wealth; he probably can't keep up with the income himself and doesn't even know himself. 😊

Anyway, talk soon. I hope I haven't said too much.

Tina

***

The next morning as I was drinking coffee, another email from Tina arrived. I clicked it open.

From: Tina Hoffmeister
Sent: December 19, 2020 10:09 PM
To: Glenda Toews
Subject: Re: Opportunities

Hi Glenda,

I apologize today was a long day and I just saw an email from Daryl showing his forwarding of $3,000.00 in your name for your additional involvement.

He said that you would be forwarding a distribution list Monday.

This is great news.

I will await your list. (Today was a long day due to to much 🏆🍺🍺🏆 *last night) but was fun.* 🐌

Daryl had once again doubled everything, so we will recalculate tomorrow.

I am going to spend Monday in the office, so I will finalize everything.

Hope your day was great!

Tina

Oh good, Daryl gave them my money, I thought, followed by, *He doubled it again? Does he do this all the time?* His generosity amazed me.

I spent the weekend working on my list. Certain names attached themselves to my thoughts throughout the weekend, and I wrote them down. Other times I thought, *What could this mean for them?* And I wrote that name down. Again, I didn't over-analyze. I prayed, I contemplated, I wrote names.

Daryl had mentioned he'd set up a fund for his grandchildren. I took his lead on this and decided to invest one pot for all my grandchildren, and following that idea, I did the same for Haney's sons.

Next December perhaps I could leave the investment in and watch it grow, or take some out and give it to my daughters so they could use it for the children. And for Haney's boys, the same idea—take some out to help in the moment, leave some in to help in the future. The idea made me smile

Then the individual names came …

Shirley

Martha and Harold

Lisa and Lavern

Kendle

Nikki

Julie
Donny
Brandie
Doug
Jessica
Barry and Rena
Matthew
Denny
Ammar
Raphael
Simon
Tracy
Cheryl
George
Clive
Noreen
Pat
Tyler H.
The Gift Fund

***

"Hi, Brandon, you're in early. What can I pour for you today?"

He sighed and looked up toward me but through me.

"Brandon?"

He sighed again.

"What's up?" I asked. Something was definitely on his mind.

"My car. It's only a couple of years old. It was acting weird, so I took it to the dealership, and they think it's the alternator."

"Ug, don't you just hate car problems?" I commiserated.

"Ya, they told me it's under warranty."

"Oh, that's great then!"

"But I still have to pay $300."

"Oh, not so great then."

"No. Three hundred dollars a week before Christmas." He looked up and off to the side, mentally figuring out how he was going to make this news fit into his life. "I'll have a double vodka please, Glenda," he finished.

"I understand why, Brandon."

He took his drink and headed to the patio for a smoke.

This happens a lot here. People come here to absorb bad news they've just received. Wouldn't it be nice to have a fund set aside to draw from? Wouldn't it be nice to be able to reach in and pull out $300 and hand it to Brandon? Wouldn't it be nice to give people a gift of hope like that? Wouldn't that be amazing!

Ahhhh, The Gift Fund. Let's make that happen!

Christmas

"The family is spending Christmas with us, I'm told. It's all good. The house is big enough. Denise's dad, stepmom, stepbrother, and stepsister from Christmas to New Years. Denise is busy baking away. I've been enjoying that, can't you tell?" Daryl said as he moved his right hand from the top of his protruding belly to the bottom in Vanna White fashion.

I slid a Christmas card across the top of the Bone toward him. "I just wanted to say Merry Christmas, Daryl. Thank you for your stories, and thank you for the opportunity you opened up for me and my family. It sure has been a great pleasure getting to know you." I smiled.

"For me too." Daryl smiled. "I have a gift for you, but it's up at the house. Will you be here tomorrow?"

"No, I don't work Christmas Eves. Tina does."

"Ah, well it will have to wait until after Christmas." Daryl hesitated a moment then added, "I think you'll like it; it's for your new house."

***

Dangling Disney characters danced within the boughs. Mickey Mouse holding a present with a red bow swung below Donald Duck swinging a golf club, with "Christmas 1999" painted in fine tip on the plaster cast mold reminiscent of a happier Christmas. A Christmas when they were all together.

The multicoloured mini lights twinkled in mock merriment.

It seemed so hollow.

Yet he had to make this moment merry for his boys, three of them: five, three, one. He didn't have time to wallow. The boys needed happy Christmas memories. He taped up another gift, tagged it, and tucked it under the tree.

The phone rang two times. He answered it.

"I just wanted to wish the boys a Merry Christmas," came her voice across the line.

"You could do that if you were here," he replied curtly, not bothering to curb the cutting edge of his voice.

She sighed deeply.

He felt disdain creep into his soul; he made a shallow effort to push it back. For the sake of the boys.

"We've been through this before. I just need some time," she said.

"Time?" he repeated "Time for what? To decide who you want to be with?"

Another deep sigh came across the line.

Quietly he whispered, "You could have picked a different time of year to find your yourself."

"I know," she said.

"You could have picked a different time of year to tell me the baby you're carrying isn't mine."

Another sigh. "I just need some time," she repeated.

"You need to pick. I'm done. I'll raise that baby as my own if you choose to stay. If you choose to keep our family together and come home, I will do that. But I'm not going to wait around for you to decide if you want me or not."

"I just wanted to wish the boys a Merry Christmas," she said.

"If you were here, you'd know that they're all sleeping."

He closed his eyes; his temple was throbbing.
"I'll call in the morning then," she said
He hung up.
Free from holding it in.
He let the tears fall.
They fell hard.

***

"That one!" I exclaimed as we stopped in front of a three-foot cedar growing by the river.

"You're sure?" Haney smiled. He knew the routine. We would wander around for an hour, he'd point out a few trees, I would scrutinize, and then dismiss them for reasons he couldn't see. The years before this had taken place at every Christmas tree farm we had ever visited, and it was no different here in the forest.

"Yes, this one. It's the perfect Charlie Brown tree, and it will be perfect inside our trailer," I replied.

"Okay," he smiled. "You're sure you're sure?"

"Yes, just dig the little guy up," I demanded lightheartedly.

Less than an hour later, I was standing in front of the wee tree listening to Michael Buble singing "White Christmas" with a box of ornaments in my hand. Between sips of wine, I hung pretty little crystals and golden birds with plumed feather tails on branches. Haney opened a box of chocolate-covered cookies and started munching.

I dug into the corner of the box and pulled out a Donald Duck swinging a golf club.

"Where did you get this one?" I asked.

Haney inspected the figurine as it swung from my fingers.

"My ex-wife. Wow, that was a long time ago." Finished with the fleeting memory, he continued, "I have some wrapping to do. I'll be in the bedroom." He popped another cookie in his mouth and started humming, "It's beginning to look a lot like Christmas."

I've Noticed a Lot of Homelessness

Lipstick smears in stop-sign red on the rim of an empty wine glass. The remnants of Christmas celebrations dotted themselves lifelessly throughout the pub.

I walked into Corky's on January 1, pulling down the sagging bits of tinsel. Multi-coloured lights that blinked "Joy, Joy, Joy" on December 23 were yawning. I grabbed an empty Vodka box and started filling it with plastic bulbs.

Daryl walked in and sat at the Bone.

"How was your Christmas, Daryl?"

"They're still there," he replied, running his hand through his hair.

"What?" I shoved another handful of Christmas balls into the box. "Don't they live in Chilliwack?"

"Her dad and stepmom do, but the stepbrother and sister don't." He didn't look amused.

"I'll go grab you a pint."

"Ya, I need it. I don't think the stepbrother intends on leaving. He keeps saying things like, 'I could get used to this kind of life; hey, sis, need some help here? You have that nice little guest house.' Denise is just trying to make life better for her family, and I can tell he's working on her. He just hangs around all day, smoking weed and drinking my good Scotch." He sighed after his screed and then continued. "And Denise says to me, 'Daryl, they'll leave in a week.' But now it's headed into the third week, and they're all fucking still in my fucking house!" He took another breath.

"The stepsister isn't so bad. I think she knows I'm getting irritated. This morning I was in the kitchen getting coffee, and she came out of her room, walked down the hall, saw me, quickly turned around, and headed back to her room." He grinned a little. "But that fucking tree planter stepbrother got into my Scotch cabinet!" he reiterated. "I went home the other night and there he was, helping himself. He actually asked if he could pour me a glass of my own fucking Scotch!" His face was animated now, and in his frustration he swiped his hand through his hair again.

I put his beer in front of him as he continued.

"I said, 'Looks like you're enjoying that Scotch,' and he says, 'Sure am. I can't afford this kind' and kept drinking it. I was like … fuck." Daryl ran his hand through his hair again. "Fuck, I need a haircut."

Probably not a good time to ask about the Christmas gift he promised me, I thought on the inside. On the outside, I commiserated with his plight. Family can be hard. It must be harder when you *know* they're using you. When you know they're using your wife.

"This kind of thing must be an issue for you all the time," I said. "Who do you trust? How do you respond when you're pretty sure people want what you have, not you?"

"I have a very small circle of friends because of this very thing, but this is Denise's family. Fucking leaches." He exhaled. "She can come and join me here for a drink, or she can stay with them up there, but I'm done with them. I'll go home when I know they're sleeping." He muttered on about midnight family swims and dangling toes in the hot tub. I saw him shudder.

"How was your Christmas, Glenda?" he asked after he'd finished his diatribe.

"Well, our freshwater tank blew out, so we had no water for a couple of days." I grinned.

"Really? You had no water? Glenda, you should have contacted me. You could have come up to the house. We would have made room for you and Haney!" he insisted.

"It's all good, Daryl. I appreciate the offer, but we survived," I responded.

"Well, so you know, if anything like that ever happens again, just come stay at the house, okay?"

"Thanks, Daryl, I'll keep that in mind. How did Denise like her gift?" I asked.

"She started to cry." He smiled "It was amazing!"

"And what did she get for you?" I asked.

"A Rolex," he replied.

"A Rolex? But you don't wear jewellery or watches." I pointed out the obvious.

"I know, the Rolex wasn't what was special. It was what she had inscribed on the back that made it a great gift." He turned his head upwards and said, "Let me see, how was it worded: 'Thank you for allowing me to afford this life.'"

Daryl seemed to think this was awesome.

I didn't.

One pint later, he looked up from his phone and asked, "Did you get your list sent off to Tina?"

"Oh, yes, I did. I told her if she and Danny were going to make my next full-time job helping people, I'd be really happy about that," I joked.

"She mentioned that you're very philanthropically minded," he continued.

"Ha!" I smiled. "Who knew I could desire more than just slinging beers." I laughed.

"You can give this all up after you turn on the football game for me," came his retort, along with a smile.

I obliged. The beer and the game soothed his strained soul, and at halftime as I dropped off another pint, Daryl looked up from his phone and said, "You know, Glenda, sometimes I drive by the Salvation Army and I see a lineup of people there and think, 'What would a million dollars do for you?'"

"That's an interesting thought." My mind immediately jumped to my guys in the corner of the parking lot. I was pretty sure that group would have a big ongoing party.

"A social experiment," he said. "Sometimes I think I'd like to see what would happen if I gave someone a million dollars. What would you do with a million dollars?" he asked.

Without hesitation I said, "I'd build my house," and grinned.

"Anything else?" he continued.

"Give me a moment to think about it, Daryl. I could say stuff off the cuff, but I'd actually really like to consider what I'd do. I've thought about this kind of thing before, usually when I've bought a lottery ticket. My question to myself is 'What *would* you do with it if you won it?' I haven't thought like that in a long time, so give me a minute." I smiled and ran off to pour the Dougs a pint.

I was pouring the beer and asking myself, *Okay, Glenda, if you really had a million dollars, what would you do with it? Hmmmm, it's not as much as it once was. After your house, what do you need? Maybe a newer car; mine is getting older. I don't need anything more than that, so what would you do with the other bit of it? Ha, I'd look for ways to make that money go the very farthest to help people around me.*

And that's what I said.

"Daryl, I would hope I'd just do what I'm doing with these investments. Help the people around me."

He absorbed the information. That's what Daryl did. He sat and absorbed information. I had watched him absorb information often. He didn't make facial expressions of any kind, and his body language was still. He looked upwards, to the ceiling. He would place his chin in his hand and stroke downward, using the action to herd his thoughts into place. Sometimes he would tilt his head to catch a new thought as it passed by. As a thought developed, his index finger would tap, on his chin, above his lip, on his cheek. His eyebrows were motionless, and he barely blinked. At the end of this process, he would either vaguely smile or bend his head down and start texting into his phone. Occasionally both. The process was intriguing to watch.

An hour and two pints later, Daryl put down his phone and said, "I've noticed a lot of homelessness here. Quite a lot, actually."

"We do have a lot of it, Daryl, you're right."

"What do you think could be done about it?"

"I've thought about that, actually. I'm surrounded by it here."

"Did you come to any conclusions?" he asked.

"Well, no. But I did think that I wouldn't use my money or my energy on the homeless we have now. If I had to place my time and energy to get the biggest return, I'd place it on preventing it to begin with."

"Hmmm." He considered the implications of the statement. "How would you do that?" he pressed after several minutes.

"We need to go to the source; we need to talk to the people who are most closely linked to the most vulnerable youth. We need to talk to our teachers. We need to see what they're seeing, and we need to use our resources to address what's slipping through the cracks."

"I think I agree with you," he replied

Ike

She sat motionless.

If I'm quiet, if I make no noise, maybe he won't know that I'm up here, she thought to herself. Big thoughts for a little girl.

Her mommy and sister had left. She had watched them, not comprehending, scurrying throughout the house. Their actions created a feeling of panic. She hung on to her doll, stuck her thumb in her mouth, and sat on her bed. She was in this exact position four hours later when she was mentally willing herself to disappear.

She could hear him downstairs.

"Where are you, you fucking cunt?" he bellowed from below.

Involuntarily she shuddered.

He smashed something into the wall. A lamp? A radio? Her momma's head?

"I'll kill you!" he screamed.

She heard him start up the stairs.

Inside she whimpered, *Mommy*.

Nobody heard her.

They were gone.

Another step. Another bang into the wall. Another howl.

"You piece of shit! Where are you?"

Her bedroom door flung open.

Her daddy staggered in.

"Wheerees yeer mootthhher!" he demanded.

She blinked.

She was five, frozen in fear.

He picked her up and held her over his head. She silently swayed as he waved her around like a blonde flag.

"Why does yer mootthher do this to meee?"

He was starting to get tired. He threw her back on the bed. Energy spent, he flung himself on the bed beside her and started muttering to himself.

He did that some times.

Endless rambling, mutters.

She put her thumb back in her mouth.

***

"Good morning, Ike. How's that new walker going for you?" I asked as he directed it into the pub.

He grimaced.

"Not so good then, huh? Let me grab your pint."

Ike headed to the back of the pub, near the fireplace. He was always cold. At one time he may have stood five-foot-five. Today he was bent to five feet.

"I'm the only person I know who made it out of hospice alive," he bragged to me five years ago when he first started coming in. "I was on my deathbed; they even called my family to come say their goodbyes. I shocked them all." He grinned. "Can you put the fights on, Glenda? Do we have to listen to the soccer match? Why does anyone want to listen to that?"

"I'll see what I can find for you, Ike. Is Jenny joining you today?" I asked.

"No, not today. She says she's busy. No time for her old man," he mocked.

I left him alone to sip on his pint.

Two hours slipped by. I took Ike his fourth pint.

"Ike, this is your last one."

"You're the only one who does that, Glenda. Everyone else brings me a fifth one, but not you. Every single time, like I'm a child."

I smiled. "Oh Ike, we've had this discussion before. You're still nice at the end of four pints. You're an ass at the end of five pints. I don't need that in my life, thanks."

He shook his head, clearly pissed off.

"Don't you remember the time I cut you off and you demanded I bring you the phone? You wanted to call the police; you wanted the police to force me to bring you another pint!" I smiled, and he smirked.

"Ya, that was dumb. I'm sorry."

"And do you remember the other time that you actually called me a cunt? You're lucky I serve you anything at all!" I exclaimed.

He was silent.

I left him to drink his fourth pint.

A half hour later, he started his muttering.

He did that sometimes.

Endless rambling, mutters.

I walked over to his table.

"Ike, you okay?"

He looked past me.

"Ike?"

His eyes regained focus. "Ya, I'm fine."

"I'll call you a cab."

"Ya, okay, Glenda."

"Your tab's been covered."

"What?" Ike asked

"A customer who was in earlier paid your tab, Ike."

"Say, that was nice of them. Next time you see them, say thank you for me, will ya?"

"I will, Ike."

The Chargers, I Own Them

"Two hundred thousand dollars."

"Excuse me?" I replied.

"Two hundred thousand dollars was what Denise gave to each of her family members as a Christmas gift, at least that's what finance informed me yesterday," Daryl said.

"Did you know about it?" I asked.

"No! Finance was doing a monthly audit and they noticed it, so they thought they should inform me."

"How does that make you feel?"

He shook his head. "I've requested a full audit."

"Well, shit, Daryl. I was just going to ask if the both of you wanted to join us here on Sunday to watch football together too.

"I'd like that," he responded.

"Well, okay then, we'll be here at 11:00 a.m.," I replied.

"I haven't had anybody to watch football with in a very long time."

"Denise doesn't watch with you?" I asked.

"Oh no, and her family doesn't watch sports either. I just usually watch alone."

"That's too bad, but I have to admit, I never got into football either until Haney took the time to teach me. I think I drove him crazy with all the questions, but at the end of the day, I now enjoy watching a game with him because I know what's going on."

"Danny and I sometimes get together and watch. I've been to a few Super Bowl parties at his house. They throw a spectacular one every year. Nelson is a New England fan. We had to attend that Super Bowl." Daryl rolled his eyes. "Tom fucking Brady."

"Haney's been a Cowboys fan for years. I think it was the cheerleaders in the '80s that had him gravitate to that team."

Daryl shook his head and snickered. "Jerry Jones is an ass." He laughed.

"Do you have a team you root for?" I asked.

"Yes, I do. My team."

"Your team?"

"Yes. The Chargers. I own them." He smiled broadly.

"Daryl!"

He shrugged his shoulders.

George

His left eye was turned inward. He couldn't remember a time when it stared straight ahead with the right one, but it did. When you're a little kid in the wrong place at the wrong time, and your mother is mad, it's best to stay out of arms' reach. If she catches you, well you might just have one wonky eye too.

He was doing okay this year. He had a stable job as a cook. His wife and he were working things out. He was able to stay away from the bottle, and the strength in his sobriety was noticed by the elders.

"Will you be a mentor to our youth?" they asked.

"With honour," he replied.

He would pick them up and take them to the gym.

He would take them to powwows.

He was very proud of how far he had come.

He was at peace.

He made cedar bark roses.

"I cut myself again, Glenda," he said.

That wonky eye, I thought.

"I took four boys to the gym today, Glenda," he said.

"Keep that up!" I replied.

One day he didn't show up to work.

Nor the next day, or the next.

Then those days turned into a year.

***

"Hi, Glenda," came a familiar voice from the corner of the parking lot.

I looked up as I closed my car door.

"George!! How are you? You just disappeared!" I replied.

"Fell off the wagon, Glenda."

"So sorry to hear."

"My wife kicked me out, but it's okay. I have my friends here." He pointed to the toothless smiles sitting beside him in the corner.

"It just got really hard."

"I'm sorry."

"I'll be okay." He grinned and then took a swig of fireball.

"Do you still have the cedar rose I made for you?" he asked.

"Yes, George! I use it as a bookmark, and I think of you every time I see it."

He smiled.

They found him dead in a park that August.

Exposure, they said.

Why Not Chilliwack?

"No Denise?" I asked as Daryl sat himself at our table.

"She mentioned that she might join us at halftime," he replied.

He shook Haney's hand from across the table just as the life-size, two-dimensional football players kicked off.

"What kind of a kick was that?" Haney exclaimed.

"A Jerry Jones pick!" Daryl mocked.

Something strange happens when you watch football with the like-minded. Somehow it makes the game a whole hell of a lot better.

The rest of the afternoon was spent in jeers, cheers, and beers, ending with a promise to do it again the next week.

Denise never ended up joining us, but we didn't really notice.

The next day Daryl arrived and sat on his barstool. "I had such a great time yesterday," he exclaimed.

"You and Haney are quite the couple. It's amazing how you really seem to enjoy each other."

"Ya, we like each other," I agreed. "There's nothing better than a good banter with your spouse."

"Well, it was refreshing to watch. I'm already looking forward to next Sunday." He smiled.

"Did you find out what happened with Denise?" I asked.

"Something to do with her family." He grimaced.

"Any news on the audit?" I pressed.

"Nothing yet," Daryl replied.

"Well, that's good! I'm rooting for her, you know. Small town girl, stepping into a different world. I just want her to have small town morals I suppose." I grinned.

"I hope you're right," he said.

"Is the family still up at your house?" I asked

"Her dad and stepmom left over the weekend and took the sister back to the ferry. I think the brother is leaving this weekend. I hope the brother is leaving this weekend. It seems every day it's 'just one more day, Daryl.' The guy's a fucking leech."

"You can always give Denise a deadline; it is your house too, and from my perspective, you've been way more than patient with the whole thing."

"Thank you, I think I have too." He smiled.

He sipped his pint and tilted his head down to his phone as I ran off to fill other beers for other people.

After the busy lunch, I pass by the Bone to check on Daryl.

"How's the beer?"

"Still good. You know, Glenda, I've been thinking a lot about Chilliwack. Denise and I have talked about what we would do if we were staying here. The valley is ripe to be picked. I'd like to build a restaurant, a smoke house, and have a string of them from Chilliwack through to Vancouver. Maybe in that five corner area. That would be the first one."

"I wouldn't put it there," I said, shaking my head.

"Why not? They're building that area nicely," Daryl replied.

"For a smokehouse-style restaurant? That kind of restaurant I'd put in that new development down at the river, by the Vedder Bridge. Let the smoke travel all up the valley, luring people in." I grinned.

"I thought that area was set for residential," Daryl questioned.

"Nope, I'm quite certain it's commercial," I replied. "And *that* place would make an amazing spot for a restaurant or pub." I grinned. "I've always thought that particular spot would be spectacular for that."

"Hmmm. I think I'll get my team to look into that area then."

"Please do, Daryl! Please make my dream come true and put a pub there! I would love that," I exclaimed.

"I just don't understand why people stay in Chilliwack. What's here?"

"You're kidding, right, Daryl?"

He looked at me curiously.

"You're the one building resorts and entertainment venues," I continued. "Do you know people come to Chilliwack from all over the world to fish? Sturgeon fishing on the Fraser, salmon fishing on the Vedder. We have hiking and river rafting and golfing all within an arm's throw of each other. If you enjoy the outdoors, we have it.

Daryl tilted his head.

Wheels were turning.

I Have Noodles

She let her body slide to the floor, crumpled in front of a kitchen cabinet. Overwhelming moments of panic had her gasping for air.

"Breathe. Breathe. Breathe."

Her body caught up to her mind, and then the thoughts returned. The black hole of "I just can't see the way out" billowed over her again. The panic resumed, and she cried. She just lay there on the kitchen floor in the fetal position, crying.

An hour elapsed.

She knew she had to get up.

The girls would be home from school at any moment.

"Oh God. I don't know what to do. Help."

The panic returned. It surged up from her chest and in tidal wave motion pulled up into her mind, rolled over, tumbling down where it laid to rest in the pit of her stomach. She started gagging.

"Breathe. Breathe. Breathe."

"The girls will be here soon."

"Breathe. Breath. Breathe."

"They can't see you on the floor like this."

"Get up."

"Wash your face."

"It will be okay."

He took the family allowance cheque again.

She had no money for food.

How a man could do this to his family, she just didn't know.

The month of food money gone.

And he'd lied.

Again.

"Breathe. Breathe. Breathe."

It would be okay.

What do you have?

"We have a roof over our head, the girls are healthy, I'm healthy, we have noodles. Yes, we have noodles. There are people in the world who don't even have noodles. I'm thankful I have noodles. I'm one of the lucky ones. I have noodles."

She got up off the floor and took a long, deep breath.

"My children are alive, we have a roof over our head, and we have noodles to eat. Others don't have this. I am lucky."

The budget was tight; it was always tight. There was just never any money. No money. Too expensive. It was all the girls ever heard. They worked hard. They had their own company; they shouldn't be suffering so.

Yet it was unending suffering.

Money would go missing.

Never any there to pay the business bills off.

She would juggle this to pay that and juggle that to pay this and she would pray the ringing phone wouldn't be someone wanting money she just didn't have.

Then he started taking the family allowance cheque.

The money she used to buy groceries for the month.

The phone rang, and she cringed.

She hated that phone.

He just won't stop drinking.

The phone rang again.

He lies about the money all the time.

The phone rang again.

This is so hopeless. How do you function when you just don't know what's going to happen next? Another wave of panic started.

The phone rang again.

"Hello?" She closed her eyes and rubbed her temple with her right hand.

The line crackled, and a faint voice with a familiar accent sputtered across the miles.

"Your dad's heart stopped. He's dead."

***

It was January 27, and I had just gotten a response from another email I'd sent off to the regional district: "No news from the Interpretation Committee."

I shook my head.

"I think we'll be living in the fifth wheel forever," I texted Haney.

"As long as I'm with you," came his text back. "Do you need anything?"

"You are a very good husband," was my reply.

"I know," followed by a happy face and a couple of question marks.

Do I need anything? I thought.

I looked out the RV window to the wintery mountain. A gust of wind had caught the tree tops and they bounced back and forth. *So weird that the trees move up top but there's no wind below,* I thought. *Do I need anything?*

I was tucked under my heating blanket; the little electric fireplace was flickering. It was toasty. *Do I need anything?*

"I have a roof over my head, we are all healthy, and I have noodles."

I smiled and texted back: "Nope, all good."

Let's Watch Football

"No Denise again?" I asked as Daryl joined our table the following Football Sunday.

He shook his head as he took off his blue jacket and hung it on the back of the chair. "It's actually starting to make me very angry. I put up with her entire fucking family for weeks, and she can't even make the effort to come and watch this game." He ordered his pint just as the Chargers kicked off.

Less than five minutes into the game, Herbert threw a pass for a touchdown.

Daryl grinned. "We knew what we were doing when we picked him up."

"That wasn't luck," Haney agreed. "He's good."

Earl wandered past our table with the newspaper tucked under his arm. "Did you see that pass? That boy has quite the arm," he admired.

"He does," Daryl agreed.

"Do you mind if I join you?" Earl asked.

"Not at all," Daryl replied

Earl put the paper on the table and pulled out a chair.

"After COVID's done, I'll have to take you to a game. We'll just jump on the jet. Sofi Stadium is pretty amazing; they did a good job on it."

My eyes got wide. Neither Haney nor Earl knew who Daryl was. I hadn't mentioned anything to Haney, and

Tina and I had made a conscious effort to not speak about Daryl outside of ourselves in the pub.

I glanced at Haney to see if there was a reaction, then across at Earl to see if there was a reaction from him. Both were intently looking up at the screen. Nothing.

The game was tight, the game was good, Daryl was grinding his teeth as the Raiders won.

He picked up his phone. "Yup," he laughed, "it was good for you! Yup, yup." Then he hung up. "That was Nelson. We had money on the game; he had to brag." He smiled.

"Playoffs here next Sunday?" Daryl asked.

"You bet." We finished our pints and headed home.

It was dark as we turned out of the parking lot. I reduced the volume on the radio. "Daryl's got some money," I said.

"I gathered," Haney replied.

"He owns the Chargers," I continued.

"I gathered that too," Haney replied. "Who is that Earl guy?"

"Ahh," I said. "He's a regular; kind of a lonely guy."

"I gathered," Haney said. "His wife died."

"Ya, I know." I smiled.

The next morning as Haney was getting ready for work, I asked, "Hey, when you found out Daryl had some money, what did you expect he should do for you?"

Haney looked at me confused. "Why should I expect he should do anything for me?" he replied as he gave me a kiss and walked out the door.

And that's why I love you, I thought, *because you would never expect it*. I smiled.

"You're a good man, Haney."

Golf with Romo?

"I had a good time again yesterday," Daryl greeted me. I slid a coaster in front of him and put his beer on it.

"Ya, 'Mr. I'm not telling anyone who I am.' I had to explain to Haney your history." I laughed. "And Earl? Well, that's up to you who you're telling who you are." I shook my head.

Daryl shrugged his shoulders and grinned.

"This morning I asked Haney now that he knows who you are, what he expected you should do for him. Do you want to know how he responded?"

"Yes."

"He said, 'Why should I expect Daryl to do anything for me?'"

"That right there!" Daryl exclaimed, pointing his finger in my direction. "That right there is an indication that he's a good person."

"Well, I knew that." I laughed. "But it was nice to know he isn't one of 'them.'" I air-quoted "them."

Daryl took his first sip. "When's his birthday?"

"Excuse me?" I wasn't sure I'd heard correctly

"When's his birthday?" Daryl repeated himself.

"June."

"Can you please ask him who his favourite Cowboys quarterback is. I bet it's Romo. Ah, but it could also be Aikman." He spoke more to himself than to me.

"I have no clue. I'll ask him."

"Do." Daryl continued. "I'm going to set up a surprise for his birthday. I'll fly one of them here. Haney can go golfing with Romo, or Aikman. They both golf, so, hmm, maybe I'll just fly them both here, and Alice too. Alice would enjoy golfing with all of them. What's a good golf course here?"

I stood in front of him, unblinking.

"What?" he said.

"You want Romo, Aikman, and Alice Cooper to come golfing in Chilliwack with Haney for Haney's birthday." I reiterated what I thought I heard.

"Why not? You're the one that says you have all these wonderful golf courses here.

I myself will not be golfing. I will be driving the golf cart and drinking beer. Would you care to join me?"

"Glenda, I need a beer here," Doug said as he wandered to the Keno machine.

I walked back to the bar, shaking my head in disbelief.

Jack

She was just ninety-six pounds. A waif of her former self.

They didn't tell you that.

They didn't tell you it increased suffering, it prolonged suffering, it created suffering.

He thought he was buying hope.

A cure.

At least a delay.

He thought he was buying time.

Time for his kids to have their mom for a few more years.

He got the few more years to be sure.

They were not good for anybody years.

Least of all not for her.

Hundreds of thousands of dollars. Every experimental drug they could find.

"Will this kill the cancer?"

It didn't.

And he, his son, and his daughter watched it not work.

And he, his son, and his daughter watched their prayers not answered.

And he, his son, and his daughter watched her wither.

She just wanted to go.

He just wanted her to stay.

She won.

***

He remarried. He pretty much had to, as he could barely cook a hotdog. She had a good sense of humour, and she was kind.

She had a headache on their honeymoon.

They caught an emergency flight back from Mexico to Vancouver.

She had emergency surgery.

They removed tumours in her brain.

Crawling out of the crepuscular, entwining its insidious tentacles deep into his soul. It hissed, "I'm baaaack."

He sat in the waiting room and dropped his head into his hands.

"Fuck cancer, just fuck it, fuck me, just fuck."

He wept.

They must have got it all because it didn't get her. It got her bits of her memory, but it didn't get her. She could still cook hotdogs, and they laughed about that.

A few hundred hotdogs into their marriage, the phone rang.

"There's a position in Vancouver. Would you like it? They sure could use you," came the voice from the other line.

He took off his jacket and hung it in the hall closet, simultaneously balancing his cell on his shoulder.

"Vancouver, you say?" He hummed and hawed. He had no desire to live in a city. "Let me think about it," he responded.

He hung up the phone and opened Google search. "Small towns near Vancouver," he typed.

Chilliwack popped up.

***

"Are you kidding me?" I said into the phone. "Look, I realize you guys are just getting used to your new delivery schedule, but could you at least send the same drivers? Every week you send different drivers. It takes too long, as they're learning a new place every week. If you just send the same drivers on the same route every week, they'll become efficient, no re-learning what each place needs. Our cooler is too small. I need kegs double stacked, and I can't do it. I have no strength to do it. I'm just a girl, and if I'm busy and I'm not there to instruct, and if they haven't been here before, they just throw the delivery all over the place and we can't even get into the cooler!"

I was expressive!

I was exasperated!

Our liquor delivery company had decided to subcontract the deliveries. The change from in-house delivery to subcontract delivery created a mess for us.

"I'm sorry you aren't happy," was the reply on the other end of the line.

I hung up, shaking my head.

"I don't know," I said to Tina. "Maybe we should just use local supply."

"Would Tony go for that?" she questioned.

"Probably not, but if it gets worse, I'll have a conversation with him.

"Can you grab the new guy; I have food to run," she said.

I turned to the doorway, where a lone male was standing. I walked around the bar to greet him. He was wearing a jacket with the liquor delivery company's logo; the logo was staring at me.

My face scrunched up.

"Hi, I'm Jack."

My face stayed scrunched up.

"If I can arrange for an in-house delivery truck to take on a Chilliwack route, would you be interested in that?" he asked.

"Um, wait, did I hear that right? Did you just ask if I was interested in the company delivering like they did in the old days? With our former delivery guys?"

"Yes," Jack said.

"Oh God, please, yes!" My face unscrunched.

Jack smiled. "I'll work on it."

Jack continued to smile as he left Corky's.

Chilliwack's not so bad, he thought, *and the weather is way better than up north!*

Chilliwack Fund

"I've been talking to Danny about creating another fund to help Chilliwack," Daryl said as I slid the morning beer toward him.

"Explain?" I replied.

"Well, as I see it, Chilliwack clearly needs help. The state of homelessness is large, and in this growing community, it will only get worse."

"I agree."

"As Danny and I work to get this fund going, I was wondering if this is something you'd be interested in investing in?" he asked.

"What's the investment?" I asked.

"I want you involved. The way I see it, I have to step away from any do-gooder stuff. If I decide to do business in Chilliwack, I can't be attached to giving money away."

"You're giving money away?" I asked.

"The city needs my help, yes."

"And you want me to help you give money away?"

"Yes," Daryl replied.

"You're going to do business in Chilliwack?"

"My team is currently exploring the opportunities, yes."

"Why me?"

"Because you already care about people," he replied. "I'd like you to be a part of the investment opportunity as well, that way your name is on it. So it's your money you would effectively be giving away as well."

"How much are you expecting that I should invest?" I questioned.

"Five thousand dollars," he replied. "The way I see it, if you invest $5,000, and I invest $5,000, with a multiplier of nine times, that will be $90,000. At the end of three months, we take half out, so $45,000, and you start influxing the funds into the community. Let the other half roll over. I like your idea of preventative focus. Use the money geared toward the prevention of homelessness."

"So in three months, I'd be giving $45,000 to help the City of Chilliwack in areas that I think will work on preventing homelessness?"

"Yes."

"That's a lot of money," I said.

"It's a big problem. Actually, I think you'll be grossly underfunded, but we need to start somewhere."

"Well, Daryl, of course this is something I'd love to do. I'm going to have to have a conversation with Haney, though. I wouldn't endeavour to do anything like this without his support, and I've invested my rainy-day fund already, so the $5,000 would have to come out of our house fund, and I won't dip into that without agreement from him. And if I have a conversation, I'll be spilling the beans to the surprise I was setting up for him for next December, but, well, I can get over that." I smiled.

"Good," Daryl replied. "I would love it if you're both involved. Have the conversation with him and get back to me."

"I'll talk to him tonight when I get home from work."

Daryl took a sip of his beer then continued. "You know, maybe I have COVID to thank for this, slowing me down enough to look around me. I never gave any thought at all to homelessness or poverty, except in order to clean it up so the resorts I was planning would do well."

Contemplating his thought, I asked, "Are you doing in Chilliwack what you did in Belize then? Cleaning up the streets so whatever you do here does well?"

"No, this is different. The infrastructure of Chilliwack is already done; it doesn't need me for that, and I still don't know for certain if I plan on doing anything in Chilliwack. The team is just investigating. The money I'm investing for the homeless problem here isn't contingent on that; it's strictly to alleviate the issue. As I said, I never gave a homeless person much thought, until now, that is."

Do You Want To?

I threw my bag on the chair and kissed Haney hello after I got home from work that evening.

"Hey, I have something I've been working on that I need to talk to you about."

Haney listened intently to all of the investments I'd been working on for everyone, the projected outcome, the names involved. His eyes got wide, his mouth hung open a little.

I continued. "The only reason I'm telling you this now, and ruining the big surprise I had for you, is because Daryl is proposing another investment, and while the investment would need $5,000 of our money, it's not just the money decision you need to be a part of, but the decision on our future. If we immerse ourselves in alleviating homelessness in Chilliwack, this will change our future. Our work will be entirely different, our focus completely different. I just need to know if this is something you want to do."

"Is this for real?" Haney asked.

"I don't know. I really don't know. You've spent time with Daryl, what are your thoughts? Do you get any indication that he's anything other than he claims to be?"

"Oh no," Haney replied, "he is who he says he is."

"I guess this is like faith, isn't it? Do you believe? If you say you believe, then step into it; if you don't step into it, then you don't really believe." I mulled the thought even as I spoke it.

"True."

"The worst-case scenario would be Daryl's a liar. What would that look like?"

"We'd be out the money," Haney said.

"Yup, but that's not the worst of it, I think. Money is money. I've spent more on Keno and lottery tickets in my life than I've invested with him, and I've taken more chances on business that took more of my money than this potential $5,000. Worse is thinking that a person could actually lie about something like this, and create such stories, and be so consistent in the stories." I was processing all the thoughts I'd be thinking for weeks out loud, bouncing them off of Haney, thankfully, because I couldn't do this before.

"His stories are so consistent, and believe me, I've been listening. When people lie, they can't remember what they lie about, and eventually things don't add up. I've been listening to him for months; one story flows to the next, to the next, to the next, seamlessly. If he was lying, he'd be brilliant to be able to keep all the facts in order the way he does."

"I don't think he's lying," Haney agreed.

"I think actually even worse than the lying is that he's becoming our friend." I continued to analyze the entire situation, bringing it down to the very worst possible conclusion. "Yes," I continued, "the very worst thing would be that our friend lying to us. That's worse than losing a few thousand dollars."

"Yes," Haney agreed.

"I guess the question we have to ask ourselves is: Do we believe him?"

I looked at Haney, he looked at me, and together we just nodded our heads.

"Anyone who spends any time with him can't help but believe him."

"So we're going to do this then?" I asked.

"Let's do it!" Haney agreed excitedly, then he added, "I have a few people I'd love to add to that list of yours. Do you think there's any more room in that investment?"

"Ha, I hadn't even thought about that! Now that you know, we can possibly add more names to the personal investment list! I'll ask Daryl tomorrow. Imagine, Haney, what this investment can do for the people we know: down payments on houses, student loans being paid, paying for school instead of taking out student loans, alleviating car payments. Oh my goodness, just think of it."

"I am." Haney grinned.

Happy Birthday, Dolly

"A fucking million dollars!"

Daryl had walked around the Bone to his seat. He was livid. He abruptly sat and ran his hand through his white hair viciously. His face was red. His eyes flashed.

I held my breath.

It was a striking moment. Witnessing the throng of his anger.

"They found a fucking CIBC account in Denise's name with a million fucking dollars that she has siphoned into it."

"Ohhh Daryl, I'm so sorry. I was really rooting for her," I commiserated. "What are you going to do?"

"I don't know. I don't know." He ran his hand through his hair again.

"Are they finished with the audit then?" I asked.

"Oh God, no, they've barely begun. I don't know what else they will find." He sighed. He put his phone up to his ear "What?" he said into it briskly.

I could never hear it vibrate; it must have been on the quietest mode. No doubt he would get so many messages it would drive him nuts to have it on at all. I was used to him interrupting our conversations this way. He got up out of his chair and took the conversation outside. He did this frequently too. I occasionally wondered about the ones he took outside versus the ones he had inside. Only briefly, though.

In less than five minutes he was back in his seat, sipping the beer I had placed there for him.

"More about Denise?" I probed.

"No, just some shit going on in Costa Rica we're dealing with." He sighed.

Probably not the time to bring up the investments, I thought. I went to cut limes, leaving him alone to mentally deal with the news coming at him.

Time washed down with a couple of pints eased Daryl's angst, and after the lunch crowd returned to their office desks, he stopped me as I was walking by.

"I almost forgot. I spoke with Tina this morning. Danny is set and ready to go with the Chilliwack fund."

"Excellent!" I replied, thankful he brought it up.

"We're good to go. Haney's on board completely; this will be so exciting, Daryl!"

"Well, it needs to happen."

"Now that I've informed Haney of all the investments I've made for others, he was wondering if there was any room for us to invest for people he knows. I said I would ask."

"Hmm," Daryl responded. "I'll talk to Danny tonight and see where that stands or if it's closed up. Generally he's pretty good at opening things for me. Tina mentioned that the Chilliwack investment would be around five times, not the nine times I originally thought."

"That's still an unbelievable return, Daryl."

"It is."

"Glenda, the bank machine's not working again!" Earl was turning red with frustration. "You need to get a new one; it never works," he vented.

I left Daryl's table to unplug the machine, praying the forced reboot would work. "Give Earl the money he needs to play the Keno to soothe the savage beast," I whispered.

When I returned to the Bone, Daryl was giggling to himself.

"What?" I questioned.

He looked upward, his right eye once again opened its gate, releasing tears. He wiped them away while laughing, shaking his head, and laughing some more.

"It's Dolly's birthday today; she's seventy-five." His shoulders shook under the weight of his own merriment. "I just sent her seventy-five bottles of Tennessee whisky."

Boys in the Bright White Sports Car

Lights flashed, bouncing off the mirrored ball hanging precariously from the ceiling. Tiny blue spots danced within swirls of green and strobes of red pulsing perfectly to the beat of the guitar. Capo on the first fret, thumb and forefinger rhythmically moving back and forth on Am.

Bump bump bump bump bump bump bump bump.

It exhaled.

The guitarist looked up. He loved this moment.

His fingers continued holding the beat. They moved on their own. They didn't need him; the fret was their home, and they were banging on the door.

Bump bump bump bump bump bump bump bump.

The crowd recognized the beat.

The crowd turned to the stage.

The crowd held their arms up, pounding their fists in the air: "Let us in, let us in, let us in."

The guitarist smiled. "Ahh, that's it, you're ours now." He gave a nod to the band and they took off.

And the crowd waved their arms in the air as the band sang "The Boys in the Bright White Sports Car."

The crowd went wild.

Cheers and beers were spilling all over the place. It was bloody magic.

A cop walked in, and the guitarist nodded his way as he walked by. The cop smiled and nodded back.

The band continued.

The guitarist smiled, and his eye followed the cop. *Ah, there he is. What's he doing over there? Is he smiling at the bouncer who's making out with two girls in the back corner? Because that's exactly what it looks like.* He laughed out loud as the band continued.

***

"Oh, sorry, did you need to go? I'll grab your bill," I said to the looming figure before me.

"I don't mean to rush you, but my tires are done. I have to go pick up my car at Ken's," he replied.

"No problem at all," I said as I tapped my finger on the POS to bring his bill up.

"I used to work here," he said as he smiled. "A long time ago."

"You did?"

"I did. Back in the day when they had some of the bigger named bands come in."

"That must have been fun," I said.

"It was. Oh, we got smashed. They didn't care back then; drinking on the job was part of the job."

His smile broadened. Turning to the back corner he said, "Over there, the night Trooper played, I was making out with two girls." He started laughing as he reminisced. "A cop walked by and watched me; he nodded and smiled."

"Those were the good old days."

He paid his tab and left; his memory followed him.

My phone buzzed.

"I'm in Seattle," read the message from Daryl.

We had exchanged phone numbers the first time we met up to watch football, and this was the first text I received.

"What the heck are you doing in Seattle?" I replied.

"Meeting with Danny. He's also contributing $5,000 to the Chilliwack Fund."

"Really?"

"We're out for drinks. Tina is here, and we've been talking about Chilliwack's needs. She would also like to put in $5,000, but she wanted to be sure that's okay with you. Is it okay?"

"Hello! Yes! Of course it's okay!"

"I'll let her know. She just didn't want to step on anybody's toes."

"No toes to step on here! This is amazing; please thank them very much for me," I typed excitedly into my phone.

'They are very impressed with how you want to help people; it's moved them to want to help too. I'll be back in a few hours."

"How are you getting back?"

"The same way I got here. On the chopper."

***

The next morning an email was flashing in my inbox:

From: *Tina Hoffmeister*
Sent: *Thursday, January 2021 7:59:13 AM*
To: *Glenda Toews*
Subject: *New investment*

Holstein Fund Management Group
1201 - 3rd Ave.
Seattle, Washington

    Dear Ms. Glenda Toews,

    Account #: Can/GT 2021010052

    Please accept this confirmation of your new investment account.

    The current deposits and balance are:

    Glenda $ 5,000.00 + $5000 (Daryl)
    Danny $ 5,000.00 + $5000 (Daryl)
    Tina $ 5,000.00 + $5000 (Daryl)
    Daryl. $10,000.00
    ———————————————————————

    Total $40,000.00

    The guaranteed investment multiplier of 6 times.
    The guaranteed payout amount available on March 5, 2021
will be no less than $240,000.00 (Can).
    I trust this meets with your satisfaction.

    Tina Hoffmeister

General Manager Account Services

***

Holy hockey sticks, I thought, shaking my head, excitement welling up within me. *Daryl doubled everything, and is that more I see? What the heck?*

I picked up my phone and texted him.

"Morning, D. Tina just emailed me with a breakdown of the Chilliwack fund. You added more?"

"Yes, I told you, you are grossly underfunded. You still are grossly underfunded to do things right."

"Thank you, this is going to be amazing."

"Don't thank me. You're the one who will be doing all the work. See you later when I come in for a beer."

Casino Shares

We were sitting around the fire—not the real crackling, roasting weenies one, but the convenient, smoke-free propane one that takes the chill off while simultaneously flicking ambience on. Ann was sipping a Caesar, I a beer. We were watching our dogs run the property.

"The casino is still not open?" I asked. "How are you managing with that?"

"I'm managing, but really there isn't any choice. If they stay closed for the duration of COVID, there isn't much I can do about it, can I?"

My sister had been serving at the restaurant in the casino for a number of years. The industry was buckling under the burden of government restrictions.

She shrugged her shoulders. "Quiggles, get back here!" she hollered to her pug, who was investigating sites a little too close to the road.

"I think I'm going to have to go and look for a job, though. My savings are dwindling. The casino is still paying our health insurance, which is great. I got an email from them too; they wanted to buy out my employee shares."

"You have shares in the casino?" I asked.

"Yes, everyone was offered them. I have some, and now they're asking if I want to sell them."

"Are you going to?"

"No, I know some girls who are selling them, but I think I'll hang on to mine."

"I think that's a great idea. I would too. If you don't need to sell them, just hang on to them."

The conversation turned to food and what great thing we ate last, as it often does.

As the visit continued, I contemplated what great joy it will be to hand her her cheque next December. All of this suffering, all of the financial difficulties, all of the burdens she is carrying today, next year will be lifted. I imagined how we would do it. I imagined her reaction. It was very hard not to tell her. I was so excited.

"Do you want another Caesar?" I asked instead.

Twelve More Names

"You have twelve more names," Daryl said as he took his seat.

"Excuse me?"

"You've been doing $100 per name on your list, right?"

"Yes."

"I'm giving you twelve names. Finance has found another bank account in Denise's name as well other funds she's been transferring to her fucking family. Three fucking million dollars so far!" He was shaking his head. "She could have just asked me. I would have given her the money. Why didn't she just ask me?" he said more to himself than to me.

"What are you going to do, Daryl?"

"It's with the lawyers now. She can have her fucken prenup. I'm done."

"What about your house?"

"It's Crystal Castles' house. She can use her prenup and buy something. I don't care. She'll be given her papers to leave. And if she wants to give me problems, we'll just charge her with theft. Three fucking million dollars?" he restated, shaking his head in disbelief.

He turned directly to me and continued. "I had made an investment for them with Danny, but now I'm transferring that investment to you. So send twelve names to Tina. Oh, and Danny said it was fine if you and Haney wanted to increase your own personal list as well. Whatever you need, he'll make it work. The simple fact that you're doing this for other people is the reason he'll manoeuvre funds around. I've told him he can move some of what I have to make room for yours if he needs. Whoever else you two want to help, he will make it happen."

I was speechless.

"Tina's waiting for your twelve names though, so try to get them to her as soon as possible so she can adjust that particular account. I want it out of their name. Fucking leeches."

The Final List

Twelve names then. So many to choose, but the burden of choice was mine. It was a burden. How do you pick? Who at the end of the year do you give upwards of $200,000 to? Do I give more to my own family? Do they need it?

Haney and I discussed who he would like on his list. With a mixture of family, some friends, we added people we worked with, thinking of ways we could extend the reach the furthest.

By the following weekend, I had emailed Daryl's Tina the following list:

Kayden
Eddie
Nikko
Andy
Noah
Matthew
Aaron
Zack
Melissa
Bill
Jasra & Jason
Arthur
Elsie
Jake
Rudy
Gisela

Denise

Sandra

Kaleigh

Al

Chris

Andy and Cheryl

Brent and Lisa

Chris

Westeck Plant 2 Employees Fund, % Haney

Elisebete

Tim

Heidi

Tandy

Karen

Dawson

Dylan

Fionn

Tina & William

Heidi S

Vivien

Kim

Robyn

Dan & Linda

Haney and Glenda's Nephews and Nieces fund, % Haney and Glenda

We had counted the total. Seventy-eight people would be helped, and contingency funds would be set up for those we may have missed or those we haven't yet met who would need help in the future. We made sure everyone we worked with had either their name on the list or would be included in our contingency fund.

This final list was emailed to Tina, with the instruction that she could close up the investments we were doing for others.

Haney and I spent hours talking about our hopes for each person on our lists. Excitement grew inside as we imagined the following December when we'd be able to present each person with their own cheque. The doors that would open for them. The financial burdens would be relieved. Every day, a surge of joy bounced in our souls knowing help was coming for them. As we heard their burdens over the following months, it was so difficult to remain quiet. We just wanted to speak it out loud: "Don't you worry, in eleven months, you'll have enough relief to cover that problem, and then you can spend your energy working on other problems."

"Hang on, help is on its way!" We were so excited; the development of it was as amazing as thinking about the reality of it.

Phil

He rolled over and opened one eye. The brass alarm clock by his bedside ticked three minutes after eight. He'd slept in.

He could hear his mother moving about upstairs, tidying up no doubt, getting ready to go to the mall. She'd asked him yesterday if he wouldn't mind taking her. She had a few last-minute Christmas gifts to pick up. He rolled over the other way, yawning, stretching himself awake. Pulling himself to an upright position, he scratched his head and gave his round face a brisk rub. He leaned over and turned on the radio.

"99.3 this is CKLG with this sure to be a classic by Led Zeppelin," came the DJ's deep voice, followed by Jimmy Page's gentle finger picking on a guitar. His distinctive tone flowed into the distinctive voice. Robert Plant started singing about a lady who's sure all that glitters is gold, and she's buying a stairway to heaven.

Damn, I gotta learn this song, he thought, grabbing his bell bottoms and slipping his legs inside.

"Man, Page and that guitar! Just wow!"

He glanced to the corner of the room, where his Les Paul Custom leaned. Ebony with block inlays and gold trim. She was a beaut, purchased last year and played daily since.

His feet turned in its direction, invisibly drawn to it by the sound Page was pulling him in with. *I'll just pick along with the song, just for a bit.*

"Sweetheart?" came his mom's voice from the top of the stairs. "Are you up, honey?"

"Ya, Mom."

"Breakfast is ready for you, and the mall opens at 9:00 a.m. Okay?"

"Ya, Mom. Thanks."

He turned from the Gibson. "Later, lady," he promised. It was December 23, 1972. He was nineteen.

He finished getting dressed, and then taking the stairs two at a time, he bounded up to the kitchen for his breakfast.

"Are you almost ready?" his mom asked after he chewed the last of his bacon strips.

"Yup," he replied as he gulped down the rest of his orange juice. "Let's go, Mom!"

He opened the passenger side and let his mother slip in. He walked around the car, jingling the keys in his right hand. He heard his name being called. Who was that? His hand tightened its grip on the keys. He glanced around. He could have sworn he heard his name. He thought he heard his name. There was nobody near except his mother, who was sitting in the car reapplying her lipstick. That was weird. He shook it off, like a dog after a dog fight, and slid into the driver seat. He turned on the car, turned his head, and started backing out of the driveway.

"DON."

His foot slammed on the brake.

It wasn't a sound; it was a thought. The thought squeezed. Enormous arms reaching around his mind, shackling the thought to his soul. He gasped.

"You all right, honey?" His mother was looking over at him, concern etched in her eyes.

"I think so, Mom; it's just weird. I just, I just have a weird feeling."

"Did you have too much to drink last night?" she asked.

"Not that kind of feeling, Mom. I just feel, well … heavy."

"Okay, are you okay to take me to the mall? We can stay home."

"No, Mom, of course we'll go. I'm good."

"Okay then."

He drove for five minutes with the arms wrapped around his chest, squeezing relentlessly. *What the hell?* he thought. *This feeling just isn't letting go. And Don? Why do I keep thinking about him? I just saw him last night?* As the name came to mind, an unobservable weight pressed it down.

"Mom, is it okay if I just drop you at the mall? I really feel like I need to go to Don's house. This feeling just is not going away."

"Of course, honey, we're right here. Let me out, and I'll walk the last bit. You go see Don."

He pulled over; his mom got out and gave a quick wave goodbye.

He turned the corner, went through one light, and was a right-hand turn from his buddy's. He saw it before he heard it—a plume of black smoke rising up in the direction of Don's house. The sound that followed was indescribable. It shook his ears, it shook his soul, it shook the world.

He rounded the corner and in front of him was his friend Don, running blindly toward the road, fully engulfed in flames.

Jumping out of the car, he leaped on top of Don. His body weight pushed Don down. Together they were rolling in the snow. Gasoline fumes reached up into his nostrils as he forced the fire down using his body to roll Don's body. It felt like they were rolling forever; if felt like they were rolling a lifetime.

The flames went out.

When Don realized he was no longer on fire, he ran back to the house, smashing at the basement window.

"They need air! They need air! THEY NEED AIR!" he screamed as he clawed at the broken glass with his burnt hands.

The fire trucks had arrived, and the firemen ran to Don, pulling him away before he did more damage to himself.

He turned his head toward the basement steps. Robert, in full flames, staggered up and out of the doorway.

The horror of it dropped his jaw.

He was frozen.

John and Robert didn't survive.

The motorcycle they were working on in the family room of Don's house exploded.

Gasoline coated all of them.

At the hospital, the nurses asked him if he could identify his friends. He nodded yes.

They pulled back the curtain.

The smell.

Oh God, the smell.

He could only identify Robert's glasses. They were melted to his charred remains.

***

"Hey, Glenda, we'll take a jug over here if you don't mind." Phil was beaming. "Two glasses, please."

"On its way!" I smiled.

I poured the beer and reached into the cooler for two icy cold pint glasses and headed over to Phil's table.

"Here you are," I said as I lay their coasters down.

"Say, would you mind getting me a tall, narrow glass?" Phil's friend asked.

"Sure, no problem. I prefer the tall ones myself. I'll be right back."

"Have you met my friend yet?" Phil asked as I placed the tall pint glass before him.

"No, please introduce." I grinned.

"Don, this is Glenda. Glenda, this is my very oldest friend in the whole world, Don."

"Nice to meet you, Don," I said.

"And nice to meet you too, Glenda," Don replied. "Thank you for bringing me the narrow glass. I have a hard time holding on to anything with these hands."

Just Stay Silent

Haney and I slid into the booth beside Daryl as Nikki flicked on the Kansas City game.

"Beers all the way round?" she asked.

"Yes, Nikki, thanks, and water too if you don't mind," I responded.

Haney and Daryl were talking football, and I glanced at my phone and saw my inbox flash. It was a message from Tina. Daryl's Tina. I clicked on it:

"I have to decide who I'm going to cheer for in this game. The next game, anyone can win, as long as it's not Brady. I hate Brady. And for the KC game, Daryl told me to pick Cleveland, with the spread. Thank God I listened. I'm five grand up because they didn't make the spread!!"

Tina and I spent the afternoon chatting back and forth—girl football via emails.

By the end of the game, her voice was becoming tipsy, her emojis were full of martinis, and her apologies of being unprofessional were typed.

As we were getting up to leave, her last message read in giggle style: *"If you could just make his wife go away, I would be forever in your debit. I've had a crush on him for ten years."*

Well, I knew his marriage was over.

I thought it best to stay silent.

Hope

"It's positive," he said. She smiled a little when she heard the words. "It's a good thing then?" he asked.

She didn't know how to answer that question. She didn't think it was horrible, but she didn't think it was good. She was fifteen. She didn't think much about anything.

"The father?" he asked.

Nope, no doubt the father wouldn't be excited about this news. The father had broken up with her weeks ago. "I love you sometimes," he had whispered into the phone. "In the moment I really do. But I don't love you all times. Sorry." *Click.*

The click echoed.

Click, click, click.

"Just like that, you twist a heart with a click."

She thought it was love. She was pretty darn sure what she felt was love. The click mocked her. "Silly child, silly child, now you are the one with child, welcome to one-sided love."

Click, click, click.

"If you need anything," the doctor in front of her said, "don't hesitate to call."

She nodded her head, thanked him, and left his office, never intending to return again.

I guess I'm going to have to tell my mother, she thought. *Make an appointment with our regular family doctor. I'm going to have to tell Theo.* The thoughts swirled. *Maybe he'll have a change of thought. Maybe he'll realize he does love me after all. Maybe we'll run off and get married and have a cute little baby and live happily ever after.* She smiled at the dream. *Yes, let's work toward that.*

Feeling focused but deathly afraid, she dialed his number. He answered. She whispered the news into the receiver she held tightly in her left hand. He was livid. "You have to get rid of it!"

Visions of happily ever after vanished.

She told her mother. Her mother was livid. "You have to get rid of it! I'm not raising another!"

Visions of whatever could be in the future were sucked back into a vortex. Her head spun.

Maybe she should tell her father. Maybe he wouldn't kill her if she did. No, he most certainly would kill her. She was hoping to have an ally in her mother, and an ally in the baby's father, be the strength holding her up as she broke the news to her father. Clearly this wasn't going to happen. She had absolutely no one.

She lay on her bed numb for weeks.

Click, click, click was replaced by, *Get rid of it, get rid of it, get rid of it.*

It was relentless.

Her mother made the appointment.

The ex-boyfriend paid the way.

She relented.

And let them have their way.

And a little life ended that day.

She would have loved to have spent the rest of her life blaming them both, but she couldn't. The choices she had made that ended with a pregnancy were hers, and to end that life, the very final say was also hers.

Nobody ever mentioned the guilt she would carry for the rest of her days.

Nobody told she would crawl under the shame for every moment of every day of all of her life.

Nobody told her she would count birthdays as the years turned and would wonder if it was a boy or a girl, and if they had brown eyes or blue.

Nobody told her she would grieve as a mother grieves the loss of her baby.

Nobody told her of the turmoil, grief mixed with guilt, that would pound at her soul like a waterfall beating against a boulder, daily, ceaselessly.

Instead, the world says it's her right to do this, and they celebrate it.

She wonders why.

They said it was the easy way. They lied.

***

"Morning, Glenda," Pat said as I turned on the lights to start the day. "How was your weekend?"

"Good, Pat. Yours?"

"Same old, same old."

I filled the ice well, laid out the bar mats, and retrieved the fruit caddy from the fridge. I turned to the remote and clicked "on." Every TV jumped to life, and Linda Perry started singing "What's Going On" The speakers vibrate. I sing along.

Perhaps in a different lifetime I could sing like her, I thought as I straightened the tables.

Eleven AM I open the doors.

"Good morning, Dave."

"Morning, Glenda."

"Morning, Phil."

"Good morning, Glenda."

"Good morning, Doug."

"Morning, Glenda."

Every morning is filled with good mornings.

The phone rang. "Corky's. Glenda speaking," I answered.

"Glenda?"

"Yes, Glenda here. How can I help you?" I replied.

"Glenda," the voice said again.

It was familiar. Momentarily familiar, like a word sitting on the end of your tongue, there but unreachable, until it hits you.

"Glenda, it's Theo."

"Hi, Theo," I whispered into the receiver.

"Is this a good time to talk?" came the voice from the past.

I scanned the room. Everyone was content.

"Yes."

"I've been thinking, lately I've been thinking a lot. I just need to say I'm really sorry for pressuring you and demanding that you end that pregnancy."

"Ohhhh."

A million thoughts in a millisecond shot through my mind.

"I always thought it was a little girl," he continued.

Oh, he knew it was a baby too, whispered in my mind.

"I always thought it was a little boy," I replied, taking the phone into the staff bathroom for a bit of privacy.

"I was thinking, I was thinking that maybe it would be a good idea if we named our baby."

Ohhh, I had never thought of that.

"I think that our baby needs a name," he said quietly.

"I hadn't thought about that, but that's a very sweet idea. I think that's a beautiful idea," I replied

"What do you think would be a good name?" he asked.

"Theo, would you mind if I thought about it for a bit?"

"Of course!"

"Give me a few days."

"I'll call you in a couple of days, okay?"

"Okay."

Life has a way of moving perpetually forward until a smell, a thought, a voice stops us in our tracks and pulls us back.

I laced up my running shoes the next morning, clapped my headphones over my ears, turned up the music, and started my run. I thought of the baby. I thought of its life. I thought of my right to even name it. As I ran, I prayed.

"I'm so sorry for taking that life."

And I started to cry as I ran and I ran harder.

A thought whispered, "If you could give one gift to this baby, what gift would it be? One gift, just one gift in an entire lifetime, what would that gift be?"

It breathed into me.

That Gift.

Clear, distinct, direct, and full.

"Hope."

I would give it hope.

And so we named our baby.

Baby Hope.

And we prayed that Hope would be blessed.

Way Out of My League

I opened my laptop and an email from Tina welcomed me:

"I'm sorry for my unprofessional manner yesterday. I had been enjoying the game at Danny and Tayna's, and Tanya and I were trying different martinis. I got a little tipsy and spoke a little too freely.

Daryl is due to arrive at our office later this afternoon to meet with Danny regarding the Chilliwack fund. I will endeavour to keep it professional with him.

Tina.

***

I was surprised to see Daryl at the pub when I opened the doors.

"Aren't you supposed to be in Seattle today?"

"I am. The chopper is scheduled for 1:00 p.m.," he replied. "How did you know I was going?"

"Tina messaged this morning and mentioned it."

"God, she's stunning." He smiled. He was clearly thinking of her image in his mind. "Way out of my league," he murmured.

It was a little painful to listen to these two separately, secretly pining over each other. Yet I hesitated to speak up. Daryl's words months ago—"I don't want to be responsible for the choices people make"—echoed in my mind on more than one occasion, and they were doing that now as I stood before him, listening to his longing.

I simply said, "Daryl, you don't strike me as a person who fears stepping into things out of your league. Look at what you've created. All of that was clearly way out of your league. Button up your personal stuff up here. Whatever lies in your future will be, but don't fear stepping into something you think is out of your league. You just never know."

"Buttoned up is done."

"What? How is that even possible." My eyes widened.

"When you have proof of theft and she has a hefty prenup and a really good legal team to fast-track papers." He grinned. "I could fight the prenup, I suppose; instead, we just deducted the money she siphoned off into her bank accounts and wrote her a cheque for her speedy departure."

"She went for that?"

"She didn't have much choice. It was that or criminal charges." He snickered. "She did ask if she could keep the Land Rover."

"And?"

"And I said fine, I don't give a fuck. I don't need to be driving around in flashy vehicles in Chilliwack, drawing attention to myself. I'm perfectly fine driving her old blue Honda. Divorce papers should be here in three weeks I'm told."

The Foundation of Hope

"I messaged Alice from the school," I said to Haney as he dropped his lunch bag on the counter.

"And?"

"And, I was talking to her about the funds that are coming and how best to help. I figured they're the ones who know where the problems lie, so they will be the ones best to direct where the funds go. She asked if we could meet with them.. I'm going there on Friday. Do you want to come?"

"Oh ya! This is exciting. I can't believe I'm excited to have to meet with the principal!" He laughed. "Is there any news from the regional district about our house yet?"

"Nothing! At least we have something to keep our minds occupied. I think I'd be going nuts otherwise! How six weeks turns into four months blows my mind."

"Crazy."

"Utterly mad," I concurred.

***

He was beaming. He was beyond beaming, if there could be such a thing.

"You'll never guess what happened, Glenda."

"In your life? Probably not, Daryl." I laughed.

"I went down to Danny's office, and then he asked me to join him and Tanya for dinner, so I stayed. We were at the little pub near the office, just starting on drinks, and Tina walked in. God, she's just stunning. Anyway, she sits down to join us, and Danny says, "Look, you too, you're driving us nuts. We know you've liked each other for years, so Tanya and I are leaving. Have a nice night."

"For real?" My jaw was open.

"Yes!" Daryl started laughing, and he wiped away that lone tear that seeps out of his eye when he's amused.

"They just left us there." He started laughing.

"God, it was amazing. She's amazing. So insecure, so timid. It's fascinating that this woman who is so fierce with numbers is so unsure of herself as a woman. She invited me back to her place, and we sat on the sofa and held hands and talked and talked." His tone dropped. "She told me about her childhood. God, Glenda, the fucking abuse; she can never have children, her fucking father …"

A flash crossed his eyes, and then he buried it.

"I'm going back tonight." He looked at me and smiled.

"You are? Why didn't you just stay?" I asked.

"Oh, I had meetings in Vancouver. Maverick has had the opportunity to buy Gateway Casinos, and we're working on a deal with Great Canadian Casinos."

"Excuse me? You're buying casinos here, in Canada?"

"Yes, the team's been working on it for some time. We just had to make sure we could get as many shares as possible. We offered to buy anyone's shares; we even sent out letters to all the employees to see if they wanted to sell their shares."

"Ah, I know. So that was you guys? My sister works at the casino, and she got an email asking if she wanted to sell her shares."

"Yup, that was us. COVID has actually helped me a lot. It's opened up the door to buy things that wouldn't have ever been available. They just can't afford to keep things going, so they looked for buyers. And, well, I have a little experience in the field." He giggled and another tear dropped.

"So you're going back to Seattle tonight?"

"Yes, I'll be back in the morning. I have some more meetings." Daryl spun his phone on the bar-top. "Oh, I forgot to mention, I was talking to Jane. She's suggesting that it would be better for us to manoeuvre in a registered foundation."

"Our Chilliwack Fund?"

"Yes, this is her thing, philanthropy and foundations. We were talking about your vision, and the size of Chilliwack, and the problems. Her recommendation was to go the registered foundation route."

"Okay then, how would you like me to proceed with that?" I asked.

"You don't. We have our legal team working on it as we speak."

"That's handy." I laughed. "What does the process look like?"

"Well, I've been informed that you will have to come up with a foundation name. They will apply for registration, and hopefully COVID won't delay the process. Jane and Ryan Renolds have worked together on other foundational areas and have been through the process a number of times. She has directed me to their legal team in Vancouver, who I've been told is the best. They'll streamline the process. You have nothing to do but come up with a name and wait."

"Ryan Reynolds?" My mind was swirling.

"Yes, Ryan Reynolds does a lot in the philanthropy area. Jane met him a number of years ago on a project in Calgary. They've teamed up on a few others since then." Daryl took a sip on his pint.

"So you want me to name it?"

"Yes. Tina and I last night were also talking about your vision. She's so excited about it too. She'd love to be more involved, if you'll have her. It's not a bad idea. She's spectacular when it comes to finances. And you'll need a strong team; even if she's not directly involved, she'll be able to vet CFOs for you."

"Daryl! I would completely welcome her help! Of course she can be involved. My goodness, if anyone is willing just to jump in like this and be as excited as we are, I wouldn't ever turn that help away!"

Daryl smiled. "I'll let her know. She'll be more than happy to hear that."

My mind was so filled with information and also with terms I didn't know. *What does vet mean? What is CFO short for?* I thought. I excused myself. *No doubt I'll have to learn a lot of things I just don't know,* my thoughts continued. *Thank goodness for Google.* I smiled, picked up my phone, and typed, "what does vet mean" into the search bar, and then I typed "CFO." Ah haaaa! I grinned with my newly-found information.

I poured another pint for Daryl and walked to the Bone. "Oh, I forgot to tell you, Haney and I are meeting with a teacher group on Friday."

Daryl looked up from his phone. "Already?"

"Well, if we're going to do this thing, there's no reason to wait." I smiled.

He nodded his head in agreement. "It should be interesting. I'll let Tina know."

"Do you think this meeting is something she'd like to attend?" I asked.

"I don't know, and I'm not quite sure if she can travel within the COVID restrictions. I have my essential service card. I have no issues at the border. I don't know if she will or even if she wants to travel, given the pandemic itself.

We can talk about these things tonight." He was quietly thoughtful.

***

An email from Tina was waiting in my inbox the next day:

"Thank you so much for allowing me to be a part of the foundation. I'm so excited for all of this, and to meet you. And I'm so happy Daryl is in my life. Do you know that when I arrived at work, my entire office was full of roses. I can hardly believe this! I don't deserve this! I could barely work. Every girl in the office is peeking in and wondering where all the flowers came from; it's so fun.

"Just so you know, I've been talking with Jane, whom I've known for years, and she's given me the contact information of the foundation lawyers. I will send them an email introducing myself, if that's okay with you.

"Also, just so you know, Daryl and Danny are working on something to truly increase your fund."

Winky emojis followed.

I closed my laptop and picked up my wine glass. I took a sip. An idea formed in my mind. *Glenda, let Tina pick the name for the foundation. If she can never have children, she will never have that opportunity. Give her this gift. Let her name the foundation.*

I opened my laptop.

"Tina, seeing as you're a part of the creation of the foundation, would you like to help me name it?"

I hit send.

"Oh my, I would have no idea," she replied.

"Well, think about it," I said, with my own series of heart emojis.

"I will," she replied.

The next morning an email from Tina greeted me: *"How about 'The Foundation of Hope'?"*

I stared at the name.

Hope.

And the prayer from a few years prior whispered across my mind: "Let Hope be blessed."

"Oh my," I whispered. "Oh my."

I opened up my laptop and hit reply: "The name is absolutely perfect. Thank you, Tina."

Western Poverty & Woodstock Seniors

"Do you think we could use some of the money for computers?" The school representative asked.

We were sitting around a boardroom table, brainstorming.

"We could outfit twenty-five classrooms with twenty-five computers each and still not have enough," he continued. "It's not like we have the Gates Foundation here." He laughed a little.

"If it all goes as I've been told, I would imagine there would be enough money for that eventually," I replied.

There were six of us around the table. We were all trying to wrap our minds around what was to come and what it would mean.

"We could outfit the clothes closet," Alice said. "So many students don't have proper seasonal clothing. We have a room here that we can set up as a 'free store'."

"What about Tim Horton's cards?" asked another. "It would be amazing to give students these cards, tell them to take their parents out for a coffee, do some bridge building."

"Save on Food cards? Their families could use food."

"There were so many wonderful leadership programs that were canceled due to lack of funding. Do you think we could start them again? If we build solid leaders in our youth, it trickles down."

"Do you think we can fund university week? Pay for students to go spend the week at the universities so they can see what it could be like for them? So many of our students haven't seen or had a chance to visit campuses."

"Leisure centre cards, bus passes, taxi passes—let's get them transportation to their jobs and get them home safely. Let's keep them off the streets and keep them busy."

"Could we start a food program? They could just go in the cafeteria line and pick their own lunch. So many don't have lunch. If we knew they could at least get one full solid meal during the day."

"Do you think we could set up a work program, so that our students who need jobs can connect with Chilliwack businesses to get jobs?"

"Some of our students live at the Cyrus Centre, the centre for youth who can't live at home. They live there and they still come to school. Can we use funds for that? To buy them necessities?"

"Christmas hampers and summer hampers? Can we fund that? During the shutdown, our teachers were taking hampers to some students we knew were struggling."

"COVID is creating more suffering than we've seen before."

The questions were fired from the different faces staring at us across the board table, finishing with Alice. "Shoes. Some just need new shoes." She sighed.

Our heads were spinning as we left the meeting. How does it get this bad? We live in Chilliwack. How are these needs not being met? How did we not even know!

***

From: Tina Hoffmeister
Sent: 2021 9:14:56 AM
To: Glenda
Subject: Foundation of Hope Fund

January 21, 2021
Holstein Fund Management Group
Dear Glenda,
As I indicated a few days ago, Daryl and Danny have been busy having some discussions about your various funds.

We all believe in what you're doing but are concerned you will be grossly underfunded.

With this in mind, we have all reduced our personal financial involvement in this opportunity and would like to add funds to the Foundation of Hope Fund.

We can also confirm that the second quarter multiplier will be no less than 9.5 times the invested funds.

Taking all these factors into consideration, we would like to add $40,000.00 to your account so that the balance of the initial funds prior to maturity is $100,000.00.

Please let me know if you are comfortable with us helping in this fashion.

Tina Hoffmeister
General Manager Account Services

***

I was plenty happy they were helping in this fashion. I knew exactly where the initial funds would be directed.

***

The Bone was filled with the Chillibowl regulars when Daryl walked in. He took off his jacket in customary fashion and hung it on the back of the barstool at the bar. He was bookended by Carl and Patrick.

"Say, Glenda, get this young man a beer, would ya," Carl said. His vocal cords, coated in fifty years of tar, rasped. "Put it on my tab, would ya."

"You didn't have to do that, but thank you." Daryl accepted the pint and took a sip. "And thank you for calling me young."

"Everyone is younger than me." Carl guffawed, and a thousand wrinkles sculpted his snicker.

"Hey, guys!" I hollered at the table of Chillibowlers. "What's in that brown bag? Why are you passing it around?"

Les quickly passed the brown sack to Dave, who crunched it up and tucked it between him and Lee.

"What bag are you talking about?" Dave chuckled.

The whole table of white hairs, the youngest probably seventy years old, were tittering like teenagers. I walked over like principal Greta McGee to see what they were up to. No need to see. I got within a foot of their table and could smell it.

"Guys!!! Really?"

The lot of them were chuckling.

"It's just a bag of brownies. I had baked some, so I'm just sharing. I'll take them back to my car now." Dave smiled, unable to contain his merriment.

"That's a good idea," I concurred. "And could you bring your pine tree air freshener back with ya? The table reeks."

Woodstock seniors. Trading their Volkswagen Samba bus for the Honda CRV, communal living for condos, and their peace signs for pensions cheques. They now swap brownies not for the high, but to ease the ache of arthritis.

I walked back behind the bar.

"Say, what do you do for work, young man?" Carl turned his head from the Keno board to Daryl's direction.

"Investments. I'm in investments."

"You seem to be in and out a lot here, but we missed ya last week. Where were you at?"

Daryl, amused by the old-timer, encouraged the conversation. "I fly in and out on business quite a bit. I was in Seattle."

"Seattle, huh?" Carl nodded. "Say, I was there once. What were you doing down there?"

Daryl smiled at Carl's candour. "Investing some money and taking a stunning woman out for drinks."

"Stunning? You really must have some money then." Carl gauffed.

Daryl ran his hand across his beer belly. "I need something to attract them," he jibed.

"Say, Glenda, can you cash these tickets in for me and get my tab? Patrick, you done?" Carl asked, nodding in Patrick's direction. Patrick nodded back. "I'll see you later, Daryl. You take care, will ya, Glenda."

"Bye, Carl," Daryl and I said at the same time.

"He's a character," Daryl concluded with a chortle.

"That he is," I agreed.

"How was your visit with the teachers?" Daryl asked.

"Oh my God, Daryl." I shook my head. "It's amazing that one just doesn't know what goes on unless you ask."

I ran down the entire conversation we'd had with the school, the help that was needed, and the story about the girl and her mom who shared shoes that Alice had told me.

"I'm embarrassed that I didn't know this kind of thing was going on here in Chilliwack. I understand a little more why the teachers would come here looking defeated.

I really know how we can initially direct funds to ease this burden."

Daryl sat listening intently.

"And the school representative asked if they could use some of the money for computers. He laughed a little when he said, 'It's not like we have the Gates Foundation helping us here.' He's right, we don't, but we do have The Foundation of Hope!" I smiled.

"It sounds like you were right, the idea of working with the schools," he responded thoughtfully.

"What's kind of scary is the fact that this is just one school. If this is a glimpse of the needs of our youth in Chilliwack, we've barely scratched the surface. No wonder we have the homeless problem we have. It will be really curious if we can develop a pay it forward mentality. If the foundation funds the needs, but we get the students to do the work. Building a sense of community and care. People feel valued when they give, and giving feels good; it releases endorphins and dopamine. Even those suffering the greatest feel naturally better when they're giving. Maybe if we concentrate on finding ways to work with this idea it will generate a longer-lasting, life-changing look for them as they move forward in their future."

I was breathless with ideas. Daryl listened to me and absorbed what I was sharing.

It was really hard to pull myself away from him, but people were coming in for lunch. Switching mindset, I started pouring pints and running food.

She Hates Red

She picked up the jar of MAC Studio Radiance and pressed the pump. One? Two? Maybe three would be needed for this bruise. She could hide the one on her arm under a sweater, but the one around her throat pushed up past the top of any turtleneck she owned.

She dotted it on and blended it in expertly. *What a thing to be an expert at*, she thought momentarily. She should have known better. She knew he wasn't in a good mood; she should have just put on the red stiletto boots he loved.

Turning into her closet, she found her scarlet lace bra, clicked it on, and straightened the straps before she slipped into her red cashmere sweater.

She hated red.

That was five years ago.

The top of her turtleneck rubbed off the foundation, and her boss saw the bruise.

Her boyfriend never returned home that night. She never saw him again. She never asked why.

She threw everything red out.

A nice-looking lawyer in the building where she worked had been asking her out recently. She kept turning him down, but he was persistent and quite charming. She agreed to dinner and drinks. The evening was fine. He wanted to see more of her, which she was okay with once in a while.

The lawyer saw her sitting in a pub with another man. The next day he approached her at work and asked her out on another date. She told him she was no longer interested in having dinners with him.

His body twitched ever so subtly. She flinched.

His eyes smoldered. She backed up and pressed the elevator call button.

Safely with four other people on the elevator, she left him on the ninth floor.

Turning toward him as the doors were closing, she saw his jaw move.

He was grinding his teeth.

***

"Hey, Grandpa."

Daryl leaned back in his seat to get a better look at the suit who'd just called him grandpa.

"Is this the guy you dumped me for?" Mr. Douche Bag leaned into Tina, brushing his lips to her ear. She shuddered involuntarily. Daryl saw it.

"Please excuse me," Daryl said. "This grandpa needs to use the bathroom." He stood up, giving Tina's hand a bit of a squeeze. Her eyes were pleading "don't go."

"I'll be right back," he assured her.

"Take your time, Grandpa. Tina and I have some catching up to do!" Douche Bag mocked.

True to his word, Daryl was back at the table in less than two minutes. Pulling out his chair and taking a seat, he flagged their server down. "Would you mind getting this gentleman's tab. He would like to clear up with you now. He'll be leaving us," Daryl instructed the server.

"Fuck you I am," the Douche retorted.

Both Tina and the server looked entirely confused.

"Trust me," Daryl continued, "get his tab."

The server ran off to do as instructed.

Daryl turned to Tina and held up his right fist, popping up his thumb. He looked at the Douche and said, "Three." Then his forefinger popped up. "Two." And lastly, he popped up the middle finger and said, "One."

When the word "one" was spoken, three very large men wearing very black leathers pushed their way through the front door. Straight forward they moved, three pairs of eyes zeroed in on the Douche standing behind Tina. Big Dude number one grabbed the Douche by the scruff of his neck and pushed him up toward the bar. Big Dudes two and three placed themselves on the Douche's right and left, like tattooed bookends.

"I suggest you get your wallet out and pay the lady," Big Dude number three said. His baritone dropped one more level and vibrated through the room: "NOW!"

Mr. Douche Bag had no choice but to comply.

The entire pub, frozen in silence, watched.

The three big dudes then escorted Mr. Douche Bag out the door.

Daryl took a sip of his beer, pausing his recantation of the events to me. I stood waiting patiently for him to swallow

"Well, Glenda, I heard the poor fella slipped on the sidewalk a block down the road, broke his hand or something trying to get back up and it got stuck in a grate. And the day after that, Tina said she was standing in the elevator when he walked up. He took one look at her, abruptly turned, and walked the other way. His casted arm was slinged upright across his chest." Daryl shrugged his shoulders, took another sip of beer, and twirled his cell phone on the bar top.

"Why did you go to the bathroom?" I asked.

"I had a call to make." He smiled and continued. "No cameras."

A Simple Phone Call

The grass crunched under my feet as I walked to the firepit. Cold and clear. Perfect fire day weather.

I ripped down ribbons of newspaper and loosely crumpled them beneath splinters of wood. Starting small, the matchsticks ignited, fanning a little, blowing a little until something red started glowing. Smoke curled upwards; gracefully the wind took its hand and together they waltzed beneath the cedars. I put a bigger piece of wood on the fire, settled into my chair, and opened my phone:

From: Tina Hoffmeister
Sent: Saturday, January, 2021
To: Glenda

Good morning,

Tanya and I are on our way to the Gates Foundation this morning.

I am very excited to be involved and doing this! It will be interesting to see the criteria they have; however, even if we don't meet it, I am sure we can arrange some sort of mutually beneficial alliance.

That is funny to hear what the principal said. Be careful what you dream! Ha! When we have people like Daryl involved, people who can move in social circles the rest of us don't, you never know what can happen! 😊

I will update you on the meeting later today!

Enjoy your day. We are getting ready for snow here. Uggggg.

"What? What the heck?" There really are no good words for shock. I was still trying to absorb the first email when the second one popped up:

From: *Tina Hoffmeister*
Sent: *Saturday, January, 2021*
To: *Glenda*
 Sorry to bother, but how many laptops would you require to make a substantial difference?

I reiterated what they told me: twenty-five for twenty-five classrooms, but that's an awful lot of computers!

From: *Tina Hoffmeister*
Sent: *Saturday, January, 2021*
To: *Glenda*

 Ok, they are talking about 1,750. So that would suffice I assume?

"YES! God, YES!"

From: *Tina Hoffmeister*
Sent: *Saturday, January, 2021*
To: *Glenda*
 Ok, I asked Daryl and he wasn't sure.
 I just talked to him and he is going to phone "buddy boy bill" and tell him you need 3,500 computers. So will leave it with that till I hear.
 We are still talking over coffee about other things they can provide. Skills training, etc.

"Are you kidding me? They are going to die! The school is going to die! I can barely contain my excitement; this is amazing!"

***

From: Tina Hoffmeister
Sent: Saturday, January, 2021
To: Glenda

Well, I don't know what to say.

"Buddy boy Bill" called during our meeting and said he just spoke with Daryl and has committed 3,500 laptops to be forwarded to this project for the beginning of the next school year.

They are also going to design a technology program that they hope could help kids enter into the computer sciences. They asked for a couple weeks to "put their thinking caps on." They were thinking a free education program at the school(s) but after hours. See what they come up with but was a great meeting!

Once all the notes are compiled, I will forward the summary to you.

On a side note, it was pretty entertaining to see their faces when Bill Gates called the lead person in his team. Was a "who the fuck are these people" moment. 😵‍💫😂

It was bizarre and a little overwhelming to see what happens when Daryl simply makes a call.

I hope this information helps with your strategic planning. Time to go for a drink

***

"Or a bottle, a whole frickin bottle of champagne!"
Who's world was I in?

Karrie

Strands of blonde hair stuck to the side of her face. Furiously she tried to push them away. A combination of sweat and tears glued them firmly, which made her more frustrated, and the added frustration fueled the fury.

She picked up a rock and held it momentarily in her right hand, arm posed like a pitcher. The stench of her own body odour wafted from her armpit. The smell was repugnant. Everything about her life was repugnant. And she was mad as hell.

"You want to fucking beat me? You breathe down my neck for a year, you piece of shit. I'm DONE!"

Her antagonist had run into the house, seeking escape.

"I'm FUCKING DONE!" she screamed as she hurdled the rock through the air into the front window.

There was a moment of victory. A moment when all the power that had been sucked out of her for the last year returned as she stared, still seething, smelling her own stench, waiting for her bully to come out of the house.

The bully didn't. The bully hid.

For a year, the bully tormented her.

For a year, she'd been crying to her teachers, the principal, the ministry, the cops.

"Help me! Help me! Help me!"

Their hands were tied, and the bully was left to bully.

The cops came and took her away. She was the bad guy now.

Surrounded by the nattering of authority and their hypocrisy.

She defiantly glared at them all.

Pushing out the sounds that were coming from their mouths, she went into herself and screamed:

"Shut up."

"Shut Up."

"SHUT UP!"

They didn't shut up.

"Fuck you all!"

She ran away.

Where the hell do you go when you're seventeen?

You run to the guy who offered you a hand of friendship via the internet. She bounced out of the hand of the bully and ricocheted into a den of vipers.

"Come here, beautiful one, try this; you'll feel better. There you go. I'll take care of you now; don't you worry about anything now," the serpent hissed.

So she did, and he did.

Mesmerized by his charm, she danced for him.

High on his drugs, she danced for him.

He hired her out, and she danced for them.

He put her in heels and clipped a long silver earring into her left ear, kissing her throat, and he placed a rhinestone necklace around her neck.

And he set her on the stage.

His pretty blonde little doll.

The necklace hung down between her breasts, reflecting the orange neon light from the Number Five Orange sign hung up behind the bar.

The music started thumping.

Bump, bump, bump, bump on the keyboard, vibrating through the speakers, vibrating through the crowd. And she started dancing.

And the music continued thumping.

And a couple of men were in front of her waving their long necks, believing tonight was going to be a good good night.

***

"Karrie," my message started, "you've shared bits and pieces of your story with me. I was wondering if you wouldn't mind sharing more so I could get a deeper understanding of your struggles in high school."

Karrie was a year younger than Danielle. Our families spent many hours together when they were children. I knew she'd had a lot of struggles as a teenager. Now that we were focusing on the high school students and the prevention of homelessness, I was eager to hear her perspective.

"Yes, just let me get the kiddos to bed and I'll spend some time writing it out for you," she responded.

"Nobody did anything about the bullying, it went on for such a long time, and nobody did a thing. I ended up running away. I didn't even know they had groomed me. They had me working at Madame Cleo's and the Number Five Orange. I had no idea I was being groomed. I was in the thick of the downtown Vancouver sex trade, and I had no idea that they groomed me for that. It wasn't until years later, when I had escaped. It was then that I understood what they had done.

Pink Diamonds

"I've asked Lyndsay to get the pink diamond I've had in storage cut. I want a necklace for Tina." He flipped his phone around and showed me a photo. "Something like this. The diamond is pretty big, so I've asked her to make sure there's enough for a matching ring."

"A ring?"

"Yes, I'm putting a ring on her as fast as I can." He grinned.

"But you're not even divorced yet." I shook my head.

"I will be in about three more weeks."

"You blow my mind, Daryl!"

"I'm going to propose." He grinned.

"You are not!"

"I am. I've loved her for ten years. Why should I wait?"

"You're crazy," I said.

"I know." He smiled.

The phone rang shrilly, breaking up our conversation. "Corky's Pub, Glenda speaking."

"Hey," a young female voice travelled through the line. "Is Kayden there?"

"Yup, hang on." I went to the kitchen and pushed the phone through the pass bar to the cook.

"Kaden, phone call." I headed back to the bar.

A moment later, Kaden was standing beside me with the phone in his hand. "They're looking for Cain, not me."

"Oh my goodness, I'm so sorry. I thought I heard Kayden," I exclaimed as I took the phone from his hand. "I'm sorry." I reiterated what I had heard into the phone.

"I'm looking for Cain," she said again.

I glanced around the pub. Everyone was a regular except for one table, a booth toward the back where a young couple was giggling with each other and getting rather cozy.

"There's nobody named Cain that I can see," I said into the receiver.

"Hmmm," she replied, "that's weird. My phone's tracking app says my boyfriend is there at Corky's."

"I don't know what to say," I continued. "Sorry?"

She hung up the phone, and I eyed the cozy couple. Could he be Cain? I picked up a tray and headed their way.

"How are you both doing?" I asked as I started clearing empty glasses from their table.

"We're great!" replied the girl. Giggling, she lifted the straw to her lips and took a sip of her Long Island iced tea. "You're awesome," she exclaimed. "What's your name?"

Sometimes they just walk right into it.

"My name's Glenda. It's nice to meet you. What's your name?"

"I'm Morgan," she giggled.

"Nice to meet you, Morgan," I said while turning to the young man who was running his hand along her thigh. "And you are?"

"I'm Cain." He smiled.

"Nice to meet you, Cain." I nodded. "If you need anything else, just let me know."

"Oh," Cain said, "do you have a phone charger? My phone is almost dead."

My inside voice said, "Perhaps you should let it die."

My outside voice said, "Sorry, no iPhone chargers here."

I excused myself and headed back to the bar. Beer glasses clinked as the conveyor belt moved them through their tunnel from unclean to clean. The motor hummed an octave lower than the Bellini machine that stood in the corner churning peach crystals into peach slurpee. Jacquie sat in barstool number one.

"Wine? Nine ounce?" I asked.

Her head nodded in agreement.

I placed the wine glass in front of her, pausing a moment, waiting for her to ask me to bring a bottle of Bud for what's his name. The long haired, long mouthed male that usually accompanied her. Her boyfriend, or husband. He told me his name once, sandwiched between sentences of "How Great Thou Art." I hadn't the heart to remember it.

She didn't ask for it, I didn't ask why.

She picked up her glass and sipped, not making a sound and looking a little sad.

I left her in the corner in her quiet reserve when I saw Earl standing at the bar with his pull tab.

"Can I cash this please?"

I smiled. "Yes, Earl." I gave him his loonie and he left.

Engagement

A Seagull opened its wings, slicing through the air it soared, scavenger sleek. I observed its cousins: some digging their beaks between boulders, others nattering, unhappy wives voicing their unhappy lives to their unhappy men. Two were pulling apart a dead fish.

"You ready?" Doug asked. He was in his dress blacks. A new black button up stretched across his chest. Delivered that morning to his room by a scrawny, pimple-faced teenager in braces and a Nirvana graphic t-shirt.

"I am. Are you?"

"The room's secure and the cameras are in place as you asked. We'll get the whole thing for you."

I turned from the gulls fighting over a fish and looked toward Doug. "The slipper?"

Swarovski Crystal. She said she felt like Cinderella; she said something like this only happens to other people, not to people like her. She says she feels like she's living a fairytale. I snuck into her closet, her shoe closet, five by ten with floor to ceiling shoes. I didn't know that many shoes could exist. I snuck one pair out, knowing for sure they wouldn't be missed. I sent them to Lyndsay with the instructions to get a pair made in Swarovski Crystal. She is my princess, and I was going to slip on her glass slipper that evening.

"The slipper is in a box under the table. When you're ready, just pop the top off," Doug confirmed.

"I don't think I need to ask about the ring, but I'm going to ask about the ring."

Doug smiled. "Tied to the slipper with a ribbon. As instructed."

I nodded.

"Sir Paul?"

"Sir Paul is set on cue. The helicopter dropped him on the island this morning. The grand piano was delivered yesterday; we set it up in the back by the bar. The staff put up a curtain panel to block it from the main seating area, so she won't have any idea," Doug confirmed. "Where is she now?"

"In our suite with Tanya and Emily, drinking champagne and doing their hair, getting ready for dinner." I smiled. "Takes her fucking forever to get ready, so it's good she's starting now."

"Why did you pick Whidbey Island?" Doug asked.

I looked up and out to the sea, jade green and calm, cedar trees in black shadows reflected in ripples across the surface. The day was icy clear, like Tina's glass slipper, ready to shatter under a puff of breath.

"We flew out a couple of months ago for brunch, eggs benedict. Tina mentioned that she would love to spend the weekend here. We're spending the weekend here." I slyly smiled. The seagull dropped something in front of me. A clam? A muscle? Poop?

***

The piano was gently playing Chopin, *Nocturne in C Sharp Minor*. We stepped into the dinning room.

One large table dressed for six, crystal glasses and silver stemware reflected the warmth of the candles linked in light from one end of the table to the other. My hand on Tina's back, I felt her breath intake as we entered.

She turned to me. "It's just lovely!" She was glowing. "Thank you for inviting everyone for the weekend, Daryl. We're having the best time!" She was giddy.

I pulled out her chair and she took her seat. Looking up, she realized that she was truly surrounded by everyone special in her life. Emily and Michael on her right, Danny and Tanya across. And on her left, her love. She just wanted to pinch herself.

She'd picked up her champagne flute and sipped as Chopin faded into something more familiar. Was that "Baby I'm Amazed"? She wasn't quite sure; it sounded different with just the piano.

Two servers dressed in white walked in. They nodded in her direction as they passed the table; simultaneously, Paul McCartney's voice started singing.

It is "Baby I'm Amazed," she thought to herself, pleased that she had guessed correctly.

The servers were drawing back a curtain.

Her mouth dropped open.

Paul McCartney was sitting behind a baby grand.

In real life.

She gasped. She couldn't believe what she was seeing. She turned to me, but I wasn't beside her. I was kneeling on the floor in front of her, holding a white box. I lifted the lid.

It was a glass slipper.

I loosened the ribbon and slid the pink diamond engagement ring from its silk.

"You are my princess, Tina. Will you be my bride?"

"Oh God—yes!" were the three words she was capable of forming.

***

"I wish you and Haney could have been there!" Daryl exclaimed when he arrived back home. "Fucking COVID. Fucking Borders!"

"Well, you don't have control over the governments closing the borders, do you, Daryl? I would have loved to have been there, though."

"Doug captured it all on video. Once he gets it cut, I'll get you a copy so you can watch it yourself. It was amazing! After the proposal, Paul pulled up a chair and joined us for dinner. He's so gracious. He even took time to sit with the staff and take photos with them."

"How did you get him there?" I asked

"Ohh … well, a trip on my jet, and a rather sizable donation to his charity." Daryl beamed.

Death Does That: It Stops the Living

"She's on to sugar daddy number two."

"Oh, that was a brutal tackle."

"But, he didn't even notice …"

"I'm trying, I just can't believe she did that. I …"

"I washed it and then of course it had to rain today."

"Ya, ya, ya, I understand …"

"People are so dumb."

"God, that was the funniest thing I ever saw!"

"I'm worth more than that, and I said …"

A thousand little snippets of a thousand little lives, murmuring as I walk by tables. Quiet ones sit loudly. Minds grinding through silent raucous sent via cell service. The human hum, moving moments through time until time is up.

"… he'd had cancer, he fought the good fight, but it got him in the end."

"… they pulled him out of the river this morning …"

"Three of them, in a car accident …"

"Why would he do that on Christmas Eve? His poor family. Can you imagine your son committing suicide for one, and on Christmas Eve for another?"

"Cancer of the stomach; it was brutal to watch."

"I heard he beat her; she just couldn't stand it any longer. It was a handful of pills washed back with whiskey."

"They took tests and tests and tests, but there was never an answer. We still don't know what it was; we just know he's gone."

"It was opioids. They found her son on a hotel bed … she got the call that morning. His poor wife … his poor mother!"

"My father passed away last night," Daryl said flatly.

The three of us were tucked into a half round facing the big screen. I had been excitedly bringing Daryl up to speed on our second teacher meeting we had attended the day before. The mood shifted. Death does that. It stops the living.

"He had dementia; he was almost ninety. It's better that he's gone. My mom won't live out the year." He was speaking more to himself than to Haney or I.

"Yes?" Daryl's cell was at his ear. "Fine. Well, Michael is going to do whatever he wants, there's not much I can do about that. Yup, yup. No, there's no reason for me to come there; it will just cause problems. Mom doesn't need that. K, bye." He picked up his pint and took a deep draw. "That was Jane. She and the kids will go to the grave site with Mom. They can't have a service, fucking COVID. Fuck Michael."

I reached out and placed my hand over his. It was cold.

Schmidttville

From: Tina Hoffmeister
To: Glenda

    Good morning,

    We have fleshed out the summary of what Microsoft is suggesting.

    They are prepared to forward 5,000 laptops. They are suggesting that the Foundation of Hope distribute 3,000 to the school system as you and your team deem best.

    The remaining 2,000 are suggested for the "learning centre." This is the location where they will provide 150 stand-alone computers for educational purposes. They will also assign a trainer from their training centre to educate two local individuals that may want become paid trainers. They are suggesting that they would split the cost of the salaries with the foundation.

    Daryl has already committed 4,500 square feet of classroom property on a site he is currently negotiating on.

    This is so exciting, and we can start feeling the momentum!

    Tina

Schmidttville. That's what I christened it after Daryl Schmidtt, who was sitting across from me delivering his update on properties he'd been purchasing throughout Chilliwack. Schmidttville was where the Corky's building stood. Three city blocks.

His team was busy buying. COVID fueled the Chilliwack sales. People were happy to get reasonable offers. Daryl was moving full-steam ahead.

Buildings on Five Corners, Midway, Airport Road, Young Street, and, of course, Schmidttville. He bought Chilliwack Golf Course and the Fraser Glen Golf Course. He was working with the local Natives considering casinos on the south, on their land. Working together building a healthy future.

"Do you have a contact for insurance? My team suggested we use a local company," Daryl asked.

"Yes, Craig. I'll email you his contact and you can forward it to head office."

"Good." He sipped his pint and continued. "Glenda, the foundation needs to build wellness centres for the Native communities. When the funds come through, I'll introduce you to the elders. You can investigate with them how best to meet their needs, maybe in the Chilliwack River Valley, maybe Bridal Falls. That project is opening up. I've never done a ski resort before. Why not? I'll build onto the casino, shovels in ground hopefully in November. We'll put up a hotel right beside it, have a breezeway to the casino, Vegas style. The airport is right there, so we'll helijet our customers to their favourite golf spots, sturgeon fishing tours, ski resorts. They can play all day, then come back here and spend their money in the casinos all night. Win, win.

"We'll build high-end townhomes around the Chilliwack Golf Course, and I'll put another casino in Abbotsford, right of the freeway, at the Fraser Glen, and attach it to the golf course there.

"The temporary foundation office could possibly go behind Starbucks in Midway. Go drive by, Glenda, see if that would work. If not, there's the one on Yale Road, or the

Envision building in Schmidttville. That location might be better. Wait, I have other ideas for that. How about by the *Progress* newspaper? Nope, that might be a little small. You'll need more space. Let's put it by the Otter liquor store. The old Block Buster video near the HSBC. We could put the foundation offices on one side and the computer school on the other. Yes, there. And how would you feel about putting the permanent foundation office on Young Road, near the career college building? They're doing an asbestos abatement there. Fuck, there must have been a sale on asbestos in the '70s. I'm paying for abatements all over town. Go check that one out. There's a creek on that property; you could put paths and fountains and waterfalls in.

"Barry is coming to do soil tests on the Corky's property. There was an old gas station in front. Those white pipes sticking out of the ground are venting, and that dirt will be expensive to clean up. He's done all the tests for the old Safeway property that was six million to clean. I'm hoping Corky's will run about three. I'll send Barry to the Young Road site, get him to pull soil samples and water samples from the creek.

"My uncle works in Ontario with the federal government, and he's found some properties by the river we can bid on—by the dog park, a row of shops with apartments above. He found the Crown land beside your property, Glenda. We could put a bid on it. Would you want it?"

"You can't buy Crown land," I said.

"Everything's for sale." Daryl smiled slyly.

"You mean we could get back the land we thought we had?"

"Yes."

Nikki

Label forward. Import Stout and rich gold whiskey ale, six deep. Cheap lager in tall cans bought by everyone who owns a truck or a pair of gum boots or both to the left. One-litre bottles of Caesar mix, regular spice to the right.

The door dingled.

One single way in. One single way out.

Full-view of the cooler from the front counter, cameras strategically placed upstairs where hundreds of bottles of wine—red, white, and rose—peer over the cast iron railing, mocking the wall of distilled below. "You call yourself top-shelf? We are upper floor!" The arrogance of wine like its bon vivant, taunting those beneath them.

"I'll just take the sherry." A pocket full of change mixed with dirt and a couple of twigs was released onto the glass-top counter. I think there's six bucks there. Can you count it, Nikki?"

"You bet, Ronnie." She started pulling the quarters to a corner, leaving the nickels and dimes to count last. She blew the twig off the counter. "Look, you have fifteen cents too much!" she exclaimed good naturedly.

Boisterous, bold, and blunt. Nikki, friend to the corner crowd, shopkeeper of the day at the liquor store next to Corky's Pub.

She slipped the sherry into a brown paper bag.

"Gotta keep that brown paper bag drinking in the brown paper bag," she ribbed Ronnie.

Ronnie smiled a toothless smile. "You're so funny, Nikki."

"Queen of comedy right here, Ronnie. Second show starts at two; bring your friends."

"I will, Nikki." He laughed, picking up the dime and the nickel with his grimed-up grips and tucking them into the front of his blue jeans. "Have a good day," he said as he reached for the door to let himself out.

"You too, Ronnie. Hey, can you give the cooler door a bit of a nudge on your way out? It looks like I didn't shut it all the way when I stocked those tall boys."

"You bet, Nikki." He put his right hand on the glass and gave it a swift shove. "Done now."

"Thanks, Ronnie. See ya."

Nikki pulled the stool that sat behind the counter, opened her phone, and checked her Facebook feed for updates. She clicked on a cat video and started chuckling as she sat down.

The door dingled.

A shadow stood over her. She closed her phone before she looked up.

It happened fast. She barely had time to register what was happening before it was done.

"Give me your money," said the voice under the ski mask.

"It's yours," Nikki replied, raising both right and left hands palms-out before opening the till and calmly handing every penny over to the human holding the gun.

He left.

He was gone in under two minutes.

Her life changed in 120 seconds.

***

"Did you see the video, Glenda?" Tina asked as she put her cash caddy down.

"What video?"

"The liquor store was robbed yesterday afternoon."

"What? Did anyone get hurt? What happened? Who was working?" poured out.

"Nikki was working. The cameras caught it all on video. It's on Facebook."

"Nooo?"

"Yes!"

"Is she okay?"

"She seems to be; she was working again today."

"Get out, really? How does she do that?"

"I have no clue."

She didn't really do it. She thought she could do it. But she really couldn't do it.

After a month of jumping at every door dingle, she quit.

"I was done with that shit. My life's not worth that. They didn't pay enough for me to put up with that shit. I be out of there like a bee in the breeze, gone, adios, my friend. I was fucked up. I'm better now, but I was fucked up then," Nikki said on her first day at Corky's.

"Well, we're glad to have you here." I laughed. "Now you can get your own soup. I was getting tired of bringing it to you over there anyway."

Well, That Was a Waste of Six Months

Six months almost to the day, the Interpretation Committee reviewing our house plans sent their findings to the regional district. I paraphrased the letter into human terms as I re-read it to Haney: "We find that this should never have come before us. The building inspector manager of the district, at his discretion, makes the decisions for properties next to Crown land."

"What? You mean the first building inspector manager was right in giving us permission to have all those windows?"

"Yup."

"We wasted six months for nothing?"

"Yup."

"Well ... shit."

"Yup."

"So we get our house?"

"Nope"

"What do you mean? They just said ..." Haney was confused.

"Let me finish the addendum from the current building inspector manager:

"... the building will still have to meet BC building code and as such will need fire rated shutters, fire rated glazing, or a curtain sprinkler system on the east side of the house."

"What? Why do we need that?"

"Apparently we need to protect the house beside us."

"There is no house beside us, and they can't build a house beside us—it's unbuildable land. The creek, the—"

"I know that, and you know that, and they know that, but the building code isn't site specific. We have to pretend there will be a building there."

"That's messed up."

"Yup."

"How much will that cost?"

"I'm looking into it now."

Government Certification

"Take the plane."

"Take the what?"

"Just take the plane, Tina. I have to stay in Chilliwack for meetings. I have the chopper for my meetings in the city. I don't need it. Enjoy the weekend with your friend and Emily."

"Just like that, Glenda, we are all on the plane. Em and I were going to drive down to Oregon to spend the weekend with my girlfriend who's having a bit of a tough time. Daryl told us to take the plane. It was insane! The three of us sipping mimosas on our way to San Francisco for the weekend, shopping, enjoying the boutique hotel. It's like I was living a dream! I got home on Sunday night, walked into my house, and there was Daryl, sitting in the hot tub drinking Scotch. 'I missed you,' he said. So he took a chopper down for the night. He's making us coffee right now then I'll drop him off at the airport before I go to work. He's crazy."

Another email followed later that morning:

From: *Tina Hoffmeister*
To: *Glenda Toews*
Subject: *Federal Government Certification*

Good morning,
The Canadian Government has reported to our Canadian legal council that they have begun the recognition process for the Foundation of Hope.
They indicated that typically the process takes thirty to forty-five days.
Upon completion, we can immediately apply to Fintrac to begin the process of transferring the funds to Canada.
I hope this information helps!
Tina

***

It always amused me how her emails flipped from child-like wonder to in control professional.

"Glenda, the Keno Machine is jammed," Judy said. Jamie sat at his table waving his beer glass for another, and Mark's head was bobbing up and down like a chicken pecking worms, his telltale sign that he wanted his bill. I closed up my phone and sighed and proceeded to save the pub people, addressing one problem at a time.

Sprinkler Systems

"Five thousand for the fire engineer to come up with a sprinkler plan plus up to $25,000 for the sprinkler system and a holding tank that has to live in our basement because we're on a well."

Haney spooned some chicken alfredo into his mouth. "Why do we need a holding tank?"

"Because we're on a well. Maybe if there's a fire it will affect the pump? I don't know."

"If there's a fire and it affects the pump, wouldn't it affect the pump from the holding tank too?"

"You know that, and I know that, but apparently it's a requirement."

"That's dumb."

"Yup. Well, if we're supposed to be getting all of this money next year, we can do that," I said.

"True."

"Actually, we could probably go back to the very first plan Joe drew up, the one with the garage with the guest area above the garage," I said.

"Rooftop hot tub?" Haney grinned.

"Why not?" I smiled. Maybe we should get Joe to revisit the first plan and see if that's possible. Could you imagine a rooftop hot tub with our view? It would be bloody amazing." I started laughing. "And if Daryl's uncle comes through with the Crown land beside us, can you imagine if we could buy it? And get what we wanted all along?"

"That would be a funny God moment, wouldn't it?" Haney said.

"Considering everything that's happened? Yes," I agreed. "Should I contact Joe?"

"Yes, let's draw it up. I loved that very first plan, and if we have the money, there's no reason why we shouldn't do it. It's just a little while longer to wait. We've been waiting this long now. What's another few months?" Haney grinned, washing down his pasta with a sip of Bud Light.

"Maybe I'll talk to Daryl and see if we can get a chunk of cash released in the October turnover instead of waiting for the December turnover."

"Good Idea."

Enter World-Changing Family

"He was my father, and I loved him."

She stepped away from the microphone.

Sparks flew up into the night sky, little fairies with lit lanterns danced through the dots connecting the moon to Mars as Lyra played and Hercules stood guard. She had a sausage on a stick. He was strumming his guitar. The fire crackled.

"I'm so sorry for your loss," said the minister, moving her from her memory.

"Thank you," she whispered, wringing the writing in her hands, paper worn from folding and re-folding the words of their life, culminating with, "He was my father, and I loved him" instead of "the end."

He was young. Forty-three. She didn't realize he was that young until she was eight years from the age herself.

Ah my, what a short little blip on this earth in her life.

Dreams, his and hers, both drowned in vodka chased back with beer.

She chose to remember the guitar, the fires, the sausages. His addiction stole the rest. She was eighteen.

Her sister was sitting in the pew, hidden by her hair. The soft, golden ringlets that framed her face at five had aged into light brown waves—thick, coarse, ruddy, and a lot. She had a twisted front tooth. Twelve is an awkward age. Her eyes, ice blue crystals flecked with indigo, were red-rimmed and puffy. One thousand four hundred and ninety-five days before this day she was twirling around the living room in unmatching socks and a blue sundress with thin shoulder straps. Strands of her unruly mane spilled victoriously from the french braid rejoicing, "Free at last, free at last!" She brushed them from her eyes as she twirled. Her sister was playing the piano, her dad his guitar; they were jamming. They were happy, she was happy, Mom was happy. A year later she was dumping vodka down the drain, wishing it would leave forever. Today she said goodbye to her daddy who had.

The wizard pulled back the curtain. He bowed low while sweeping his right arm to his side, inviting them to take their first steps on the golden path of sorrow. The sisters looked at each other. The elder held out her right hand, the younger grasped on to it with her left. The wizard stood behind them and pushed.

There is never a shortcut down this thoroughfare, though many try. The sisters were no exception. When their own steps found that all those things they thought would work didn't, they each let go, and let God.

Braces untwisted the tooth. Jesus untwisted the heart.

As they healed they helped, and they found husbands with hearts to hear, and the years were full and good, and their homes were blessed with babies—five for the elder, four for the younger. And their hands had to stretch across counties because the elder was in Kyiv and the younger was in Germany. And their mother was in Canada pouring pints in Corky's.

***

"We need to talk," I messaged the girls
"What's up, Mom?" asked Danielle.
"Ya, what's up?" asked Taylor.

"This is what we're doing in Chilliwack."

And out came all of the everything we'd be planning, though not their surprise fund. Mommies always need a little secret up their sleeve.

"What?" said Taylor, laughing.

"You're kidding," said Danielle. "You're like friends with the richest man in the world? Hahahahaha." And the tears started rolling.

"I think there may be funds to help you guys with your projects over there. We have one fund called the Community Fund; this fund is separate from the foundation fund. I can draw from it and we could use these funds for your dreams of helping humans over there. I don't know how much. But there should be some, so start dreaming."

And our girl group chat's name was changed to "World-Changing Family."

And the World-Changing Family began dreaming Daryl big.

Jigging Cod

The beach had a name, the boat had a name, his uncle had a name, but none of that was important. Jigging cod—that was important. Jigging cod with his uncle—that was important. Uncle rolled his words the way the ocean rolled waves on a windless day: long, slow, deep in colour with a bit of froth on the top. He loved to listen to him. He was seasoned. Everyone is seasoned when you're ten years old, but Uncle was seasoned more than most. Skin bit deep by eastern gales, cracked lips cracked jokes, and crevassed folds flanked deep blue eyes that winked the good nature the sea endlessly tried to beat out of him.

When they finished, the fishermen would gather, a fire lit, lobster chowder ladled into big bowls. They would eat until they couldn't move, then leaning back in their chairs, they would listen to the fiddles, sea shanties, forecastle shanties, the chantie. Uncle would slip him a sip of beer. The chill of the sea ebbed, mollified by maritimers. He fell in love with the sea then. He's been in love with the sea ever since.

***

"How come you never mentioned this to us, Glenda?" John, surprised, sipped his rye and continued. "What if Trish and I wanted to invest too? Is that something we could do?"

"I don't know. I could ask, but I wouldn't have approached to invest ever. Any investment is risky, and I don't want to be a doorway to that risk for others."

"But you were comfortable investing?"

"Yes, I have no problem investing for me, but I don't want to be responsible for you." I smiled.

"Well, if you wouldn't mind asking, I'm game. If it's good enough for you guys, it's good enough for us," he continued. "One day I want to retire, and I would love a house by the sea." He nodded to Trish. "We would like a house by the sea." Trish smiled at her Johnny. "Tell us more about the Foundation of Hope."

And I did.

"Could we give back to that too?" John asked. "I mean, really, if an investment provides a livelihood for us, is there a way for us to pay it forward too?"

"What an amazing idea, John," I replied, deeply touched that even now, he and Trish just wanted to ease other's burdens too. "I'm sure there are things that we can work on together through the foundation to put your desires to use, even if it's just plowing snow in our parking lot." I laughed.

"Hey, before we go, could you put the old guy's tab on ours?" John asked.

"Whose? Old Ike's?" I nodded in the direction of Ike, who was sitting silently in his own thoughts at a table by the fireplace.

"Yes, him, just don't tell him it's from us." He smiled slyly.

"I know the drill, John." I laughed. "Consider it done."

Ted Lasso

From: Tina Hoffmeister
To: Glenda Toews
Subject: Re: Ummmmm what is going on?

Just so you know, Daryl just transferred $115,000,000.00 to your foundation account!

Not the growth account, because Danny could never make that work, but to the account that will be listed as the foundation principal account.

***

I messaged Daryl: "What's going on? Tina just sent an email saying you dropped a bunch of money in our foundation account?"

"Ya, Jane thinks I'm dying. I sent the same amount to her accounts as well," came his reply.

"Why?"

"You're grossly underfunded. Once you start building wellness centres and setting up the foster care transition apartments you were talking about, even what I've just deposited won't be enough. And Jane? She can use it for whatever she sees needed. She had mentioned that she never thought of going directly to the schools like you and Haney did. I believe she's meeting with some this week."

"When is this money expected?"

"Not sure. I have to talk to Tina about Fintrac. I can imagine there could be some issues with that. I'll get her on it."

"Okay. I think it's time to stop, though. It's a little overwhelming, and I have to catch my breath."

"Okay, sorry, sometimes I forget.

***

"Hey, can I buy you a beer?" Daryl asked. I was finishing up for the day.

"Ya, you know, I think I'd like that. Let me do my cash and I'll be right back down."

There was a pint of Canadian waiting for me when I returned to the Bone.

I pulled out the barstool and took a seat.

"I think we're okay for funds for a while, so maybe stop depositing them, okay?"

He smiled and shrugged his shoulders. "As I said yesterday, I forget. I realize that I just move forward in the same manner as I do with everything. I apologize."

"Well, you see everything in BIG. I'm truly just looking to get some immediate aid to the school. When do you anticipate that to happen?" I asked.

"As I understand it, you're still waiting for the government certification of the Foundation of Hope. Once that is done, we can start the process of moving some funds up. They have to clear Fintrac, and that could possibly take a month or so. It's hard to say with COVID delays. Hopefully around May?"

"What about the community fund? Are we able to manoeuvre money, even ten thousand? That way we could at least start."

"That's a good idea. I'll check with Tina." Daryl sipped on his pint. "What would be your first steps with that?"

"Well, besides starting a breakfast program, we'd like to take the students shopping. The students can pick out the clothing for the closet, then we would take those who did the shopping work out for lunch. I'm trying to think of ways that the work is done by those who would be receiving help, so that there's a feeling of having contributed, having earned it themselves. Like Christmas—you know how people sign up to be sponsored for gifts?"

"Yes, Jane and the kids do that a lot."

"Well, how about if those people who've signed up for the aid also are given funds to do the shopping for another family. That way they also get the joy of giving, the joy of picking out gifts and giving to another family in need? They do the work, and we foot the bill."

Daryl absorbed the idea.

I continued. "Help is often freely given, but in giving, sometimes we overlook what we're taking away. It's a little more work to do it this way, but I think the idea can have a longer reach. Imagine, the family who is always on the receiving end out of need, allowed the opportunity to be on the giving end. Giving is good for the soul."

Daryl picked up his phone. "Nelson, Glenda just shared a concept with me that I think we should implement ..." The conversation was brief but to the point. Daryl laid his phone on the table when they were finished.

"Speaking of money, Haney and I were wondering if we could take some of our investment out next October instead of letting it run the full year. I have a house to build." I smiled.

"That shouldn't be a problem. Just talk to Tina, but you shouldn't worry about that. You know I'll just give you the money you need."

"Ha," I laughed at him. "I didn't consider you an option."

"I know what wage the foundation will be paying you; you'll be good for it." He grinned.

"Well, if you want to finance the build, I'll just leave our money to turn over for the full year. But I'm not taking your money unless you make sure to take the money back. I'll ask Tina to take whatever we use right off the top of our investment and give it back to you."

"Sure, whatever you want. Speaking of your house, I have a window for you. I thought about putting it up in my house, but I think it would be more fitting for your place. It's a hunter scene, sixteenth century I think, I'm not sure. I'd have to ask Steffanie; she has the history of it written down somewhere."

"That would be amazing! How big is it? I'd need the measurements soon so I can give them to Joe."

"Three by three? Maybe three by four?"

"Can you imagine, install the stained glass then write on the wall its history! That would be so cool." I was mentally designing in my head.

Earl walked by. "Hey, would you mind if I joined you two?"

"Sure," Daryl replied.

"Did I tell you about Ted Lasso?" Earl giggled a little as he pulled out his barstool. "That Ted, I tell you." And he laid down his newspaper and laid the latest episode on us.

Sucking the Breath Out of God

When the righteous move forward, bands of righteousness flow, like ribbons, like tentacles. Silk shards the skin and leaves the heart hanging by a bloody bow.

"Perhaps the churches can help. I mean, truly isn't that why we have the church?" I suggested it to Alice. We were having a drink in the corner booth at Corky's discussing the eminent needs in the school.

"When we think of community and having the community involved in giving to each other, isn't this something we could explore? Churches helping school needs? And then the Foundation of Hope supporting those supporting others?"

Alice shook her head long and slow, pulling a memory from my mind as she did so.

I sipped my beer and stepped back to when I was fifteen.

"They kicked me out." Barb said as she pulled on her jean jacket. We were getting ready to go to the mall.

"What do you mean they kicked you out? How do you get kicked out of a Christian School?" I replied, naively.

"I had some alcohol. They didn't like that. I broke a code of conduct or something like that."

"That's weird. Didn't Jesus turn water into wine?"

"I guess he wouldn't be allowed in that school either." She grinned and winked.

I took another sip of beer and stepped back into another past;

"As you and Haney have been spending a lot of time together, the church needs to ask if you had an affair ..." An email sent in the "love of Christ" by the pastor of the little church I went to.

And the silky ribbon sliced.

"You saw my life. I laid it open for you all. Please tell me, when did I have time for this affair? When I was on my knees crying, begging my husband to get help? Or maybe when I was searching for ways to feed my daughters when money went missing?"

Do we sit in pews and stand behind pulpits searching for sin, hoping to please God?

I decided that we wouldn't be attending church anymore. I didn't have the strength to chew through the ribbon. A year later the pastor came to my house to inform me that the little church we once loved had withdrawn my membership and my oldest daughter's membership. We were kicked out.

It doesn't make sense.

God says, "Take care of the widows and orphans." Jesus came for the lost and the hurting, yet mankind beats mankind over the head with the Bible and rejoices in rejection.

"You're right, Alice, perhaps we leave the church alone to do its own thing." And we ordered another round.

Religion sucks the breath out of God.

Day of Reckoning

"Gotta go," he proclaimed, gulping down the last inch of draught and slamming the mug on the bartop.

He was at Cooters. They have flat-chested waitresses, a burger called Big Chubbs, a sandwich named The Cooters Club, and an abundance of deep-fried swimming in ranch sauce. It's located midway between his home in Honeytown and Mike's Mobiles Homes in Wiser County

Cirrhosis of the liver is on a barstool nursing his JD on the rocks. Heart disease is sitting at the table in the corner reading the single-fold, plastic-covered menu, and Diabetes is licking the grease off his fingers as he finishes up his basket of bacon cheesy fries. He contemplates having another mug of beer or a piece of key lime pie. He decides on both. There are deer heads hanging on the wall and a couple of big guys dressed in black shooting pool. Americana 2021.

"We still meeting tomorrow?" Billy, a good fifteen years younger, was looking up to the man he'd been looking up to for the past thirty years. A current flashed between them.

Shared secrets of shared sins with a deep desire to do it again, and again, and again. Fifteen years of "again." Billy looked at Bob, eager to hear that tomorrow would be another again."

Bob's lip curled in a sinister twitch. His left eye pulled into a wink, then broadly he grinned. His breath, pungent, a mixture of stale tobacco rinsed in stale beer, loomed out as he leaned in, so close the stubble on his chin scratched the skin of Billy's ear. He whispered, "Stew's girl." Billy flushed. Stew's girl was fresh, untouched, tight, and twelve. He felt himself harden.

The White Boys Club. Established in 1851. Established by the Lewis Family Father.

The town glances sideways and speaks only in hushed tones regarding them. Mothers tell their children to stay away from Lewis children, their sons are not to date. Lewis daughters and their daughters are to run from Lewis sons. Bile rises in the throat when one passes a Lewis on the street.

The sins of thy father are heaped upon every Lewis child, boy or girl. One forced to damage, the other the damaged. If either knew their destiny, they most certainly would have found a way to never be born. Each cry out to God. And when God doesn't stop it, they stop crying out and go numb. God is dead, and so are they.

In 1973, Bobby was taken to the barn off Lincoln Way. Bobby's dad fueled him with whiskey and introduced him to his sister. Bobby was fourteen, his sister three years younger. His Uncle Owen stood by. "It's what we do." his papa commanded. Taking a swig, he passed the bottle to Bobby. Bobby drank deeply, the heat of the whiskey fired up his throat, fired up his belly, fired up his mind. "We need to prepare her for her future. We need to show her what to expect; it's our duty as the males in the family."

The three of them prepared her fully. Fueled by the whiskey, cheering each other on, they started in a freakish frenzy. The second round, a little slower. Papa and Uncle Owen were spent. Bobby had the endurance to go a third round; his soul was stolen. He hungered for more, and he did.

Bobby was initiated into the Boy's Club that night, and he, his brothers, his sons, and their sons have been preparing their daughters ever since. They savour this right. They make sure the girls are prepared well. They do it often. They enjoy it. And the sins of the father fold over generation after generation.

Bob smacked Billy on the back and he turned toward the door.

"See you tomorrow, Billy."

"Ya, Bob. Tomorrow."

The Billy Bob goodbye.

Bob jumped in his truck. New in 1989. It was silver in 1989. The sun and the wind and the rain have beaten the silver into dull gray. The wheel wells are rusted. The 4x4's engine roared to life with the turn of the key. Bob backed it out of Cooters and turned east on Lincoln Way. The sky was spitting. He turned on his wipers and they started slapping time with Janis as she belted "Bobby Mcgee" over the radio. He sang along.

Red and blues flashed in his rear view two miles from home; reluctantly, he pulled the truck to the side of the road. Gravel crunched beneath the tires as he pulled to a stop.

"Shit," he muttered, "why the hell am I being pulled over?"

He turned down the radio and rolled down his window.

"Get out, with both hands up where I can see them," the trooper number one stated. His gun was drawn.

"What the fuck?" Bob uttered in disbelief. "Why the hell for? I ain't done nuttn' wrong!"

"I said get out, hands up where I can see them," the trooper repeated himself.

"Fuck." Bob pulled the latch, and the door popped open. He slid out, both hands in the air as instructed. "I ain't done nuttn'," he insisted as trooper number two turned him and pegged him against the truck. Bob's face was pressed into the glass. Another "fuck" escaped his lips as he turned his head to the left and rested his cheek against the wet window. Trooper two cuffed him, walked him to the cruiser, and slid Bob in the back seat.

"What the FUCK!!" His face was red in rage now, and "fuck" was discharged in a spray of spittle. Trooper one started reading Bob his rights.

"What is wrong with you people? I ain't done nuttin' wrong!" As the words were spoken, he saw trooper two popping the front seat of his truck forward. "Leave my fucking truck alone. You ain't got no right digging through my things!" he demanded. The vein on the right side of his neck was bulging, throbbing as his blood surged.

Trooper two emerged from the truck with a clear bag of something white. "What the hell is that?" Bob was livid. The sky opened and rain poured. Bob could barely see out of the cruiser's window. He was frothing in frustration. "What the hell did you just pull from my truck?" he screamed, demanding an answer.

Trooper two handed the bag to trooper one. "Tag it," he commanded.

"Tag what? What the hell could possibly need tagging from my truck?"

"Your kilo of cocaine," stated trooper two.

"What the hell are you talking about? I don't have coke. I don't do coke. This is bullshit!"

"Looks like you're selling shit," trooper one stated, "a lot of it by the looks of it." Trooper two was headed back to the cruiser carrying four more bags.

"Five kilos," trooper one stated. "That's good for forty years, even for a first timer."

Blood drained from Bob's face; his mouth gaped open.

The troopers called a tow truck and headed to the station. Bob fumed in the back seat as he spent the thirty-minute drive trying to figure out how the coke got in his truck, who put it there, and how he was going to get out of this shit mess he was in.

Back at Cooters the big dudes dressed in black sank the cue ball, swallowed their last swallow, cleared up their tab, hopped in their Jeep, and turned east onto Lincoln Way. They passed a gray truck and a police cruiser just as the sky opened and the rain poured. They saw the trooper carrying the bags of white from the truck. They smiled.

***

From: *Tina Hoffmeister*
To: *Glenda*
Subject: *Re: good morning*

I know Daryl wants vengeance for my past and also to "eliminate scum," so they are not preying on others.

I told him you can't clean out all the scum, and he looked at me with dead eyes and said, "Why not?" That was a, well, ummmmm I don't know answer moment! 😾

How does a person respond to that!?

I love he wants to fix the world ...

I don't know, sometimes I just want to throw him at everybody, but ...

On a side note to this conversation, I hear my POS father back home is in jail for selling coke He got caught with a lot ... like enough to keep him in jail for life. Makes me go hmmmmm.

I don't want to know, but I really hope Daryl had something to do with it, but I will never ever ask him.

Kind of a godfather moment. Don't ask me my business!

***

"Tina and Emily are taking the plane to Ohio today," Daryl said shortly after he sat at the Bone.

"Yes, she messaged me about her father," I replied, reading Daryl's face.

Could he indeed have arranged kilos of cocaine to be stashed in a truck? I had no doubt he could. How I felt about that was what I was weighing. Rule followers tremor when rules aren't followed.

His face offered nothing. It was no more expressive, no less expressive, than all the days before. I didn't know if this was a good, bad, or a thing that is indifferent.

I concluded that it was far better for the coke to put him in jail, that jail is where he should have been years ago, girls are safer with him locked up, and that sometimes when rules don't protect innocent people, people must.

"Why are they going to Ohio?" I asked.

"They need to say their piece."

***

From: *Tina Hoffmeister*
To: *Glenda*
Subject: *Morning*

Good morning,

Sorry I didn't talk much yesterday. Was a full day, as I'm sure Daryl told you.

My sister and I are on the plane headed to Ohio to put this behind us once and for all.

We're going to try to see my dad for the last time ever.

So I may or may not be very chatty, but I just wanted to let you know.

Daryl is going to Chilliwack, so if you see him, take care of him.

I think he is hurt I don't want him to come with us, but I have to do this on my own.

***

From: *Tina Hoffmeister*
To: *Glenda*
Subject: *Re: Morning*

Well, we are here.

All checked in, waiting for my cousin to come over.

We will see my dad tomorrow I guess. The lawyer has it all set up. I had a chat with my therapist from the Caymans. I was stunned she is here! But then I always forget I am engaged to Daryl, and anything seems possible.

My sister ran to the store across the street "unattended," and that got us a lecture from Doug.

Will be interesting when we go out for dinner and drinks tonight!

***

From: *Tina Hoffmeister*
To: *Glenda*
Subject: *Re: Morning*

Yes, this is the cousin that tried to help us and hopefully leaves her man and comes home with us. He beat her bad a week ago, so time is up. If she doesn't, then perhaps I have to have a conversation with Daryl. 😳🤭

We haven't seen her in about six years but talk every week so.

Yes, there is a lot of support. All my sister and I have done is hug and cry. We don't have to worry about anyone showing up and running our lives anymore. So it is good.

She has talked to the therapist as well, so that helps.

***

From: *Tina Hoffmeister*
To: *Glenda*
Subject: *Re: wishing you well*

It's over.

He thought we were there to help him with lawyers, etc.

When we told him we were there to applaud him being in jail and rotting there, he tried to create all the fear he had before.

I didn't work. For the first time I saw him as the pathetic little person he is!

Apparently he is in protective custody because he had been beaten twice since his arrest. I say good to that

Now we can move on!

***

From: *Tina Hoffmeister*
To: *Glenda*
Subject: *Re: Morning*

So my cousin is coming back with us tomorrow.

She is going to stay with me/us.

We were having drinks at the pub, and one of my sister's exes came up to us and started yapping, called her a cock tease whore. He apparently raped her when she was fifteen. I had no idea. At a school dance.

She told him he was a piece of shit!

319

He said, "Really, you know you want this," grabbing his dick, then there was Doug. Threw the guy in the floor, stepped on his head … told him to apologize. His friends started to come to him, and there were six of Doug's guys with FN guns telling them to go home! The guy who Doug was stepping on peed his pants!

God, where were these people years ago. Very different world

I asked Doug, "Are you worried about the cops, etc.?" He just laughed and said nope. Barney Fifer would be cute to see this.

***

Tina and Emily arrived back in Seattle with Roxy. As Tina washed off the Lewis name and became Hoffmeister, so it was with Roxy. Whoever Roxy was before was left in Ohio. The name change didn't stop her from looking back.

The past is a part of the present. Screaming. Not out loud, but in affliction.

A Chopper & A Yacht

"We're looking at the end of May. The Foundation of Hope should have its registration, and the first draw of funds will likely have made it through Fintrac. Tina's essential service application is expected to be processed then as well. I was thinking that we should plan a stay on the boat that weekend. We can go together to the HSBC downtown and get debit cards and Visa cards released for the foundation accounts. We can meet with the legal team and get your name signed on all the appropriate paperwork and have a party on the boat. I'll see if Jane and Christine can join in. I'd like for you to meet Nelson and Robbie too, so I'll see if they're available, but for sure Jane and Christine, because you're all a part of the do-gooder team." Daryl spun his cell phone on the bartop as he thought to himself out loud.

"How exciting! I can't wait. I can't wait for all of it!" I grinned.

"The legal team mentioned that in order to process the foundation paperwork faster, it would help our cause if we had the Gates on as our Foundation Consultants. I spoke with Bill and he has agreed that he or Melinda would be up for this."

"Get out! We have the Gates as consultants? This will be completely amazing!"

"I'm going to see if they'll be able to come up for our boat weekend too. I don't know, though; they are laying low with COVID. I'm not sure coming to Canada is something they want to do, but I'll ask."

"I can't wait to meet everyone." I started getting goosebumps on my arms. "I guess Haney and I will drive to the city that weekend—"

"Drive? Oh, we won't drive. We'll take the chopper downtown. I don't drive there." Daryl laughed. "Way faster on the chopper."

My eyes got wide. "Well then, that will be a weekend of a hell of a lot of firsts for us!"

***

"Mom!" exclaimed Danielle and Taylor on our World-Changing Family chat. "That's so exciting! You're going on a chopper? And a yacht? And the Gates might be there? What are you going to wear?"

"Ha, I was thinking I should get a new blazer, maybe some new jeans. All of my good clothing is in storage. I wouldn't even know where to dig to dig it out, much easier to buy new, but not too much new. Tina says she's taking me shopping, and we're going to Holt Renfrew. She says it's one of her favourite stores. And she's come up with another name for the community fund. All the fund accounts were starting to get confusing, so we were chatting, and because the community fund is a non-registered, casual fund, we've decided to call it the Shoe Closet. One because we both like shoes, and two because the idea is to help fill closets.

"Taylor, would you and Raphie start working on a Foundation of Hope graphic for us, that we could use as a letterhead, or business cards, that kind of thing?"

"Oh geeze, yes! Do you want one for the Shoe Closet too?"

"Why not? That would be so much fun. We'll surprise Tina with it!"

The girls and I had an afternoon of fun finding outfits on the internet that we thought would be suitable to meet "suits" with.

Later Taylor private messaged: "Raphie and I were talking, and we were wondering if you wouldn't mind asking Daryl if there's some place that he could recommend where we should invest. We have our tax return coming, and we think it would be good to invest it rather than spend it."

"I don't know, Taylor, but for sure I'll ask, though."

Abandoned Babushka

"ти де, ти де, ти де? Where are you, where are you, where are you?"

She rolled around on her little cot mumbling the words wishfully, hopefully, mournfully. Each day folded into the next with little change. She would close her eyes in the daylight, and they would open in the dark; she would close her eyes in the dark, and they would open in the daylight. She could tell the seasons changed by the one glass pane, arm's reach from her cot. Some months the sun shone in; most months it was covered in ice.

The layers she was under did nothing to ease her distress. The layers on top of her mattress did nothing to cover the smell. She had no choice but to come to terms with lying in her own filth. Sometimes the lady came to change her diaper; most days she did not. Her body hurt, but she could do nothing about it. Her mind hurt, but she could do nothing about it. Her soul hurt, but she could do nothing about it.

And she cried out to her son: "ти де, ти де? Where are you? Where are you?"

Maksim found her like this on one of his visits to the village. A little old babushka. Abandoned by her son, left to live alone in a tiny hut with no running water and an oven but no one to keep the fire. He walked in. He gagged. The smell.

Once a month since, he drives up near Chernobyl with a small team to check on this village of grannies. Once a month he drives to other villages with other grannies. Ukraine is full of tiny little villages of babushkas, deserted by their adult children, left to lay in their own feces, left to die. The Ukrainian babushkas receive a small stipend from the government; the Russian babushkas receive nothing and rely only on the mercies of others.

Maksim would love to create Meals on Wheels, to open a recovery house to aid the men who desire to quit drinking. Ukraine suffers under alcoholism. He would love the men in the recovery home to be the force of the Meals on Wheels for the babushkas. He dreams.

Maybe tomorrow; today, they need blankets and sheets and pillows.

"Mom, it's atrocious." The empathy poured from Danielle's words on our chat. "As we pack up to move, I'm collecting all of our blankets and sheets for Maksim to take to the grannies, but it won't be enough. They need so much more."

"How much more?" I asked.

"It seems insurmountable," she replied.

"Okay, let's start small. I'll send you $500, and that could buy some, right? Try to find a local shop in Ukraine and buy from them. Support their local economy."

"Thank you, Mom! I'll get on it right away. When do you think the community fund money will come?"

"Shoe Closet," I corrected her.

"Yes, the Shoe Closet funds. They are really needed here. Those grannies have to walk to a well to pump their own water, and they have to walk to the forest and cut their own wood, and the ones who can't move—oh, it's terrible. In one village they said a nurse comes to change diapers. She is paid to change the diapers, but she doesn't come, and they lay in their filth."

"I'll talk to Daryl."

"Thank you! We could set Maksim up. He could get a building for the recovery centre, he could start the Meals on Wheels for the grannies, he could get running water into their homes, build bathrooms, and get rid of bed pans and outhouses."

"Yes, this is definitely something that money could fund. We would just have to figure out the best way to get the funds in there. I'll talk to Daryl; maybe he has some ideas."

Give

I sat in front of my computer with my pinky hovering over the "enter" button. Fifty years ago this button didn't exist. The carriage return lever of a typewriter had only the power to change where text would go. Today, one of the smallest bones in my body has the power to move text and to bring change. If I hit the enter button, I immediately send $500 from my bank account into another's, and that $500 has the ability to bring a tiny bit of change to humans across the world, in a different country, in a little village, to humans I never knew existed and will never meet. My pinky has this power. My pinky will only move if my mind commands it to, and this is why it is hovering and not pressing.

It's never easy. It's most often a struggle. It's entirely uncomfortable.

I always desire to hang on to what I have.

There can be the greatest need in font of me, and I have the ability to address the need, but I always have to battle the dragon in my mind, two voices at war in my head.

"Surely they don't need your help, Glenda. Surely someone else will do it. Surely they will figure it out themselves. You shouldn't give your money. You don't know that tomorrow you won't need it for yourself. You do know you could use that money to buy new tires, right? You do need tires, Glenda."

"Glenda, you must. Money is here to help, not horde. Remember those times before? Remember how much it helped? Remember how you felt when you followed this path? You know it's the way to go. You have enough to buy tires plus give. You aren't a horrible person if you keep your money, but it's better for you to be able to give."

I don't know where this dragon came from, but it's existed in me for as long as I can remember. I battle it because it's a worthy battle.

Like daily exercise and eating vegetables, there are healthy practices made for the flourishing of human life. Giving is one of them. Like daily exercise and eating vegetables, I don't always enjoy to first step. Fulfillment only follows the act. Fulfillment is inevitable. There has not been one instance when I've ever regretted giving; perhaps this is why it perplexes me that I struggle to do it. I enjoy the end result. I love the end result.

I contemplated the foundation and toyed with the thought that maybe there would be no joy in giving. Joy perhaps only follows after a sacrifice.

What sacrifice would it be to give away money someone else had acquired? How would I make this endeavour joyful? I didn't know.

Deeply I contemplated what millions of dollars injected into the community could look like. Would it help? Would it hinder? It could do both. The prospect of the responsibility was daunting. What would it be creating?

As I contemplated, I realized the Foundation of Hope would have to endeavour to use its funds to inspire others to give. Bolster up, not take over. Could it destroy otherwise?

Maybe humans need their internal struggles.

Maybe we need these struggles because as we overcome them, they strengthen us.

Maybe each internal battle is like the first strum on a guitar. The whole thing feels entirely awkward and uncomfortable in your arms, and it's only after hundreds of hours of discomfort that beautiful music emerges, and it's only after hundreds of hours of discomfort that the practice becomes easier, more efficient, less calloused.

Maybe the Foundation of Hope would fund the guitar and the guitar strings so to speak while helping those to teach and aid our youth to muddle through learning the notes, providing encouragement and congratulating the callouses, so that they will be equipped to create beautiful music.

Give so that others also may give.

Don't take away their choice.

Don't take away the battle of choosing one way or another.

Let them work through it so they experience their own joy.

"Blessed is the man who strives against his own selfishness; he will taste in its fullness the joy of accomplishment" (James Allen).

My mind chose to move my pinky. I hit the enter button. The sword pierced the heart of the dragon, and I stood over it victoriously.

Money for Grannies

From: *Tina Hoffmeister*
To: *Glenda Toews*
Subject: *Re: Official*

I'm wondering who else you want as a signatory on the account for the foundation accounts. Yourself and the lawyer naturally, but would you like Haney to have a signature as well? We are suggesting that all payments over $10,000.00 require two signatures. Should Haney be a signatory, that may ease the creation of locally generated cheques you wish to distribute.

Just some food for thought.

***

"Did Tina message you? She was asking me about signaturors over our coffee this morning, and I suggested she contact you directly about that."

"Yes, she did, Daryl, thanks. Did you have any idea about the ETA on the Shoe Closet funds? We're sending some money over for sheets and pillows for grannies."

I spent the next ten minutes filling him in on what Danielle had reported to me. His face didn't change expression, but when I had finished, he pulled out his wallet, opened it, and peeled out four one-hundred-dollar bills and told me to use it.

"So the Shoe Closet funds will be a while then?"

"I'll talk to Tina and see what we can do about getting you some debit cards. You could at least start with that."

He seemed flustered, weighted in vicissitude, the world dropped on his shoulders.

"Daryl?"

"Yes."

"Its not your responsibility to save the world because you have the funds to do so. It's our responsibility, each and every one of us, to respond to the things we see and use what we have to help."

He nodded in understanding.

"I'll check with my team about Ukraine."

"Thanks, Daryl."

Karen

"Good morning, Karen."
   "Good morning, Bob."
   "Morning, Karen."
   "Good morning, Jen."
   "Good morning, Karen."
   "Good morning, John."

And so her day began, in much the same way as it had begun for the fifteen years before, and beyond those fifteen years with other Bobs and Jens and Johns. Greeting the ordinary with good.

This day as in all the days, the good drifted in and scents drifted around, wrapping each in turpentine, steel, and cedar, finished with just a little dab of fertilizer. Dior J'adore Hardware Store.

Tills counted. Paperwork rustled. Orders picked. Shelves stocked.

From a distance, the whirring of a forklift could be heard, followed by the sound of stacking. Stacking had a sound. Tiles encased in cardboard *whooshed* and bundles of wood cracked.

Bob was restocking a roll of chains. The end let loose, and Marley was released: "I wear the chain I forged in life; I made it link by link, and yard by yard; I girded it on of my own free will, and of my own free will I wore it."

Karen slipped into her desk, sipped her mug of coffee, and watched her computer wake up.

The kitchen designer, once in a quiet corner of the store, moved recently to the middle of the store. A desk was tucked between plumbing parts to the right and electrical essentials on the left.

"Excuse me, are you busy? Would you mind telling me where I can find the paintbrushes?"

The voices clinked like Marley's chain, interrupting her concentration as they dragged their needs through the hardware store, culminating at her desk with a steely rattle.

Clink, clink, clink.

"Did you hear me now? I need a paintbrush. Are you busy?"

Karen chewed over what she would need to do in order to look busy. Creating kitchen designs on a computer simply doesn't appear busy enough to the consumer. As the chains rattled, she contemplated the wisdom of the decision to place her desk here, in the middle of an aisle. Her thoughts were interrupted.

"Excuse me, you don't look busy, would you mind telling me where I can find nails?"

***

"Hey, Karen, how was your day?" I place her wine in front of her.

"Full of chains, full of chains." I looked at her perplexed. "It was fine, Glenda." She smiled.

"Tough day at the office?" I asked. She nodded. "What would you like to be when you grow up?" I asked.

"You know, Glenda, I love designing kitchens, and I love my job, but I would absolutely love to teach low-income families how to cook healthy meals with low-cost food items."

"Excuse me?" Her response came out of left field: specific, thought out, immediate, and unexpected. I was stunned.

"I would love to open a kitchen and teach families how to cook."

"What a bloody amazing idea, Karen!"

"Right! I just don't have the energy to apply for the grants and start it up. That's not my passion. My passion is in the teaching to cook. Can you imagine it, though? Have a room full of islands, with parents and their children working together learning a skill then eating it together, maybe with one long table, a community table, where everyone eats together. A community kitchen."

I got goose bumps.

From the ordinary, good grows.

***

"A community kitchen, Daryl!" I said excitedly. We were meeting over a beer to discuss foundation plans. "I mean, her idea is spectacular. This is something absolutely the foundation can set up, then we hire her away from her job and give her this dream job that will be amazing for our community."

His expression didn't shift; it rarely did. He listened intently.

"I have some buildings we could put it in temporarily. Maybe the old IHOP at the Travel Lodge. I'm leasing it to BC Housing now, but maybe we could make that work there."

"You bought the Travel Lodge?"

"A while ago."

I shook my head and laughed at him. He smiled.

"I was thinking more in the downtown area, within walking distance from lower-income families. Set it up like Master Chef and add one long community table where everyone can join together and eat together what they've cooked, gather together, be together. She really had a great idea. I've told Taylor and Danielle about it. Taylor and Raphie love the idea so much they're looking to see how the idea could work in Germany."

Daryl looked up to the left and then started tapping his index finger to his chin.

"Maybe the old Envision building would work for that," he said to himself, out loud.

"Oh, Tina needs a mission statement for the registration of the foundation. Would you be able to get that to her this week?"

"Absolutely! I'll work on that tomorrow and get it off to her."

"Barry was at the foundation site. It will be about a mil to clean up."

"A million dollars?" I was stunned. No wonder that piece of property stood vacant for a while.

Phil walked by the table. "Hey, you two, would you mind if I joined you?"

"Not at all," Daryl replied, moving his beer and coaster over and clearing a spot for him. The men started men talk, reminiscing over their old cars, and then it evolved to guitars.

"I still have my Les Paul Custom." Phil smiled. "The ebony is as shiny as it was the day I got it."

"God, if you ever want to sell that guitar, let me know. I would buy it. Two things I want but don't yet have: a Super Bee and a Les Paul Custom." Daryl grinned.

"That won't ever happen. I will never sell that guitar." Phil smiled and sipped his pint.

The Shoe Closet

You can almost hear it grow. The earth yawns as it wakens from its winter slumber. It blinks one eye open. It blinks another eye open. It rolls over and reaches up to the sun as it breathes green. Spring had arrived.

I opened my laptop and contemplated the Foundation of Hope's mission statement. How do I condense the desires into a couple of paragraphs?

Petey laid on my legs sandwiched between my laptop and my lap snoring. The sun was peeking over the tree tops, the leaves in brilliant contrast from the week prior fluttered in the breeze, a lone large one waved "Hello." It would have all been perfect; it was all perfect, until Petey farted. Pulled out of reverie by gas.

"Petey!"

He snored on.

"It's a good thing I love you, you little shit."

I began typing:

"The Foundation of Hope's purpose is to eradicate homelessness in Chilliwack BC.

"Our vision is to prevent homelessness rather than respond to it.

"Recognizing that over 21% of the city's homeless population are from ages fifteen to nineteen years old, our intentions are to immerse ourselves into the needs of this age group, understanding that if we provide stability, direction, housing, and hope, the youth of Chilliwack can enter into adulthood stronger and in a better position to remain housed for the rest of their lives.

"To reduce pain, to build relationship/community, and to encourage a pay it forward attitude within this age group will be the primary focus; meeting their basic needs, the bedrock.

"The Foundation of Hope will be working alongside the community, the teachers and counsellors, the community programs already in place to fund what is working, to evaluate programs that were successful but were canceled due to lack of funding, and restart them, as well as initiate our own programs aimed to alleviate the expense of trades/post-secondary education.

"The City of Chilliwack's population is approximately 100,000 in a fairly closed environment, giving us a greater ability to monitor the outcome of the involvement of the Foundation of Hope. Ideally our future will know how many dollars and what kinds of programs are needed in a city this size to effectively reduce or to eradicate homelessness."

I read and re-read, satisfied with the result. I sent it off to Tina.

Taylor was online. "Mom, I'm working on the logos. How is this one for the foundation?"

"How is this one for the Shoe Closet?"

"Fantastic! I'll send them to Tina."

"So fun!"

Tina responded in less than five minutes: *"Your daughter did an amazing job! Tell her I think she needs to be paid in 'shoes!' Send her to the Holt Renfrew site and pick two pairs. I will order them and have them shipped out using my Crystal Castle Credit Card Daryl surprised me with last month."* A series of shoes and happy face crying emojis followed.

"You're kidding?"

"Not at all."

"Okay, I will."

I transmitted the message. Taylor had a difficult time picking out two pairs of shoes. "Mom, they are $1,000 each! That could buy groceries!"

"Accept the gift graciously, Taylor, and enjoy them," I typed my reply.

A message flashed in my inbox from Tina: *"I informed Daryl I'm buying your daughter shoes, and I think you should have a matching pair also. He told me to order Haney a pair of Dallas Cowboys cowboy boots, so I'll do that too. He's going to give them to him when we all go to the game."* More happy crying emojis followed.

I closed up my laptop. "They are nuts, Petey." I laughed; he yawned. "Let's go explore spring."

We returned from our walk just before noon. It was Friday. I had given up my Friday shift a year before. Long hours on my feet were taking a toll, and they were threatening strike action. I reduced my workload to keep them happy. I contemplated future foundation work. My feet for sure would like the new job.

I opened my phone and a message from Daryl flashed: "Join me for a beer?"

Hmm, why not? "Where?" was my response.

"I'm at Characters."

"I'll join you in an hour"

"See you then."

***

Daryl was alone at a high top in the corner, typing something madly into his phone when I arrived. I glanced at the bar and gave a nod to a couple of our regulars, who nodded back. I noticed Jack, the liquor logistics director, sitting at the end of the bar. I smiled; he smiled back. I turned and joined Daryl.

"What's up?" I asked, pulling back the barstool, draping my leather messenger bag over the back.

"Can you get a bigger bag?" Daryl laughed.

I smiled. "I carry a lot of shit around," I said, defending my choice in handbags.

"What's Haney up to?"

"He had to work today, poor guy. Are you going to Seattle tonight?"

"If the ceiling lifts." He turned and looked out the window. Typical spring on the coast: one minute sun, then rain, sometimes a little snow. Right now he was looking at the clouds that had rolled in over the last hour. "It's a little low right now; maybe later tonight. Tina has 'wine Friday' with Emily, Roxy, and Tanya tonight anyway. If it lifts, I'll join her when they're done."

"I will never get over how you use a chopper like a taxi," I said.

The server arrived and I ordered a pint.

"I hear I'm buying fucking shoes." Daryl laughed.

"Tina said." I grinned then added, "Happy wife—"

"I just can't wait to see Haney in fucking Dallas Cowboys cowboy boots." He laughed, amused with himself.

"Well, I'll enjoy my boots, that's what Taylor decided on—a cute pair of tan heeled boots and a nice pair of black with a more practical heel boots, and Tina says we're all getting matching, so it works for me." I grinned. "Thanks for the boots, Daryl, you're a gem!"

Daryl laughed and shook his head. "I heard from my team regarding Ukraine. It's exceedingly political, and we have to be very careful about how we aid. I've been toying with some ideas. I've talked to Bill and Buffet, and we're creating another fund."

"Buffet? As in Jimmy?"

Daryl chuckled. "As in Warren."

"Get out! Daryl."

He just smiled.

"Anyway, they're going to run it through Berkshire Hathaway. Billy is going to set up a website. This fund will have investors actually investing in Bill's projects, the batteries he's working on, and ... this is why I'm bringing it up, the water filtration system they are working on. It's a pump and filter in one. Anyone can pop it in a river or creek and, voila, instant perfectly safe water. This will be ideal for Ukraine."

"What's it called?" I asked.

"The pump filter?"

"The fund, the website—what is it called?" I shook my head.

"They haven't got that far. We were just brainstorming over the weekend. I'll just call it the superfund until they get it sorted out. They asked if you wanted to be a part of it too, or if your daughters wanted to be involved."

"For sure I can put a thousand into that fund. I'll ask the girls what they want to do. Maybe Taylor would like to put some of their income tax return money toward that."

"Sure, I could split it up put a thousand in the superfund for her, and the rest I'll put into gold."

"Gold?"

"Yes, I had my team investigate what would give her the biggest return fastest. They informed me gold. Our mines are doing well, and have you seen what gold is getting per ounce?"

"You have gold mines?"

He smiled. "And a diamond mine." He chuckled again "Where do you think Tina's pink diamond came from?"

I rolled my eyes and shook my head again.

"Anyway, they informed me that her investment into gold would likely give her a monthly draw of approximately $1,200."

"That's what they live on. Daryl, do you know what this will mean for them? Do you know how much this will impact their lives?"

"I'm aware."

"When will the first draw be?"

"Thirty days from the initial deposit."

"How will she get it?"

"I was thinking about that. I'm thinking that we put the gold into the Shoe Closet account, and you can transfer it to her monthly. Would that work for you?"

"Yes, I could do that, no problem. Where will the Shoe Closet account be?"

"Where do you do your banking?"

"Prospera, a little credit union in town."

"Okay, I'll go there, open an account, and then transfer that account to you."

"Great! When will you do that?"

"I have an appointment on Monday."

"Perfect. I'm not going to tell her how much she'll be getting. I'll just send it when it comes. It will be a nice surprise."

"We can do the same thing for your other daughter too," he added.

I thought for a moment. "No, Daryl, I like the way you do things. You give when others are willing to take the first step themselves. If Danielle chooses to ask, the way Taylor did, then I would include her in the gold, but if she's not willing to step her own foot forward first, then I don't think it's fair to include her as well."

Daryl nodded his head. "I agree."

From: *Tina Hoffmeister*
To: *Glenda*
Subject: *Re: Warning*

I am wearing the pink. My sister said Daryl has never seen it all together on you, so you should. I think she just wants her hubby to see it! 😂

Daryl speaks so highly of you and your family. I know he has his team looking at the rules and regulations of Ukraine to end this despicable situation, but like he says, we now have Russia, the Ukrainian government, and now the USA because of politics, so … This is just surreal; he thinks so far ahead of "just send the money."

He was talking with the Richard Branson to get him involved. I overheard him say, 'Why the fuck do you want to go to space? We need to fix the problems on earth first!"

I was kinda startled when Daryl told me tonight that Warren just made the top six 100+ billion billionaires.

Me being me researched their wealth, and Daryl has ten times more wealth than them all combined based on what I have seen.

I am happy with all of us. So much good coming. You are a great woman, and I love talking because we can yammer about Daryl and his silliness, and I don't share that with anybody because they don't know him like we do!

Links to Landsberg

"We've found a perfect area for the coffee shop. An area in Landsberg, by the river, they are developing. Beside it will be an area where we could put the community kitchen. It would be amazing, one beside the other! Let me know the minute funds are available and we'll start." Excitement jolted through Taylor's typed words.

I looked up from my phone, across the bar to the Bone, where Daryl was reading something on his phone. I walked over and interrupted him.

"Taylor has found a spot for the coffee shop and their community kitchen. Let me know how your appointment goes today; she's eager to begin."

"I was there already. The manager was exposed to COVID; he's in quarantine."

"Uggg, really? That's shitty. Well, I guess not much can be done about that." I sighed. It would at least be another fourteen days.

"Where's the development?" Daryl asked, redirecting my disappointment.

"Landsberg. Let me get my phone. She sent me a link."

I enlarged the screen and hit "translate to English." Daryl leaned in and we inspected the map.

"Could you please send that to me. I want to forward it to Steff."

"Of course, Daryl."

Little Doug

An orange cat was licking its paw, gnawing on its own claw. It whipped its head to the right so suddenly that it startled the crow cawing from the power pole on the left.

"Black Crow Cawing." He smiled and took one last puff on his smoke before butting it out in an overfilled ashtray sitting on an overfilled coffee table. A McDonald's cheeseburger wrapper, ten weeks old, fell to the floor. He peered over his Gretsch, thought about picking it up for a half second, and a half second later was strumming his guitar, cheeseburger wrapper forgotten. That happened a lot. He forgot a lot.

As he strummed the Gretsch, his gravel rock star voice started singing "Black Crow Cawing" in his mind. It was the only place he would sing. He watched the orange cat through the patio door as he strummed. A tabby cat joined him, leaping from the balcony rail, a feline Fabrice Calmels. He played, they danced.

"Here, kitty kitty, come here, kitty kitty. Where are you, kitty kitty?" a voice scratched from next door. The tabby lifted its head, responding to its name. Kitty Kitty. It leaped over the balcony rail, leaving the orange kitty alone to resumed licking its paw.

He stopped strumming and stood up, momentarily holding the position to anchor his gait before he dare step forward. Gout pulled him to one side, Fireball to the other. He leaned his hand on the wall as he leaned the Gretsch in the corner. Neither fall. He considered it the victory of the day.

He'd drink a little less and care a little more if he didn't have a ticking time bomb in his head. Aneurysms do that, and he has a few. One ruptured once. It wasn't fun.

The couch awaited his return. Picking up his pack of smokes and a lighter with a Jack Daniel's logo etched on the side, he staggered back to his sofa and fell into it. His body thanked Jesus for him. He opened the pack, pulled out a smoke, lit it with Jack, drew deeply, and exhaled, observing the smoke melt. Respire desire. He's the only smoker who never thinks of quitting. He flicked on the tube and started watching something that caused him to nod off. Burning fingers jolted him awake. "Shit! Gotta be more careful." He put out his butt, laid down on the sofa, and slept.

***

"Has anyone heard from Doug?" Tina messaged over our work group chat.

"I came in this morning, and the pub is a mess! Tony and I have been madly trying to clean it before we open!"

Privately she messaged me. "I'm going to kill him! It's the day after St. Patrick's Day in an Irish Pub, and he ties one on so bad he can't get up? He just messaged me. He said he slept in! What the heck!!!"

***

"Sorry, Glenda, I slept in."
It was a few days later.
"Doug, the day after St. Pat's Day?"
"Ya, I know, bad day to have done that one."

"Ya think?" I smiled and shook my head. "The floors are pretty sticky still. Are you able to give them a little more attention tomorrow?" I asked.

"I'll try."

"Try? Okay, Doug, you're a shitty cleaner, and I get you have health issues, but this is a business, and we need it clean."

He smiled. "I know, Glenda."

"Are you staying for a beer?"

"Yes."

He stayed for the day.

He was moving a little more slowly than his already slow self. That combined with his no-show after St. Pats Day had me a little curious. When I got home, I clicked on my phone and scrolled to the work camera, clicked on recordings, and watched him work. Ya, that's what I thought I saw today too—he's not moving his left arm. He's dragging the mop with his right arm only. What the hell, Doug?"

He was putting the mop away when I came in the next morning.

"Doug, you're not moving your left arm. Did you have a stroke?"

"I think I might have."

"Have you gone to the doctor?"

"I think I might have to."

"Would you please?"

"I'll think about it. Glenda, please don't tell my brother if he comes in."

"I won't, Doug."

"Thanks. Glenda?"

"Yes, Doug."

"Would you mind carrying a bowl of soup to the bar for me. My hand isn't working so good."

De Ja Vu

COVID, like the battle of Cambrai, came round a second time.

Restaurants and pubs with outdoor decks brought in tents and heaters. Cluster in the cloister was permitted on the patios. Those that could, did. Those that couldn't, didn't. We didn't. Almost exactly one year to the date we'd shut our door for the first wave of COVID, we were doing so for the second.

We packed up the bar and kitchen and hoped for the order to be done in two weeks over two months.

Fathomage

The architect amused himself. A room here, a room there, and let's connect it by a hallway and add another room there and another room there. Voila! Now, what shall we do with it? Ah ha, why yes, let's make it a pub!

And so Characters was born.

And not much has changed about it since.

The pool table was moved a few years ago, and someone thought it a good idea to fill the space with comfortable club chairs. It was. The rooms on the other side kept the old Characters charm. Worn banquettes on worn carpet, surrounded by worn wooden tables with worn wooden chairs in the upper room, tall tables toward the patio where everyone gets a barstool in the lower room. Quirky knick knacks stare at you, or you at them. The characters of Characters prefer this side.

An abundance of young pretty waitresses dressed in black Lulu Lemons come and go like the pints they serve. Some of them smile; most of them don't. Today one of them dropped a cloth on the patio floor.

Jack sat at a table under a heater looking at his phone as he took a draw off his pint. *The heater is nice*, he thought to himself. *Might have to get one of those for my patio.* The second thought piggybacked the first one. He saw the cloth go down. There it sat, and sat, and sat. The girls kept walking around it. Nobody picked it up. It annoyed him; it amused him.

Daryl was sitting at a table for two just outside the patio doors, watching the same cloth on the floor. Seven times the waitress walked by it. Seven times it was left there. He looked up and noticed another man at another table was watching the same cloth.

"How long do you think it will be before someone picks it up?" Daryl asked.

"Well, I couldn't say for certain, but they don't appear to be too rushed about it, do they?" Jack responded.

Fathomage, from the deep it came.

The seed, the cloth? Their common cognition?

Nobody could say exactly how it arose, yet it did. The burst of laughter.

And Jack, the director of liquor logistics, met Daryl, the richest man in the world.

And from a burst of laughter a friendship was born.

Just like that.

Princess Tina

Isn't it the dream of every little girl? Certainly it must be. Cinderella whisked off by the prince? Little girls grow up. Princes are hard to come by. The fairy tale must change.

The desire never does.

"Follow me," whispers Sidney Sheldon. He places his hand on the small of her back and guides her down the romance aisle of Barnes and Noble. "Over there," he breathes into her ear.

Enter the trillionaire!

***

"I feel like a princess," Tina's words read.

"Where are you going to get married?" I typed back.

"I know it sounds silly, but I've always dreamed of getting married in the Disneyland Castle. Every little girl's dream, right?"

"Ah, the Neuschwanstein Castle," I type in, and I attached a photo from our visit there.

"That exists?" came her reply.

"Yes, the Disneyland Castle was developed from this one," I assured her.

"Well, I have the slipper." She giggled over the email.

***

"Your love wants to be married in a castle," I said to Daryl when I saw him the next day.

He looked up from his phone, startled. I repeated myself. He looked up, tapped his index finger to his chin, and said, "I'll talk to Steffanie."

***

"We are getting married at the Neuschwanstein Castle, Glenda! You must be a bridesmaid! You and Em and Tanya! We all have to go to Milan! Drink Champagne and pick out our dresses! I would like it candlelit. Won't that be beautiful? A candlelit ceremony in a Castle!"

***

"I spoke with Steffanie, and we're going to rent out the whole village near the castle for the week. Your whole family—your daughters, their husbands and children—will be invited. We'll set up a kids' area, like a mini-Disneyland for all of the children on the day of the wedding, with proper supervision so all parents can enjoy themselves at the wedding. Mark your calendar, Glenda. It's set for July 15, 2023. The wedding will be in the castle, but we'll have the reception in the gasthaus in the village. We won't have a head table. Tina and I want to sit with our guests. You and Jack will be in the wedding party. Maybe we'll get Haney to be an usher and your daughter can sing. I'll see if I can get Alice to sing with her. Could she sing "Ave Maria"? Tina wanted that song. I wonder if we could get a Cinderella carriage. Hmmm, I'll have to get Steffanie on that one.

"The guest list is growing. Word has gotten out that I'm getting married, and I've been getting messages from people who want to attend. Obama and Michelle will be seated with us at our table. I was talking to Biden the other day. He mentioned he would like to be there, but that probably won't work. Alice is in charge of the music. He was laughing the other day because of the messages he's getting. Elton John got wind of the event and messaged me, so he'll be doing something. I don't know what. Alice said they're working on something together. Jon Bon Jovi is coming. Do you know what would be fun? Let's have all the musicians do karaoke! But they can't sing their own songs. They have to sing someone else's song. Alice can sing an Elton John song, and Elton John has to sing one of Alice's. Ha ha ha, that will be amazing. We definitely are going to do that, maybe two days before the wedding. You can ask Stephan King all the questions you want, Glenda. He's coming too. Jack messaged me and asked if we wanted a show there a couple of days before—Gilmour Jack. I have to talk to Steff about that, something about flight zones because of the laser light show. They want to do the full show, and I told him I thought the idea was marvelous. Have you seen their show, Glenda? I'll find it on YouTube for you. Pink Floyd always puts on the best shows."

Madame CEO

From: *Tina Hoffmeister*
To: *Glenda*
Subject: *Re: Whew*

We are in the Caymans!
It's amazing!
The main house is huge!
We went to corporate headquarters to meet everyone. God, he's amazing to watch!

He has a weird and uncanny ability to pull people in. The people he knew he remembered life details. Which was weird, because he has been away so long, but he knew random tidbits.

With new people, he would see a piece of children's art, or a wedding ring or an engagement ring or something, and he would lead the conversation, ask questions.

He learned so much from people that I'm sure they don't know they gave up. But when he left, I was standing with Lynds, and you could see everyone talking. New people going "That's Daryl?" Old staff saying, "God, I'm glad he's back."

It was sureal, the fact he just seemed to joke and goof around with everyone ... always a crack off or something.

It really was an unbelievable experience that I have never seen in a corporate type environment.

The thing that shocked me and made me love and respect him more was he talked to everyone! Stopped at all the desks, talked to new people, old staff, everyone.

In the bars, restaurant etc.

You really get why they are all so loyal.

The freedom allowed to think outside the box is incredible. I think that because people don't feel like they are "under the gun," they respond better and work harder. The fact he has built a team where everyone—and I mean from janitorial, dishwasher, whoever—share in the success gives them a sense of family and team and pride of ownership!

Nobody seemed to be "just doing a job."

Even Ronaldo saying to me, "New eyes, new perspective are very important, and that breeds our success!"

I think he has created a group and culture of "with the success of the company comes success of us personally, our community, our world."

I don't know when that started or if it was there from the start, but it is a lot to think about.

I don't know how to describe it best, but it's like the company is a living, breathing thing. Everyone working together, sharing ideas and suggestions, and ALL divisions working toward a common goal.

It makes me wonder what is really going on in Daryl's mind all the time, because this is definately HIS company. The morals, the drive, the intensity is there but so relaxed.

I'm not sure this makes sense, but you'll see when you're there.

I have no idea how Daryl does it. Guess it has been his whole life. It is fun and exciting, but it takes time to wrap your head around.

I think the way his company runs is hard to figure out too. So casual with TRILLIONS of dollars involved yet so relaxed.

At head office you can tell who was meeting with bankers, lawyers, etc. that day because they dress up. Everyone else just did their thing. It made me wonder … here we all dress up but may never see a client or do anything but work at our desk.

I wonder who is happiest. Having said that, I understand we are nowhere near the company Daryl is, so … kinda confusing!

***

Subject: *Re:* **From:** *Tina Hoffmeister*
To: *Glenda*
Subject: *Certificate of charity BC*

Hi Glenda,
I wasn't going to say anything, but Daryl said you need to know that the Government of British Columbia has signed off on the Recognition of Charities BC.
This means that upon receipt of the certificate to the lawyer's office, as well as the receipt of the Foundation of Hope BC registration number, we will be finalized for the provincial certification with the Government of Canada next in line.
We will know more from the Canadian Federal Government later today.
I find this tremendously exciting!
Congratulations on passing step one!

***

From: *Tina Hoffmeister*
To: *Glenda*
Subject: *back in Seattle*

Back in the office now.
Caught everyone off guard wearing a new Caymans sundress!
Danny just laughed and said, "I see you have been hanging around the Crystal Castle Holdings Int'l group!"
I think people were just surprised! Not used to seeing me dressed so casually.

But hey, when you get off a jet, why go change?

As for the transition back and forth, I told Daryl we definately have to plan differently. I think I need to be home for a night to get "acclimated" to being back in this office.

Waking up in the Caribbean then coming to work is a lot. Well for now! 😵😂😂

***

From: Tina Hoffmeister
To: Glenda
Subject: get ready

I can't even begin to describe how happy I am!

This is a culmination of months of so much good happening! Meeting you! Becoming part of a new life!

From last December things have exploded! From accounts to help people move forward, to the gold fund, to this!

Plus helping my sister, my cousin!

Then there is Daryl! Fuck, I love him so much! Look at us go! How do you feel?

I know you haven't seen all the paperwork and such, but that's being put together now that we have these numbers!

Get ready for trips to Vancouver! I hope you like helicopters! Because Daryl has meeting set for all of you Tuesday, May 18. That's when your head will explode! Madame CEO!

The certificate is at the lawyer's. He's going to the bank to show it to them this afternoon. They will complete the provincial registration etc. and then I can send funds.

Fifty million dollars is on its way to the account of the Foundation of Hope. Bank is submitting all documents to the government Fintrac division, so here we go!!!!

Negotiations

"We're in negotiations," Daryl said.

The two of us were sitting on the patio at Major League Pub under a heat lamp, consuming beer COVID-style.

Daryl smiled. He was refreshed and sun-kissed. The weekend with Tina in the Caymans reflected in his demeanour.

"Landsberg?" I asked, sipping my pint.

He smiled again. "We just have to convince Markle that a casino on the bank of the river is in the city's best interest. It shouldn't be difficult. We've worked with this government on a lot of things. The only pressure is there is an election coming up. We'd like something signed before that. Steff has been hard at work. Right now she has four of the six sites under contract. We just need the two by the river; it's very close though, I'm told."

"Taylor will be shocked." I laughed.

"We'll find her a spot for her coffee shop." Daryl pulled the site plans up on his phone and pointed out the areas he thought would be suitable for their intentions.

"Hey, what's going on with the debit cards and the Shoe Closet account?"

"There was a white card in my mail to go to the post office to pick up registered mail. I'm assuming these are the cards from HSBC."

"Really? Daryl? You knew you were meeting me for drinks today!" I laughed. "You could have sat down and surprised me with the cards. Geeze."

A sheepish smile crossed his face. "Sorry, I didn't think. I had other things on my mind. Remember, I was up at 3:00 a.m. for my meeting with Steff. They must have tried to deliver them when I was with Tina. I'll get them tomorrow."

"I know, you have a world of issues you're thinking about. Sorry. But what about the Shoe Closet account? What's going on with that?"

"Your fucking manager. First he's exposed to COVID, then he had to check with head office about something, then he got COVID. Fucking COVID, fucking small towns. It's like pulling teeth to get anything done here. Nobody wants to make decisions, or they can't make decisions. I don't know. I'm so frustrated with them, I think we need to take it to the HSBC, have a real bank deal with it."

"Okay, let me know what you need me to do."

"I will. I think you and Haney will have to go open an account there. I'll talk to downtown and we'll figure it out. I was at your work last week." Daryl grinned.

"Corky's? We're shut down. Why were you there?"

"Well, I thought as I'm looking to buy that property, perhaps I should buy Corky's too. I had a meeting with your boss."

"You met with Tony? You're going to buy Corky's?"

"We're in conversation. His valuation is way too high, so we'll see if he comes down. Anyway, that guy you call Skeletor—"

"Mark?"

"Yes, Mark, the one who drives the HellCat, he was pulling away from the liquor store just as I was walking out of Corky's with Tony. He looked a little surprised." Daryl grinned again.

"Yes, he would be shocked to see the two of you together." I smiled thinking of Mark's reaction. "I thought you already owned the Corky's property?" I continued.

"Not yet, very close, though. We had to make sure we could clean up the site in front of it at a reasonable cost first. We can, so now the talks continue. I don't expect we'll have any difficulty, though." He was reveling in his "ace up the sleeve" smile. "Anyway, legal informs me that all documentation is just about finished on the foundation side of things. We should have no problem moving forward with our boat weekend."

"And Tina? Will she be able to make it over the border?" I asked.

"They foresee no issues regarding that. Her essential service card is nearly complete. As I understand it, Tina has set up appointments with legal and with HSBC for June 17. Are you and Haney available that weekend?"

"Yes. Of course, Daryl. Our lives are pretty much revolved around where the foundation needs us to be!"

"Good, I'll let her know."

Tex

"You'd better explain why my returns are not as I expected them," he drawled. Tex sat under his cowboy hat.

"Absolutely. Here you can see—" Tina began.

"Honey"—he leaned back into the white leather sofa, spreading his legs and draping his arms across the back—"I don't need no Barbie doll explaining man things to me. How about you walk those purdy little legs out of here and go get me yer boss."

"Excuse me?"

"You heard me, doll."

"I have your figures right here. I can explain—"

"I said"—his eyes flashed black, then narrowed—"I don't need no woman explainin' man things to me, so take your pretty little ass and that big fake rock you have flashing on your finger out of here and git me your boss."

A chill seized her, crawling right up into her fingertips, leaving them numb. She instinctively stepped back.

"Well?" he continued.

She nodded in his direction. Turning from him, she walked to the glass door that separated her office from the hub of Holstein Management. Her numb fingers opened the door. She exited and walked straight to Danny's office.

"I'm having a problem with Tex," she said. Danny looked up from his desk as she entered. "He doesn't want 'this Barbie doll, this woman' explaining 'man' things to him."

"What?" Danny replied incredulously.

"He called my engagement ring fake." She spun it around on her finger; the personal attack pushed her toward tears. She straightened up, took a deep breath, and let it out slowly, regaining her composure. Glass offices hide nothing.

"How much does he have invested with us?" Danny asked.

"Just over a mil." Tina replied.

"Okay then. Stay here."

Tina took a seat by the window that overlooked the city of Seattle.

Danny left the building that housed Holstein and walked across the street to the bank.

"Hi, Danny. What can I help you with today?" Barb asked as he stepped up to her desk. Barb was Curt's gatekeeper.

"Is Curt in today?"

"He is."

"Great. Does he have a moment?"

"For you, Danny, absolutely. Give me a minute."

A few handshakes later, Danny was exiting the building with a bank draft of $1,350,010.45 laser-printed and braille-dotted tucked into his breast pocket.

Tex was flipping through a copy of *The Wealth Collection* when Danny opened the door.

"Your entire investment, paid out, in full. Sign the release," Danny demanded.

"Excuse me?" Tex questioned, the heat of anger flushed in his skin.

"You heard me. We will not do business with you." Danny was firm and matter of fact.

Tex realized he had no hand in this, so he picked up the silver pen and scratched his name on the bottom of the release. Taking the bank draft, he made a big Tex exit.

"Tina," Danny said upon returning to his office, "why don't you pack up and head home? The day is almost done anyway. Go pour yourself a big glass of wine and let Tex go."

"You know, Danny, I think I will. That one got under my skin a bit."

She drove her silver Audi ten minutes up the coast to her home. The house sat on a bluff overlooking the Seattle coastline. Built in 1890 by a sea captain, she had been slowly restoring it, being careful to keep the old-world charm. She pulled into her driveway. A black Mercedes was parked in it. She glanced around and saw nobody, so she headed to the front door. It was unlocked. With a bit of trepidation, she entered her home. The sound of Daryl's laughter coming from the back yard eased her angst.

"Whew, it's Daryl." Relief and joy simultaneously ran through her. Dropping her briefcase and handbag on the blue leather sofa, she moved quickly outside to see her love. *He just couldn't have picked a better day to surprise me!* she thought as she stepped through the back door.

"Well hello there." Daryl grinned as he saw Tina step onto the back patio.

Tina couldn't believe her eyes.

Daryl was sitting on the edge of the hot tub with his pant legs rolled up, feet dangling in the warm water. He was sipping a Scotch. To his right was Mackenzie Scott, and to his left Mackenzie's new husband, Dan. The three of them turned to Tina and waved.

"*Fuck, Glenda,*" came the email from Tina. "*I come home from work to find Daryl and Jeff Bezos' ex, Mackenzie, and her husband, Dan, all dangling their feet in my hot tub, giggling like kids. What kind of a life is this?*"

Schrem Building

"*Wir haben es nächste woche für Sie.* We will have it ready by next week."

He spoke in hushed tones. Even walls hear whispers. *Achtung, Feind hört mit.*

The General nodded. "*Nächste woche dann.* Next week then."

The meeting was brief, to the point. Both were busy men.

Karl tipped his hat toward the General. "*Für das mutterland.*" The General nodded in return. Both men turned in the opposite direction and left the corner they were standing on.

Karl's black boots made no noise over the cobblestone. A fresh layer of snow covered the streets, the stones silenced in a tomb of snow. Karl didn't give it a thought; his mind was already on tomorrow. How much could they get done? One hundred workers in one hundred hours? "Yes, yes," he said aloud as the numbers came together. "It can be done." He smiled only then.

***

"Did Daryl end up buying the development in Lansberg?" Taylor messaged me from Germany.

"I think so, but I'm not quite sure if the deal is complete."

"Could you ask if Development Three belongs to him? The village is in a bit of an uproar. The developers want to name the building 'Karl Schrem.'"

"And?" I waited.

"Karl Schrem was a Nazi. He worked with the Nazi Party and supplied them; he ran a factory of some kind."

"Ohhhhh, ah, hmmmmmmm. What the heck? Does that make him a Nazi?"

"Yes, here he would be considered that, as he helped them. The whole village is freaking out. A building named after a businessman who aided the Nazi Party is like honouring that part of history." Anxiety in Taylor's reply was audible. "Do you think you can find out if that belongs to Daryl? And if it does, could you ask him to change the name?"

"I think, let me first message Tina, and I'll get her take on it. Maybe she can investigate and we won't have to bother Daryl with it. He'd be livid if he found out one of his buildings was named after a Nazi, ugggg!"

***

From: *Tina Hoffmeister*
To: *Glenda*
Subject: *Re: Development Name; Karl*

OMG!

Can I send this to Daryl? He is going to explode if that is his group!

I would be dumbstruck if Steff was doing this.

Daryl's dad's brother was run over on the sidewalk by the SS after mouthing off about Hitler at the pub, so …

Even if it's not him, I am sure he will make sure there is a name change!

Taking Care of Business

"The issue is being dealt with." He hadn't even sat down before the words exited his mouth.

"Which issue?" I replied.

"Landsberg. You can tell your daughter we will rename the building. We didn't name it. It was the previous developer who had the names selected."

"Ahhh, Tina mentioned it to you then."

"Yes, she did. Please thank your daughter for bringing this to our attention. They are working on it as we speak."

"I'm glad she did too. It's really weird how stuff like this happens," I said, shaking my head. "Who would ever think that you sitting here in a pub in Chilliwack could reach into a different country where my daughter is to find out information like this that could impact something you own. Kind of cool though, isn't it?"

"As I've said before, I don't know what wheels in the universe were turning to move us together, but it is very interesting, I agree. Everything is set for next week. It even looks like Tina will be able to join us on the boat. She's very excited about this."

"Oh excellent! I really can't wait to begin, Daryl. The sooner the better. Did you pick up the cards?"

"Oh fuck." He breathed in deeply, pushing back his annoyance. "Didn't I tell you about that?" Shaking his head, he continued. "I went to the post office and they wouldn't give them to me. I didn't have proper ID.

Apparently my Cayman driver's license wouldn't work. I needed something with my house address."

"What?" I was stunned. "So give them something with your house address—a bill, your car insurance papers, property insurance."

"I don't have anything!"

"What do you mean you don't have anything?"

His blue eyes peered from behind his glasses straight at me. "Glenda, I don't pay bills! Other people pay my bills. I don't own anything. Everything is purchased through Crystal Castle. I even contacted HSBC and had them fax over my information to the post office so they would release the cards to me, but they wouldn't do it. They said they need something with my name and that house address. HSBC finally gave up and told them to return the cards to them and they'll courier them out."

I shook my head. "That's ridiculous."

"I know! Anyway, we'll be there next week. Maybe we'll just pick up the cards there."

"True, we can do that."

"Oh, and apparently my cars are ready."

"What cars?"

"I had ordered a couple of Alfa Romeos, an SUV for Tina to drive around in when she comes to Chilliwack. I don't think she would appreciate crawling into my Honda." He snickered. "And I bought a sedan for myself, but I'll leave that in the city, I think. Anyway, both are in that new brilliant red. God, that's a beautiful colour. They should be ready for pick up next week." He grinned.

"Well, we could drive them back instead of taking a chopper."

"That's what I was thinking. Hmmm, maybe I'll bring the sedan back and park it in the garage too. Ah, we'll see." He was clearly thinking out loud. "We'll have two more," he said to our server as she passed by our table. He swallowed the last of his pint and pushed his glass aside. The afternoon was pleasantly warm, and Daryl eased back in his chair, opening his body to the sun the way a cat owns the sunbeam it lies in.

"Corky's should have revamped the patio and stayed open," he stated in a sigh. "I miss the heat. God, what am I doing here?"

"Good question. Why stay? Why not go back to the Caymans?"

Daryl smirked. "I have to be where we're building up. I have too much going on, and, well, the team is excited again. Everyone was getting a little bored. Even Ronaldo said he was contemplating retirement before we started the Fraser Valley. Now it's exciting again. Different problems to overcome, different government to manoeuvre through. I'm headed to Victora tomorrow to meet with the rule makers regarding full disclosure of the government portion of lotto money. It bothers me that they have it under general revenue. Somebody somewhere is lining their pocket. When the casinos reopen, we'll be changing the way it used to be." He smiled broadly at the thought.

"Bringing a little Gambino in, are you?" I laughed.

"Maybe." His eyebrows lifted ever so slightly. "Day after tomorrow I'm in Ottawa and then Montreal."

"Why there?" I asked.

"I have casinos in Montreal, and I need to talk to government in Ottawa."

"This is a little bigger than you let on, isn't it?"

"Maybe." He smirked again.

"What's going on with the computers and the manual the Gates Foundation was working on?"

"Hmmm, good question. I'll message Tina. I know she and Melinda have had a number of conversations. The Bill thing certainly hasn't helped, has it? We've been waiting for that to die down a little before we proceed with the fund that would be helping Ukraine. Bill, Bill, Bill." Daryl shook his head, not in personal judgement but rather in being delivered another issue that needed to be dealt with. "I know Melinda has been lying low since the news of their divorce came out, though she and Tina have spoken and she fully intends on continuing her commitment with the foundation."

"Oh, that's good. I was wondering. I knew the foundation would continue with or without her, but it will be so much better with her. Have you spoken with Bill lately?"

"I have. I told him his timing could have been better." One of Daryl's eyebrows moved slightly, his tell of amusement. "I make no judgement on my friend. I just don't want his decisions to fuck up our plans."

Our server dropped two full pints on the table, spilling a little over the side of the glass. Beer puddled on the table, and she quickly turned away, ignoring the mess. Visibly annoyed, Daryl picked up his pint and took a deep swallow of his lager. Shaking the excess liquid from his fingertips, he glanced at his phone. "Excuse me, I have to get this." He put the phone to his ear.

"Hi, son, what's up? I would suggest you let them know you aren't doing it alone and you have us behind you. They're looking at your age and your experience. If you need me to get involved, I will. I've noticed some information leaking into the media, so you'll need to get that scrubbed. Yup. Yup. Sounds good. Love you. Yup. Bye."

"Nelson?" I asked.

Daryl nodded.

"Still working on the Flames deal?"

"Almost there." Daryl smiled. "Have I showed you this yet?" He pulled a picture up on his phone of something that looked like tile. Vibrant moss green striae with earth brown, sliced and polished into a creamy sheen. "It's petrified wood! They pull it out of the ocean up north. My contact at Peterson Stone Works is supplying this for our renos in the lobby of our casino in the Bahamas. It's $1,000 a square foot, but it's so amazing. I've spoken with Lisa Peterson about using it for the reception desk for the foundation. They're making it as we speak. You should put some in your build." Daryl grinned.

"At a $1,000 a square foot?"

"Just in your foyer," he insisted.

I did quick mental math and chuckled. "I'm not spending $100,000 on tile for our foyer, Daryl."

"I'll buy it for you, but you have to put it somewhere in your house. Foyer, back splash, bathroom, I don't care."

I laughed at him. "If you're buying, I promise you I will find a place in our build for it."

"I need to get your window to you too. Where do you think you'll put that?"

"I was thinking actually in the powder room. It's a place where every visitor would see it," I suggested.

Daryl looked a little incredulous. It was clear he didn't think the powder room was an optimal spot for a piece of sixteenth-century stained glass.

"Our house is contemporary, Daryl. I need to find a place where this historic piece is not drowned out by that noise."

He said nothing so loudly. His eyes, unblinking gate keepers, peered through me. No lines creased his face. His nose, narrow, direct, clear, an enigma. Large consumption of alcohol over a lifetime doesn't author a nose like this, yet it didn't seem out of place or out of the ordinary. Daryl wasn't ordinary, even his nose acknowledged this. He picked up his pint and sipped like he knew my thought and mocked it with a sudsy exclamation point. Two light brows lay motionless on his waxen frons, moving seldom on a brow remarkably smooth. One would assume Botox was involved. That would be out of character. This man's care of his own appearance is that it was clean, unadorned, orderly, unsoiled. Standing in a wax museum he would be mistaken for a sculpture rather than a spectator, a statue not a squire. His hands soft, his fingertips elegant, evident they had escaped a lifetime of anything manual. His mind a map of neurons connecting, bouncing, intertwining within themselves, producing more neurons that bridged information to idea. Layers of thought, pressed by a half a decade, created his own diamond. When he chose to let you see it, it sparkled, bedazzled, or cut. I sipped my pint. Was I sitting with a Saint or Satan?

"You're right, Glenda, you see different in me, but I will never let you see into me," his stare spoke.

I believe it's safer for me if I don't. My thought lingered a moment, etching itself in mise en garte script. As the pen finished off with a flourish tail, Daryl picked up his phone.

"Well hello there!" His voice softened, a smile tugged the corner of his lip as he listened. "Your mom could help with that, you know." Gentleness drifted over him and eased his being. "You'll figure it out, honey ... yup, yessssss. I love you too, bye." Smiling, he set his phone face down on the table.

"Christine?" I asked.

"Yes, she's just making final plans at home before they come to the boat," he replied.

"I really can't wait to meet her. You speak so highly of your kids. You're so proud of them, it truly makes we wonder what they're like in real life."

"You will like them, Glenda." He flipped his phone over, saw a message, and picked it up to read.

"Tina says that Tanya has taken the Gates manual home to read. She should be finished with it over the weekend. Hmmmm, that's a little odd."

"I agree. But Tina did say she and Tanya were looking into how they could help the schools down there. Perhaps it's just doing a little homework." I smiled. "I do hope she's done with it soon, though. I have all the time in the world to read it right now."

"Yup, you need to take advantage of that. You're going to be very busy very soon. What will you be doing tomorrow? Quiet mountain day for you?"

"Yes, I plan on doing more online research. I need a good grasp of what our community is doing and how best to direct funds when they arrive."

"That's a good plan."

"How long will you be gone?" I picked up my pint and sipped.

Daryl leaned back in his chair and folded his arms across his chest. "I should be back the day before we go to the boat, if everything goes as planned. I may even have to take a side trip to Seattle." He grinned mischievously. "I need to move the Marlin."

"Excuse me?"

Unfolding himself, he leaned back in, picked up his pint, and took a long sip. "When we were in the Caymans, Tina wanted a souvenir, so I found a replica marlin and had it shipped to her house. The last time I was there, I hung it on her mantle."

"I bet that went over well." I laughed.

"Well, she did tell me to make myself at home in her house." He was laughing. "The next time I was there, it was gone. So that was short-lived." He chuckled. "I found it outside, hung on the shed. So I brought it in and hung it over the bed." He was grinning foolishly, pleased with his marlin-moving skill. "I probably need to go there and move it into her shoe closet. God, I've never seen such a room in my life. Do you know that in the corners she even has shoe racks that turn, like Lazy Susans? Has your daughter got her shoes yet?" he asked. "Tina is going to bring yours up with her and give them to you on the boat."

"Taylor hasn't said anything, so I'm going to assume that she hasn't, and yes, Tina and I already discussed my shoes. She wanted to know if I wanted them shipped to me. I told her I'd rather they come in person, with her." I grinned. "Shoes are things. I'd rather see the gift giver. So I'll wait until she makes it to Canada."

Nodding, Daryl continued. "I hear she bought herself the same kind as the both of you. I don't know where she's going to put them, though; her fucking closet is full."

He's Not Good, Glenda!

"With genuine thanks and warm regards, Glenda."

I put the pen down and re-read what I'd just written. Satisfied, I tucked the card in its envelope and sealed it shut. I had genuinely enjoyed writing these thank you notes, one for the Gates and the other for Jane. Both had helped enormously with getting the Foundation of Hope off the ground, and I was exceedingly grateful for their expertise and their desired to help. I knew the Gates wouldn't be on the boat, so I would leave the card with Tina and have her deliver it to Melinda. I was looking forward to giving Jane her card personally.

Now what kind of gift do I get for Tina?

The thought was daunting. Clearly she needed nothing. Clearly she had funds to buy whatever she desired. Clearly she had high taste. Clearly I could fail.

Perhaps I could connect it with the foundation? Yes, let me think on those lines.

We had passed emails back and forth on interior design for the foundation offices over the past eight weeks: an earthy colour palette of black, gold, and teal mixed with wood and stone had emerged. We were going to be looking for local artists to supply us with art, showcase it for them. If someone wanted to purchase pieces, we would make that happen. Wood chainsaw carvings of bears and eagles would be purchased from local artisans and placed throughout the space, again with the intent of creating connection with the community. I looked through the Stolo gift shop. Ethnic Native pieces filled shelves, and a beautiful blanket caught my eye. A simple but stately design woven in mixture of black, teal, rust, and gold. I knew I wanted this blanket lying over a chair or sofa in the office.

I'll buy two, I thought. *Perfect for a chilly night on a boat, and connected with the one for the foundation office. Yes.* I was pleased with myself. *Yes, the blanket and a nice bottle of local white wine, simple but very meaningful gifts.*

Thursday had arrived. Pensively I considered what I should pack. It was just a weekend, but I would be meeting suits. Comfortably professional I concluded and started pulling pieces of clothing together in my mind, mixing and matching mentally.

I sent a quick email off to Tina: "Today is the day!"

I did have most of the day to pack. We weren't due to head for the chopper until late afternoon, then dinner at Carderos, a night on the boat, and the following day set with suit meetings, lawyers, bankers, and some shopping. The itinerary had been set the week before.

I pulled my little overnight suitcase up onto the bed and started pulling out pieces of clothing that I had ordered in my mind. I was laying the combinations of clothing on the bed when I heard my phone signal incoming message. Picking it up, a message from Tina flashed in my inbox.

Re: TODAY!!!
From: Tina Hoffmeister
Sent: Thursday, June 17
To: Glenda
Subject: Re: TODAY!!!

Daryl was hit by a truck.
He has a broken jaw a concussion and they are removing his spleen.

***

On Thursday, June 17, 2021, 8:39 AM Glenda wrote:
I can't believe it

***

From: Tina Hoffmeister
Sent: Thursday, June 17
To: Glenda
Subject: Re: TODAY!!!

He is not good, Glenda.

Montreal

"Fucking government." I shook my head as I thought about how corrupt the government really was. Slimey smiles, slimey hands stuffed into suits. They sicken me. I boarded my plane in Ottawa oblivious to my surroundings. My mind was weaving information. I trust nobody. Every time one of them opens their mouths, I mentally make notes of where I'll be directing Doug next. When I landed in Montreal, I had fully formed a plan. I sent a quick text to Doug.

"What's your desired turn around?" the captain, Tim, asked as I gathered papers scattered in front of me up into a pile as I prepared to head out.

"Here tonight, return to BC in the morning, land in Abbotsford. I'll chopper to Chilliwack, pick up Glenda and Haney, and chopper back to Vancouver. Is the hanger available in Abbotsford, or are you going to head back to Millionare after you drop me in Abbotsford?"

"I'll head back to Millionaire," Tim stated.

"Good. You'll be close if I need you."

Tim nodded. "I'll be ready for you to board on your return to BC at 8:00 a.m. tomorrow."

"That works. Thank you."

I descended the steps. Lyndsay had set up car service for me and they were there. God, she's perfect. She's always ten steps ahead of me. I slid into the back seat of the black Buick Enclave.

The Enclave turned left onto A20 and headed east. In under thirty minutes I was in the offices of Casino de Montreal.

I leaned back in a black leather executive chair in their boardroom, folded my arms across my chest, and listened to them speak. As they spoke, I wove, mentally manoeuvring in my mind. Had they the ability to peek inside my mind, those speaking would have been stunned. Instead, they rambled on, oblivious to how their very own words were being used as thread, creating new fabrics. A new future of gaming. I glanced at my phone: "Exactly as you thought." Doug's words scrolled before me.

I stopped hearing the blonde who was speaking and gazed up, eyes hovering for a moment through the window overlooking the Olympic Basin. I brought my left hand up to my chin and started stroking my beard. The speaker noticed the distraction and stopped. I turned quickly to the speaker. "Continue, please. I'm listening." I then picked up my phone and typed: "Fire them."

I placed the phone back on the walnut table, turned my attention fully to the speaker, and smiled. She smiled back. I was smiling because I had fired 30 per cent of Great Canadian upper management, the 30 per cent who were greasing the palms of the government. She was smiling because she had my attention again.

Meetings done, I checked into my hotel, threw my blue jacket on the bed, and headed back out. The evening was warm, and I needed a beer. The Flames were playing, so I walked across the street from my hotel and found a sports bar. Slipping onto a barstool, I ordered a pint from the bartender, who looked like a teenager, and lost myself in the hockey game. During commercials, I texted Doug, and I texted Tina. I needed diversion. If I didn't have the game, if I didn't have Doug and Tina, I would have wound a thousand threads of thoughts into another thousand threads of thought. Once it starts it's difficult to stop. I welcomed the distraction.

The game finished, the night got dark, and the beer started tasting like water. I sent one last message to Doug, asked for my tab, flung a few bills toward the bartender, and left. Standing on the corner waiting to cross the street, I felt my phone buzz. I pulled it up to my face to read the message as I stepped off the curb. It was from Doug. It said—

The next thing I remember was waking up in a hospital room. I could taste blood, and my vision was blurry. I pulled his hand up to my eyes. My glasses were gone. For a moment I panicked. The nurse by my side saw I was conscious and feeling my face.

"Would you like your glasses?" she asked as she placed them on my face. "One of the lenses had popped out of the rim, so I put it back in for you." She smiled and placed them on my nose.

"My phone?"

"Right here." She handed it to me. "Amazing that it wasn't damaged. They said it must have flown right out of your hand. A passerby picked it up, along with your glasses, and gave them to the ambulance attendant."

"A truck ... a mirror?" I said.

"Yes!" The nurse assured me that I was remembering correctly. "You were hit by a truck mirror."

"It flung me around."

"It appears so," the nurse agreed. "We are monitoring your brain for injury, and your spleen has been damaged. Your jaw will hurt—twenty stitches they counted.

My mind was fuzzy. I opened my phone and snapped a photo of myself. I sent it to Tina.

"I have a bit of a problem," I typed. After hitting the send button, I felt myself slipping out of consciousness. Vegas lights glittered around me, and a deep voice from the past frothed: "You don't know who you are talking to!"

What the fu ... I didn't finish the thought; I was out.

***

From: *Tina Hoffmeister*
Sent: *Thursday, June 17*
To: *Glenda*
Subject: *Re: TODAY!!!*

I'm in Montreal. Lynds is here.
I will keep you updated. I am so scared.
They took him straight into surgery last night. He was in recovery before I got here.
His spleen is removed and he is asleep. They're going to keep him sedated today and then assess him tomorrow.

***

I slipped onto the chair, stunned. If a mind could think one hundred thoughts at one time, mine was there. Questions erupted from the chasm of nescience: who, what, where, when, how? Trying to answer the unknown with the unexplained—fruitless, I knew, yet I found I couldn't stop reaching into it.

Was it so bad? Could Daryl actually suffer brain damage? Oh my God, what a tragedy that someone such as him, at this time when he's trying to do so much good, be struck down in this way. Why, God? What is it that I can't see? Why would such a thing happen and at this precise point? Really, God?

"Please let his brain not be hurt," I prayed simply.

Then my mind pulled me into the pit of selfishness. The cards, the help for the school, the meetings with the lawyers and bankers, the boat, the dinners, the helicopter, meeting everyone. Poof, just like that, gone. So very near, on the cusp of reaching my fingers around this new future. I could feel it. The excitement, the desire, the hope snuffed out. Not for ever, but for now, and my heart sank further.

Combined with concern was the realization that I was forced to continue to wait.

I crumbled.

Relief

"Please don't do that again, Daryl. You scared the crap out of me."

"It's not like I controlled that." He laughed and winced, instinctively putting his right hand to his left side, as if holding it would ease the pain a ripple of laughter created. He was looking remarkably well considering ten days before he was being observed for possible brain damage. A small scrape on the bottom of his chin, a finger cut up and bandaged with gauze, and a gouged up knee were the only remaining visible vestige of his ordeal.

They kept him in hospital for five days and then released him to recover in his hotel room. Yesterday they had removed his stitches and cleared him to fly. He was sitting across from me in booth 12 in Corky's. COVID restrictions once again lifted, allowing for indoor seating.

"Why didn't Tina come? She was in Canada. They let her in for a medical emergency. Why on earth did she go back to Seattle?"

"Glenda, do you have any idea how much work she had backing up because she was sitting with me in Montreal? Danny told her to take the time she needed, but she knew what she was leaving in his hands. She's far too conscientious to have put it off longer than needed."

"But geeze, Daryl, I've been dying to meet her. You would have thought she would at least have dropped you in Chilliwack and left tonight."

"I'm sorry, Glenda. She really couldn't put off the work she'd put off for a week."

I sighed. He continued. "She didn't even get off the plane. They just touched down, I kissed her goodbye, got off, and they took off again. She says she's going to work until Wednesday and then fly back up. You'll meet her soon enough." He smiled and winced again as he straightened out his knee. "She's going to have to get here quickly. She has my wallet."

"Excuse me?"

"She had all of my things; she packed everything up. We didn't even think about it as I got off the plane. She was already looking ahead to what her day would be, as was I. I simply got off the plane. I messaged her when I went to pay for gas and realized I didn't have my wallet. Sure enough, she found it in the bottom of her bag. She said she'd try and come back up tonight, but she can't use the plane. The pilot has too many hours already, so I suggested she use a chopper. She's a little nervous, as she hasn't done that before."

He glanced down at his phone. "Shit," he muttered under his breath.

"Shit what?" I asked.

"It's Tina. She said there are no choppers available. Something about a shortage due to the forest fires."

"Yes, while you were away, BC caught on fire; it's been terrible."

He sighed deeply.

"Well, I've got your beer."

"Ya, thanks." He trailed off in thought.

"What's up, D.?"

"The reason I had to make it back to Chilliwack so quickly is because I have a meeting with my insider regarding the Bridal Falls development today. He didn't believe that I had been in an accident. The Natives are pretty untrusting with white men, understandably so. I need to get some cash to him."

"Why do you need to get him cash?"

Daryl smiled at my innocence. "It's how we get things done, Glenda. I give him cash, he makes sure to leak things to the press."

"So ask him to wait until Wednesday."

"That won't work. He already doesn't trust me, and my accident didn't help. He's leaving tomorrow, it's tonight or—"

"Or what?"

"Or I start from scratch trying to gain their trust all over again. I've come so far …" His voice trailed off for a moment and then continued. "I suppose I could go to the house and pawn a TV."

"Daryl, that's ridiculous! How much do you need? I'll go get some cash for you."

Relief washed across his face. "God, Glenda, you don't have to, but it would certainly be very helpful."

"All good, you have other things to deal with. I can help with this. How much do you need?"

"Three thousand should be enough. I'll message Tina and have her wire you up funds. Could you please send her the account number you'd like it deposited in?"

"She could e-transfer it too, or even PayPal," I suggested.

"We don't do PayPal due to a security breach we had a few years ago, but I'll get her to check into transferring as well."

"I do need to run it by Haney. I don't touch anything out of that account without him knowing about it."

"As it should be," Daryl replied.

I ordered another round of beer as I texted Haney and waited for his response.

Haney was visiting his parents, but if he was home, he wouldn't get my text message. Our cell service was so limited it barely existed up on our mountain. Normally we used Messenger or WhatsApp, as both ran via WiFi. Strangely, only Daryl's texts made it on our mountain. I joked with him often. "What kind of cell service do you have? Nobody's texts make it up our mountain but yours ... and all your memes and gifs—*poof*, no problem."

He shrugged his shoulders and smiled. "Security takes care of that. They just tell me to reboot my phone once a day, and I do as I'm told."

Haney messaged back. "If you're comfortable doing that, I'm okay with it too."

I was happy to have funds to help Daryl, and I was happy to have a husband who was good with helping too.

When I returned from the bank, Daryl informed me that Tina would be sending me an email to get the specifics for the wire transfer. She needed a swift code, address, etc. "I've told her to wire you $4,000."

"Why would you do that?" I asked.

"Because you're helping me out, and to thank you for your kindness. Also, I've spoken with HSBC, and they're sending someone here. We'll just do the foundation's banking at this HSBC. They said they will be sending someone out on Monday."

"And the legal paperwork?" I asked.

"Josef will be bringing out the paperwork himself."

"Josef?"

"Yes, Josef, one of the lawyers we've been using for the foundation."

"When is he coming?"

"He's just left for vacation and will return the first week of August. We'll get the paperwork signed then."

Daryl started looking a little pale. He had barely finished his first pint, and the second one I had ordered an hour before sat untouched. I had forgotten he was still recovering, and then I felt guilty for pummeling him with all the questions.

"What time is your meeting?" I asked.

"I have to be there at 5:00 p.m."

"It's almost that now, Daryl. We should finish up here," I said.

He asked our Tina for a glass of water and finished it before we stood up. He put his arm around my shoulder and gently hugged me. I squeezed him back.

"Thank you, Glenda. You have no idea how much your friendship means to me," he whispered quietly.

It's True!

"Mom, you'll never guess what I just read!" Taylor exclaimed over WhatsApp messenger.

"Have no clue," I typed in. I put my phone down and stood up, stretching.

A smokey haze hung thickly in the air, stealing a crisp morning. I walked to the coffee maker to pour another cup and returned to my leather chair, pushing Petey to one side. "We share, big guy," I said, scratching his floppy ear. Sipping from my mug and staring out the window, I contemplated the destruction of fire and the need for forest fires for the natural order. "One of the ways our earth takes care of itself." I sighed. "Problem is, it's harmful to humans." My mind was toying with the paradox of humans needing an earth to do its natural thing in order for it to sustain itself so they could live on it, and the fact that the very thing the earth was doing to help sustain itself was harming humans when my phone vibrated.

"It's in our local newspaper. I'm going to go and get it and read it to you. I have to translate it, so give me a bit, would you." Taylor continued. "So basically in English, it says this:

"The new Developers of the Landsberg build out will be holding a contest to allow all of the community to decide what they would like to call the buildings of Development 3.

They assure the community that the name Karl Shrem will not be used."

"Get out!" I exclaimed. "Amazing."

A shiver ran through me, followed by a jumbled mess of thought:

He really is who he claims to be!

Good God, I haven't thrown all that money out!

We really are going to be helping the schools, the kids, all of Chilliwack!

He really was hit by a truck and truly hurt. Oh God, I'm a horrible person for wondering if that was really true or not!

I sat completely stunned. Every doubt that had crossed my mind, months of planning built only on a foundation of trust, swirled in front of me and then released itself into the ether of reality. For the first time since December, I exhaled.

"Isn't it, though?" Taylor agreed. "Mom, Daryl really is who he says he is."

And both of us in that moment, she in Germany, me in Canada, slowly came to grips with the reality of what she had just read.

"It's one thing to hope, isn't it, Taylor?" I typed. "Quite another thing to know."

I continued. "A contest? Let the people choose? Ha ha ha, this sounds completely like Daryl, doesn't it?" I laughed—giggled, really. A joy mixed with relief giggle.

"Completely amazing," Taylor typed.

"How does that make you feel, Taylor?" I asked. "That you mention something to me, and I pass the information forward, and just like that, change happens?"

"Awe," she stated simply.

"And," I continued as I thought of all implications, "exceedingly responsible for our own words."

"Ya, wow, I never in a million years would have thought that little me could impact something such as this. It's a really weird feeling."

Not so Friendly Glenda's

"Do you know Jack? The liquor logistic man?"

I wiped the Bone top, laid a coaster in front of Daryl, and placed his pint on it.

"Of course I know Jack." I laughed. "I love Jack! He arranged for my old delivery guys to return to this route."

"We've been hanging out quite a bit." Daryl spoke in confession style. "I met him at Characters on the patio over a cleaning cloth on the floor that nobody would pick up; anyway, he sees a lot of things on the streets. When the foundation is up and running, I'd love for you two to connect so that you can get some aid to him for when he encounters these issues."

"Sure thing, boss." I smiled.

"He's so funny. We were having a beer at Characters the other day, and he said, 'So my wife and I occasionally go out for a bite to eat. Kate enjoys a good Monte Cristo sandwich, so when she wants one of these, we head over to the Airport café. They make the best ones. She's craved the Monte a number of times over the last few months, so that's where we've been. It's interesting to me that every time we're sitting in the cafe eating our sandwich, we see a chopper come in, land, and I see you step off that chopper. Not just once, or even twice, but a lot. You say you're in investments, which I don't doubt, but I have to wonder, with your suntan and all, that helicoptering might have a little more to do with investments than you let on.'

"That's funny, Daryl." I laughed. "How did you respond to that?"

"Oh, I just smiled and said 'maybe.' I do like him, though; he's smart. He likes hockey and football, and he walks a lot."

"You like that he walks a lot? Have you been walking with him?" I laughed out loud at the image of Daryl walking for health purposes. Nope. To the bathroom, yes. Further than that would be considered manual labour.

"I"—Daryl ran his hand in that Vanna White style down the front of himself—"would do nothing to ruin this. I do not walk." His exclamation point was a grin. "When all of the COVID regulations lift, I would love to have you all come to the house for a barbecue."

"I'd love that, Daryl."

Earl wandered by, newspaper tucked under his left arm, eyes turned upward toward the Keno board. "Just a baby beer please, Glenda," he said and then wandered to the middle of the pub, where he took his seat.

"He's funny, isn't he?" Daryl observed. "He's always telling me about his dead wife." He trailed of for a moment and then continued. "Anyway, Tina and I were talking, and we thought it would be wise to get a set of keys for the house made up to give to you."

"You want me to have keys to your house?"

"Well, yes. It would be helpful to me if someone I trusted could check on things up there when we're travelling, and if anything goes on or if you need extra space as you're building, you can just stay in the guest house."

"We're fine in the trailer, Daryl." I laughed at him. "But thank you for thinking of us. I'm hoping we would never need to use it, though it's certainly nice to know the offer is there."

"I'll get Tina to get them cut. The gate has a code, and the guest house has a code, so we'll get your own code for those two."

I nodded. The post-COVID lunch crowd started to trickle in, putting a pause on our conversation. I started pouring pints.

Standing behind the bar, rimming a glass with salt for a Caesar, I saw our landlord and another man walk in. "Tony?" he asked me.

"Upstairs," I replied

A quick nod, and he turned on his heels and headed up the stairs. The other fellow followed.

That was odd, I thought and then turned my head to observe Daryl observing them. *That's odd too*, I thought.

Daryl was sitting at the Bone facing the bar, staring at his phone. When the landlord walked in with his friend, Daryl glanced up from his phone, his eyes following them, a hint of amusement playing in the corners. His head turned toward them as they moved through the pub.

I walked past the Bone. "I know them." Daryl's voice amused, lilting, a smirk starting to form.

"That's the landlord," I said.

"I know," he replied.

"He didn't notice you when they walked in."

"I wouldn't think he would. I'm not present for most negotiations." He smiled. "I do know that the other man with him is the money behind your landlord."

"What?" I said incredulously.

"Your landlord has investors; the other man is one of the other investors. I wonder if they're up there trying to talk Tony into a package deal," Daryl voiced curiously.

"You know way too much shit, Daryl." I laughed.

"I know." He smiled.

Carl walked in, pulled out a barstool, and nodded at Daryl. He coughed a couple of times, cleared the tar from his throat, and said, "Say, young lad, haven't seen you around these parts in a while. Where you been?" Without waiting for an answer, Carl turned to me. "I'll take that bottle of Kokanee when you have time, Glenda." Turning back to Daryl, he continued. "Your investments keeping you busy?"

"You could say that." Daryl smiled.

"Say, Glenda, put a beer for Daryl here on my tab, would ya. He looks thirsty. And could you run my cards through?"

"Yes, Carl." I smiled. When I returned with his beer and Keno tickets, he continued, "Say, Glenda." Another cough was followed up with a loud honk blown out of his bulbous nose into a napkin. "Say, Glenda," he started again, "have you seen Patrick lately?"

"He was in yesterday, Carl, but not today. Not yet, anyway."

"Well, if he comes, you make sure you put his beer on my tab, you hear." He finished wiping his nose with the napkin and tucked it into his breast pocket.

"I will, Carl."

"I'm going to have to take a rain cheque on that beer, Carl," Daryl said. "Thank you, though."

"What's wrong?" Carl snickered playfully. "I'm not good enough for you?"

"Not today," Daryl teased back.

"The beautiful girl always wins. I can never compete against her," Carl bemoaned blithely.

Daryl laughed, swallowed the last of his pint, threw cash on the Bone to cover his tab. "No beautiful girl today; tomorrow, though."

"Always tomorrow," Carl gauffed.

"Bye, Daryl, see you later," I said.

Daryl walked out the door as Jenny came in.

"Your usual, Jenny?"

"Please, Glenda. How are you today?"

"Good. And you?"

"Dad's in the hospital again."

"Awe Jenny, sorry to hear that."

"They don't know what's wrong with him. He was really dehydrated and we thought for sure he was going to go last night, but then we trickled water in his mouth and today he's cracking off jokes again. That guy!"

"Nine lives that one."

"No kidding. Hey, was that your friend Daryl that I just passed coming in?"

"Yes, that was Daryl."

"People say he's loaded."

"They do, do they?" I smiled.

"It's just what I hear." She smiled shyly.

"Say, Glenda," Carl's crusty voice cut in, "can you ring this through, see if I got anything? And I'll take another beer when you've got time. Who's that who's in hospital?"

"Old Ike, Jenny's dad. He comes in sometimes, sits in the back, uses a walker."

"Gaaaa," Carl commiserated, shaking his head, "we all need walkers! Hope the old guy pulls through." His voice trailed off as his watery eyes looked up at the TV to watch the Keno numbers drop.

Phil walked in carrying a brown cardboard box.

"Beer?" I asked

"Yes, please." He smiled. "These are for you and Tina, some of Sierra's cupcakes."

I opened the box and saw four perfect, individually dressed cupcakes. Designer cupcakes. Cupcakes you can't wait to sink your teeth into, but you don't want to because they're too pretty.

"Oh Phil!" I exclaimed, "these are AMAZING! I'm going to have to order more from her!"

"She makes fabulous cheesecakes too, and her cakes! Her cakes are a work of art. If you ever need one, just order. I can bring it in for you."

"Thanks, Phil. You must be so proud of her."

"I am." He grinned. "Oh, hey, Don just messaged. He's coming. Would you mind pouring us a pitcher?"

"Glenda, can I get my bill please? I got to get back to my dad." Jenny had her card out ready to pay.

Big and little Doug pulled out their barstools just as Jenny was swiping her card. "Oh, hey, see you guys later. I got to get back to my dad; he's in hospital."

"Sorry to hear, Jenny," little Doug said as I put his pint in front of him. "Give him my best."

"Will do. See ya."

"That old Ike, he just keeps going, doesn't he?" Little Doug was shaking his head in amazement.

"He's that old guy who comes in with the walker, sits in the back, right?" big Doug asked, clarifying which Ike we were talking about.

"Yup, that's the one," I said. "He's a spark plug, that one." I laughed, putting their pints in front of them.

"Had a chance to talk to that Daryl guy you've been hanging around with, Glenda, over at Characters. He was there the other night sitting beside me and Cin, and we started talking about stuff. Turns out he knows my uncle, the one that sold that pub in Vancouver. Apparently Daryl was the one who bought it. I'd never have believed it, but the guy certainly knows the pub business downtown. The guy sure knows his stuff." Big Doug stopped talking long enough to sip his beer.

Jacquie came in and sat down at the edge of the bar, ordered white wine, and opened her phone. Weird boyfriend nowhere in sight.

"Thank you," she said quietly when I placed it in front of her.

Doug stopped talking freely. It often happens when newcomers sit at the bar. The vibe shifts. The vibrato of a regular, squeezing itself silent, studies the stranger intently. As an eagle examines his river with talons clutched to a birch, the regular scrutinizes from his bastion, the barstool. Woe to the foreigner if he is a predator. Woe to the stranger if she is searching for prey. The regular, the protector from perverts, will heave out the haughty, scan for the liar, the cheater, the trickster. The bar's gatekeepers keep watch over the spirits that enter, welcoming the witty, snubbing the smug.

The Dougs silently sipped their beer on the bulwark.

Jacquie picked up her wine glass, her phone, and her coat and moved herself from the bar to the Bone. The Dougs unconsciously breathed relief and resumed their chit chat. Big Doug's Keno was done, so he left to purchase another.

"I think I know what you're doing, Glenda." Little Doug leaned in toward me, speaking in a hushed tone.

"What I'm doing?"

"Yes, I think I know why you've been spending all that time with that guy Daryl."

"You do?" I smiled, curious for his explanation.

"You and him are working together to open the Friendly Mike's pub back up."

"That's a great guess!" I said with a little laugh. "It would make sense, wouldn't it, me having my years of experience here, Daryl with his years of experience in Vancouver. Yup, I can understand why you think that."

Little Doug glowed, for sure he thought he fit the last piece of his puzzle together. The Rubik's Cube solved, he leaned back in his barstool. Victor!

"But that's not it."

His face fell.

"Nope, but it was a good guess. What would we have called it?" I laughed

"Not so Friendly Glenda's," little Doug mocked.

"That works!" I smiled.

Searing Sorrow

She leaned forward as she poured a shot.

A hundred feelings mixed with a hundred thoughts swarmed again. The shot was supposed to take care of it; the shot was supposed to soothe it. The fire of Fireball. She tipped her head and threw it down her throat and then studied the legs of the liquor on the glass. Will it purge? Will it purify? Intrinsically, she knew the outcome. She knew it would feel great for a couple of hours. Feelings would be mollified. The lingering edge of sorrow sat petulantly at the head of the table. It whimpered, whined, or wailed according to what it was eating. Shut it up with Fireball. Shut it up, shut it out, she shot back another until the mewl was bearable. It didn't cure, but it made the moment tolerable, and right now that was all she could manage. Sorrow did that. Left you to manage.

The legs pooled into a puddle on the inside of the glass.

"This isn't helping!" a searing scream ripped through her mind "I'm sad, I'm sad, I'm sad, and it's not going away! I'm so sick of being sad!"

She threw the shot glass across the room and screamed, "FUCK YOU! Everything I try to do doesn't help. Everywhere I go, everyone I talk to, everything I think, I'm stuck in this horrible pit of sorrow, and damn it, I WANT OUT!" And the anger burned like the whiskey in her belly.

"Oh God, how do I get rid of it? Please make it go away!" She was demanding, crying, and praying all in the same breath.

Sentenced to a prison of sorrow, sucked deep into the swamp of sorrow, she was Artex. As a child she cried that Artex died, and today she understood how. Stuck in it and getting sucked down, hating it and being comforted in it at the same time.

"I will surely die if I stay here."

Then get out, whispered the air.

"How do I get out?"

Think.

"I can't think. I'm so tired of thinking; it hurts to think."

Remember.

"Remember what?"

An image from the past scrolled across her mind, and someone hit the play button.

She was standing with a couple, downtown east side Vancouver, she bought them coffee. She was fourteen on an outreach with her church youth group. They were dirty, they were drug addicted, they were thankful for the warm java they held in their hands. As they sipped, they spoke. "Don't ever start. No matter what happens in your life, just don't do it, not one time. Heroin will steal your whole life the minute you open the door and let it in."

The warning was understood, but it was the look of gratitude in their eyes that reached into her soul. Helping felt good. Helping felt wonderfully, astoundingly good.

That.

"That."

Remember how that felt.

"If I go out and help people, perhaps that will make me feel better."

What have you got to lose?

"Not a stinking thing."

Three months later she was tasting hummus with women and their children in Ramallah. She thought she was helping them, but the reality was that their plight helped her. Being a woman in Muslim territory was hard. Horrifyingly hard. They lived it. She was thankful she was just visiting.

***

"Будьте здоровы. God bless you!"

The wrinkles were etched deep into her skin, crinkling deeper at her eyes. She grinned a toothless grin. The granny from Chernobyl was holding new sheets and pillows Danielle had placed in her arms.

"пожалуйста, позвольте мне дать что-нибудь для детей. Please let me give something for the children." The granny was insisting. She pulled out a coin. "для конфет. For candy." It was her last coin.

Danielle watched her five children play in the front yard of the little run-down villages. It was hard for them to enter some of the huts; the smells were difficult to bear. She was proud of them. They were wise not to mention it; they were happy to help give the pillows along with their mamma and papa.

The drive back from Chernobyl to Kyiv was long; they were tired but full of joy. Danielle sent off the pictures she had taken to her mom so her mom could share in the joy too. Then she leaned her head against the van's window, closed her eyes, and let her mind drift into the past. The images on a timeline flickered. Fifteen years of helping people in dozens of map dots throughout the globe. Their faces, their lives flashed before her. She smiled. Another image, a photo of her and her dad standing in front of the van that took her on an outreach to Vancouver when she was fourteen. She missed him. She remembered that sorrow when he died. It still hurt to think about him. Remembering has a way of stirring sorrow up. Titus, her four-year-old son, looked up at her just then. Reaching out his pudgy little hand, he pinched her tummy. "I love you, Mommy." He grinned. A surge of love and gratitude flowed through her.

"Thank you, God, for helping me remember what it felt like to help people."

Amazon

"It's okay, honey." He laughed a little into the phone as he stood up to take the conversation outside. "Awww, it would have been a fun surprise ..." His voice trailed off as he exited the building. I could see him outside, smiling and nodding as he paced. One can never be entirely motionless when talking on the phone, and Daryl was no different. He finished the conversation, put the phone in his pocket, and reentered the building.

"It was so cute," he said to me as he took his seat. "Tina wanted to surprise us today, so she flew up."

"Really?" I said excitedly.

"Yes, she said she had everything packed—your shoes, the Gates manual, the engagement photos. But they wouldn't let her into Canada."

"What? Didn't you get her that essential services card yet?"

"Yes, she has it. The border security guard said she needed a negative COVID test. She didn't know she needed it, and they sent her back. She's crying." Daryl laughed a little.

"You're laughing, she's crying?"

"I'm not laughing because she's crying. I'm laughing because it was a very sweet idea," he said, sipping his pint. "She feels like a failure and that she's let everyone down."

"That's ridiculous. How can she let us down when we didn't even know she was coming? And it wasn't within her power to cross the border."

"The test, she feels badly that she didn't even think to check about COVID tests. Hang on," he continued as he pulled his phone out of his pocket. He read the message and looked at me. "She wants to know if the wire arrived? Did the money come through?"

"Not yet," I said.

"That's strange, hmmmm." He put his head down and started typing, then stopped, considering the length of message. He pulled the phone to his ear and called her once again, removing himself from the table, taking the conversation outside for privacy.

"Would you mind resending the swift code," he said as he returned. "She may have got that wrong, she said, and now she feels like a double failure. I told her to relax, it's not a big deal, but she was crying anyway. I told her to go have a glass of wine. I'll take the chopper down tonight. She seemed to cheer up a little."

"Well, it would have been great to have her here, but at least you can go there."

"Maybe I'll get her to come back with me tomorrow," he said as he eased back into his barstool.

"That would be great too!" I exclaimed.

"Hey, do you know any body shops around? I have to get the Honda looked at. Someone backed into it when it was parked at the airport."

"Did they at least leave a note?"

"No."

"I hate when people do that. I'm sure your ICBC will cover the damages."

Daryl looked down at his phone and read a message that had come in. "Sylvia's here at the HSBC in Chilliwack as we speak." He smiled, phone still in hand, ready at any moment to respond to the world with his fingertips.

"Finally!" I breathed. "You should invite her here for a beer afterward. I would love to meet her."

"I'll ask." He immediately put his head down and began typing.

Sylvia had been sent out from head office Vancouver to the HSBC Chilliwack branch the week before. Miscalculation of time and an unexpected traffic accident delay had the meeting postponed.

"Hmmm." Daryl put his phone to his ear "Yes," he said as he stood up and exited the front door for privacy.

He returned, concern etched in his face. "The Caribbean." He sighed. "If it's not a hurricane or an earthquake, it's a fucking volcano erupting."

I left him alone to chew on this news. The last thing he needed was a waitress from Chilliwack badgering him with questions.

He ran his fingers through his hair and stared sightlessly upwards, then he glanced down at his phone, read what it was telling him, and began to chew on his cheek. His pint was almost empty, so I pulled another and took it to him.

"Sylvia left. She said the bank manager here in Chilliwack has some serious issues. She's headed back to the city to sort them out." He looked and me briefly before he glanced back at his phone and pulled it to his ear. "Yup," he said.

His face eased and his tone lifted. He smiled broadly. "Thank you. Well done." Finishing the call, he held the phone in his hand, staring at it.

"Good news? Finally?" I asked.

He started giggling and shaking his head from side to side. A lone tear dropped from his right eye. He turned his head upwards as if to acknowledge God, then back down at his phone. "I just bought Amazon." And his body started quaking in laughter.

What Is Thanksgiving?

Deals are often put together in unique situations. The fact that the purchase of shares from Mackenzie Scott to Daryl's Crystal Castle happened while dangling their toes in a hot tub in Seattle is no different.

Together Mackenzie and Daryl pulled power away from Jeff, and that made them smile. They both disliked him for different reasons. The hot tub deal brought them close enough to push Jeff off his throne, but not quite enough. The quite enough came after Doug did his Doug thing and dug up something Jeff would prefer the public not know. That bit of information, whatever it was, caused Jeff to reluctantly step down from top spot in Amazon. In public it was done with grace. In private, Jeff's abdication was less than amicable.

"Mackenzie would like to donate $50,000 to the Foundation of Hope," Daryl informed me the day after the Amazon deal was complete. "And it looks like I'm going to have to head back to Vegas tonight."

"Why?"

"Amazon is buying MGM. MGM the film portion is all connected with the Vegas portion." Amusement flashed across his eyes. "I'll be back day after tomorrow."

I shook my head again. "I'd be exhausted if I were you, flying here, there, everywhere."

"It's my life, Glenda. It nearly killed me *not* doing it."

"What's going on with the HSBC? Did Sylvia get that all worked out?"

"From what I understand, we'll run everything out of head office. She's not comfortable with the management in Chilliwack, but you and Haney will need to go there and open bank accounts. We'll do everything downtown but transfer funds into those accounts here. She also has new debit/credit cards made up for the new accounts downtown, and I'll be picking them up in person when I get back from Vegas."

"Sounds good."

***

From: Tina Hoffmeister
To: Glenda
Subject: Re: HSBC cards

So my love just informed me that using Amazon he just bought MGM studios for 8 billion dollars! 👩

Doing that also increases his control in Vegas back up to 55 per cent of the MGM RESORTS INTERNATIONAL.

I am having a very bizarre time! Nowhere near what I expected! I'm sure Daryl has filled you in! I'm now apparently partners with him in 68 per cent of the MGM Group. Me?! Little me?! So much to say. Going to meet Daryl for a private lunch! We have alot to discuss!

***

"Fucken border!" came the text from Daryl the day after his announcement of his purchase of Amazon. "They wouldn't let me back into Canada. They said I was running fever. Fuck, fuck, fuck! My fucken COVID test is negative, but they still won't let me in.

Daryl was exasperated.

"The cards, Daryl!" I texted back. "The school is waiting for the help we promised them."

"I know! These are part of the things that stress me out," came his reply. "I'll take my temperature in the morning and try again."

Frustration.

Our moving forward was constantly being delayed by others, the weather, the universe.

I laid my phone down and tried to shake that frustration out of my being.

I was angry.

Yet who could I be angry with?

Who do I direct my anger at?

When circumstance thwarts expectation, when hope is hung in front of you never being met, the effects are not only mentally exhausting but create enormous stress on the physical being of a human.

Are we made to hope for things never to come? Or is the wait for the hope fulfilled greater when it is fulfilled after a longer wait?

While I hoped for the latter—indeed, I looked toward that, I couldn't help but feel a level of cruelty generated by delays.

It was the paradox of this perceived cruelty associated with the aim of helping people that I struggled to wrap my mind around. Daily I found myself suffocating under the weight of hope, yet hoping for the Foundation of Hope.

"God, make it stop!" I cried as I felt my chest twinge in a pain I knew was brought on by the stress of this wait. "Help me endure this!"

I went for a walk.

"How do you feel about living up here, Glenda?" my mind spoke to me.

I was walking through a grove of cedars, branches draped perfectly to draw the eye across the river to a single tree.

"I'm so entirely thankful to be able to live here," I responded.

Immediately the feeling of contentedness surged through me, and my body relaxed, my mind relaxed. An old verse, familiar but forgotten, breathed: *"In prayer and thanksgiving, present your request to God."*

I was always presenting my requests to God.

I had no problem doing this.

Greedily, hungrily, lovingly, hopefully, in joy, in anger, in tears, in need …

But "thanksgiving?"

I contemplate what I normally do: "Dear God, thank you for my children, my grandchildren, my husband, my dog, my job, etc." Then I present my request as if it was a formula I needed to do in order for God to "work."

As I stared through the cedars, I recognized that there was a physical change in my whole body when I thought and acknowledged what I was sincerely grateful for. Once again, I was amazed at the complexity of God.

"Do this because it is good for your body and your mind.

But it only works if it's done correctly, as I created you to do it."

I thought about my previous prayers of "thank you for my health" and considered all my health does for me. It was then that I understood how thankful I was for it.

I was now entirely grateful to understand what thanksgiving was, and what it did for the physiology of my being, and in turn thankful to God, who made me with inner chemical tools of serotonin and dopamine to cope, and instructions on what to do to activate them.

Prayer and thanksgiving are intrinsically needed for healthy human flourishing. Daily I started examining my mind for at least one thing I was sincerely grateful for and allowed the chemicals in my body release within this. Including deep thankfulness to God, who heard and responded to my prayer: "Help me endure this."

Stuck

"Three negative COVID tests. I wish they fucking would have told me I needed that yesterday when they didn't let me in. A bunch of clowns, border services. Apparently the rule is after presenting with a fever, they need three negative COVID tests before they'll allow you to re-enter Canada," read Daryl's text the next morning.

"That doesn't even make any sense," I typed back, aghast with such ridiculous rules.

"Why do you think there's such up roar with the Canadian government. Other countries have rules that make sense, but here, it appears that the border agency can pick and choose and decide what they want, when they want, without question. I'll just wait it out. I'll visit casinos down here and take my daily COVID tests as they demand. But Nelson said he can help us out. He needs to come to BC anyway, as he's scouting cell tower areas. I'll send the plane for him. He can stop in at HSBC downtown and pick up the cards. Tina had a cheque made for you for the wire transfer that didn't go through. I was bringing that back with me yesterday, and today. I left it in the safe on the plane, so Nelson can deliver that to you too. Are you around this weekend?"

"Yes, Daryl."

"The plane will pick him up tomorrow morning. He should make it to Chilliwack by one in the afternoon. Is it okay if I give him your phone number?"

"Of course, Daryl. I really look forward to meeting him."

Nelson

"Just don't spill that shit on my dad's plane!" Nelson reminded buddy number one as he poured a healthy portion of Crown Royal into crystal shotglasses. "He'll kill me."

"Awe, relax," buddy one replied. "Lift 'em up, boys!"

And they did.

Nelson and two of his buddies sat in white leather club chairs on the Gulf Stream. raising their glasses off the sleek walnut table in cheers fashion.

"To boys weekend!" said buddy one.

"Here, here!" agreed Nelson and buddy two simultaneously. The three men tossed back their shots and chased it with a swallow of Alexander Keiths.

"This is going to be EPIC!" buddy two proclaimed.

"I'm so stoked your dad got stuck in Seattle!" buddy one said.

"Ya, it's been a while since we did this," Nelson agreed

Just then the captain came out of the cabin.

"Boys, there's a bit of a delay. A tornado of all things, just a small one hovering close by. We can't fly till it's gone, obviously."

"So what does that exactly mean?" buddy two asked.

"We'll be delayed."

Nelson mentally addressed the news with time expectations and messaged his dad to let him know that they would be arriving late and to let the bank know he wouldn't be there as expected, and to stand by for expected time arrival.

This done, the boys started their party on the plane.

"Just don't drink all of my fucking booze," Daryl texted Nelson after receiving the delay text. "I'll message Glenda to let her know to expect you later."

The three of them had a healthy buzz going by the time the Gulf Stream was able to depart. Nelson savoured a beer on the flight but declined more shots the buddies kept offering, He was a big guy, and he could consume copious amounts of liquor. He *had* consumed copious amounts of liquor in his life, but never when he had to drive. An unspoken honour nodded in his sister Stephanie's memory.

A rented SUV awaited their arrival. The three of them climbed in, and Nelson directed the vehicle to the HSBC. He picked up the bank cards and tossed them in the black satchel with the cheque and house keys he'd pulled from the plane's safe. Traffic was busy, and he clicked on Google Maps to see what the roads to Chilliwack were like. The plan was merely to drive to Chilliwack, drop off the satchel to dad's friend Glenda, and have a boys' weekend at his dad's house.

Traffic looked thick.

"Dad, we're going to wait out rush hour at the Hard Rock Casino. We'll head to Chilliwack when it dies down," he said over the phone.

"I'll message Glenda that you'll be in later."

Glenda received the message of delay from Daryl at 3:00 p.m. Mentally calculating their arrival and realizing they were on a boys' weekend, she suggested they stay in Vancouver and come in the morning.

"Why don't you just stay the night on the boat, have fun, and head to Chilliwack first thing in the morning?"

Daryl texted Nelson back after getting the suggestion from Glenda.

The three boys partied hard and well into the night.

At 9:00 a.m., Daryl messaged Glenda to let her know they were just finishing breakfast and to expect them by 11:00 a.m.

Nelson and buddy one and two sliced through their hangovers with orange juice and bacon. Nelson was crunching on a piece of toast when he clued in about the time.

"Damn, guys, we have to get going!" he said, brushing crumbs off of his shirt while standing. "Shit, Dad's going to be pissed. He's such an ass about being on time."

"So hard to leave this boat, though," buddy two proclaimed.

"Right!" Nelson agreed. "But we got to go. I've got shit to do."

In under ten minutes the three of them were standing in front of the SUV, applauding themselves for accomplishing this feat in record time. Nelson was opening the hatch to throw their bags in when he noticed a flat tire. He walked around the vehicle and ran his hand through his hair in frustration. Not just one flat tire but four slashed tires.

"The fuck?" escaped in exasperation. He called the car rental place first to arrange for another vehicle, and then opened his phone and started typing: "Dad, we're going back to the boat to wait for the rental service to bring another car. Sorry, nothing we can do. Who the fuck does this kind of shit?"

Daryl read his text and let Glenda know.

"The rental company is enroute now, so they should be on their way within the hour"

"Slashed tires! What the hell next?" Glenda exclaimed to Haney. "Bloody f'ing bizarre! Oh well, let's just go into town and start our shopping. Daryl says they should be here by noon. We'll just head to Corky's for lunch and meet them there."

The car rental place, true to their word, delivered another SUV.

"Thank so much, guys. Hey, I'm really sorry about the tires," Nelson said. Truly he felt poorly about leaving them to deal with this tire issue. He and the buddies climbed in. Leaving the parking lot, they turned left onto West Hastings and right into a traffic jam.

Nelson slammed both hands onto the steering wheel. "Fuuuuuuuuccccckkkkk," he hissed.

A hint of headache played behind his left eye. He could feel his pulse beat through his neck; he could feel himself turning red.

Buddy one looked at Nelson. "Dude, you're turning red."

"Fuck off," Nelson flipped off.

Buddy one smiled. "Let's just go back to the boat and wait it out there." Buddy one really didn't want to drive to Chilliwack and was enjoying the finer things of life right there in Coal Harbour.

Nelson sighed deeply and laid his head back on the headrest. "Why the hell is traffic all jammed up anyway? It's Saturday. This doesn't even begin to make sense." While he spoke out loud, the words were for himself. To add anst to his anger, he couldn't see ahead for the cause. He took another deep breath.

Buddy two rolled down his back window and hollered to a teenager with blue hair in a black hoodie who was walking from the direction they wanted to go. "Excuse me, hey bud, is there an accident or something up that way?"

Eyes looked up from under the blue fringe, and his hand went to his ear to pop out an ear bud. "What?"

"Is there an accident or something up there?" Buddy two repeated himself.

Blue hair shook his head no. "Naaa, it's a blockade. The Indians are blocking shit again. They've got all main streets blocked."

"Thanks, man," buddy two said as he rolled the window back up. "Well, there you go, your answer."

"Fuck," Nelson breathed, fumbling for his phone. "My dad's going to be pissed," he said while dialing his number

"Hey, Dad, we can't get off West Hastings; there's a fucking blockade." Nelson reiterated their newest problem into the phone.

"Go back to the boat," Daryl instructed. "Take out the jet skis or something and wait it out there. It can't go on forever."

"Thanks, Dad, we will if we can get the fucking car turned around."

Glenda and Haney were walking through the store when her phone rang. "Hey, Daryl, why are you calling me? You never call; you always text," she said curiously.

"There's a fucking Indian blockade; they can't get out of the city. I told them to enjoy the afternoon on the boat and come when it's done, but it probably won't be until tonight," his voice said over the cell waves.

Glenda could feel her eyes roll in annoyance. "Just send them up to our place then. I'm not staying in town that long." She hung up and took a deep breath herself. *I think I'm going to write some of these delays down*, she thought. *It feels like we've had at least twenty of them. I'm sure I'll laugh about this one day, but not today.* Out loud she said, "Let's go for a beer!"

The afternoon progressed, and the boys did exactly what Daryl had prescribed—jet skiing until the captain rang the boat bell calling them in when news of the roads clearing arrived. Nelson gathered his things and his buddies and headed back to the SUV to begin their trek to Chilliwack. Enroute, buddy one said, "Hard Rock, boys?"

Buddy two looked at Nelson. Nelson looked at buddy one. "Well, I am hungry," Nelson justified. "We haven't had lunch, and it's almost dinner." The three boys grinned and turned the SUV in the direction of the casino.

"The boys are just stopping for dinner and should be there before 9:00 p.m.," Daryl's text to Glenda read.

"It just feels like I'm constantly waiting around for something to happen that never transpires; it's getting really exhausting," Glenda replied.

Inwardly she started fuming—seething, actually—as she read the text. *Really? Your dad asks for a favour, he provides his plane and his boat and an afternoon of jet ski fun for you and your friends, not to mention his booze, and you thank him by ditching the one thing he's asked you to do—make a delivery. Or you delay it again by stopping in at the casino for something to eat.* She churned these thoughts through her mind as she sulked.

"Dad, would you fucken just calm down!" Nelson said into his phone. "I've got your fucking shit. All of the delays weren't anything I could help. Why are you freaking out on me? Ya, so maybe we shouldn't have stopped at the Hard Rock, sorry about that. I'm at your fucking house now. I've thrown all your shit in the safe. You deal with it. I'm not talking to you anymore!" With that, Nelson hung up the phone, leaving Daryl on the other end chewing his cheek in anger.

Glenda was still mid-sulk when her phone rang. It was Daryl. Picking up, she wanted to say "What?" but instead she said, "Hello?"

"I'm absolutely livid!" Daryl's voice echoed Glenda's feelings. "I just got off the phone with Nelson. We had a huge fight and I told him to fucking forget about tonight and he can fucking get those cards to you tomorrow, then he told me he put the stuff in the safe and said, 'You deal with it.' I'm just seething."

Glenda took a deep breath. "It's not worth it, Daryl."

"What?"

"It's not worth it. I'm frustrated with the whole situation, you're angry with him, now he's angry with you. He's your son! This shouldn't be creating anger and fighting and friction."

"You're right."

"Just let it go. If he can get the cards to me, great, but it's not worth your guys' relationship, so just let it go. We've waited so long already, another week won't matter."

"Okay."

Nelson and buddy one and buddy two enjoyed their Sunday at Dad's place. The buddies flew WestJet home Monday morning, and Nelson headed east to scout out cell tower sites. He arrived far too late on Monday to deliver any cards. He jumped on his WestJet flight home by 7:00 p.m., having somewhat made up with his dad.

The plane arrived home at 8:00 p.m., and by 9:00 he'd pet his dogs hello, grabbed a quick snack, and was attaching headphones on his head. He clicked "start." *The House in Fata Morgana* had mixed reviews, and he was eager to make his own.

For F' Sake!

"We're staying in Taylor's basement until we figure out what we're doing next," Danielle messaged. "Most of our things have been given away. The people here need them, and it's a lot of work to haul everything back from Kyiv to Germany. Maybe we'll stay in Germany, maybe we'll look into moving to Austria. We'll see. Have you heard anything about the funds yet? The super fund?"

"Nothing, all in limbo. It's exhausting. I get tired of waiting, but I feel like such a pest asking. Daryl's so busy with all kinds of things, ugggg."

"Let us know when you know."

I signed off with three thumbs up.

A new messaged from Daryl flashed on my phone: "We are leaving Seattle now."

"We?"

"Tina wanted to come, so we're on the plane waiting for take off."

"Good luck," I typed and put my phone down.

You'd better prepare yourself, Glenda. Those cards won't be coming today or tomorrow or for a while. They'll be turned around at the border, I thought. During Daryl's three negative COVID test wait, Tina had the stomach flu. I shook my head in disappointment at her lack of forethought.

Five hours later, I received the text I had been expecting: "Turned around. Tina has a fever."

"Maybe just take her temperature first next time," I suggested.

"In retrospect, yes, we should have done that, but what could I do? I couldn't say no when she said she wanted to try coming, could I? I'm just going to spend the night and come by myself in the morning."

***

I could feel his angst through the text message the next morning: "They won't let me in AGAIN! Apparently anyone presenting with someone with a fever has to present three negative COVID tests before they can cross. I'm stuck here for four, maybe five more days."

"You mean because Tina had a fever and was with you on the plane, you need three more negative COVID tests before they let you in?"

"Yessss," he hissed.

A surge of anger toward Tina filled my being: thoughtless and selfish and now we have to wait longer. I breathed deeply, trying desperately not to allow the anger to overcome my mind. My email inbox flashed:

From: Tina Hoffmeister
To: Glenda
Subject: 🔒

I hope you had a good night and cozy sleep! I'm so angry with border services, but a bit of me is happy that I get my honey with me for another four days. We are at one of Maverick's casinos right now. I'm drinking martinis, and Daryl his beer, and he's introducing me to all of the people who work here. I just saw someone I used to date at one of the tables here. Eeeeeek, the look on his face when he saw us walking around the casino with security. Eeeeeeek! Well, I have to go. Have a wonderful night!

***

Sure, Tina. We have a school waiting for help and delayed promise after promise, but go ahead, enjoy your f'ing martinis.

And I was entirely perplexed that she didn't see how cruel this was.

The Duffle Bag

"Put it in the trunk," he said, pulling his keys out of his full grain Nappa leather jacket. Like the growling muscle resting on rubber, it still had its new smell. The jacket was rusty brown, the car jet black. The owner of both was young and white in a fitted tee and jeans that cost $100 per tear

He wore a silver cross strung from a brown cord around his neck, and a titanium spinner ring on his index finger. The aroma of expensive cologne mingled with Nappa was attractive. All accessories painstakingly picked turned the twenty-eight-year-old from an average five into a ten. He smiled, revealing perfect, even, white teeth, the only thing he didn't have to buy. He pressed the button on the black fob, and the trunk sprang open, His contact slipped the duffle bag in.

"You're good to go," the contact said.

"Yup," Nappa Leather replied. "I have buyers lined up, so hopefully I'll need another bag by the end of the month."

"You know where to find me," Contact smiled. He loved doing business with Nappa Leather—no games, no run around, no money problems. His word was his word, and he appreciated it. Even in this industry a level of trust was admired and hard to find. *Yes*, Contact thought, *very hard to find.*

Five minutes and a fist bump later, they were both driving down the freeway out of Abbotsford. Contact turned right to Vancouver, Nappa Leather left to Chilliwack.

The DEA of the RCMP in an unmarked Ford Explorer in unremarkable white turned left to follow the duffle bag, skillfully squeezing in between a grey minivan and a silver crossover. Nappa Leather, head down, scanning for the perfect playlist., didn't notice the Ford taking its place three cars back. Technology blinds life.

The stereo started pumping rap, reverberating syllables over and over. Nappa Leather's head moved in beat. Up went the volume and down went his foot on the gas, picking up speed to a strong, controlled 120k. It was nothing for the Explorer to keep up while keeping back. The cops smiled.

Nappa Leather took a right off the freeway at Prest. His eyes scanned the rear view out of habit, unconcerned. How many times had he made this drive? Honestly, he couldn't count. Once a month for three, maybe four years now? He remembered the initial drives, filled with paranoia, internally shivering as the adrenaline coursed through his body. Quotidian trips followed, his concern with them, complacency was created. Nappa Leather should have been watching his own back in his own rear view. He slowed down for the roundabout and then he noticed it. A glint? An inner voice? Intuition? All of the above? He could feel their presence like a foreboding, looming unshakable. He didn't look back; instead, he directed the car like Tom Cruise directed Darkstar, manoeuvring the machine with precise, deliberate control up the mountain, the roads of his youth. Ryder Lake.

Nappa Leather had an advantage over the Explorer. Familiarity. The winding road he knew like the back of his hand; the fact they were unlit was his to advantage. He could tell you when the next pin curve was coming, not by sight but by timing. Quickly he pulled away from the Explorer, losing them swiftly in the dark bends.

His breath caught up with his adrenaline. He breathed deeply, partly from martial arts practices, partly out of relief. He guided the car out of the mountain using Thorton Road, pulling his foot off the accelerator as he declined. A deer stood dead centre. Unblinking and unthinking, Nappa Leather pulled left to avoid it. The deer walked away; the muscle car did not. It was stuck firmly in, crunched between metal gate and the brick pillars that held them up.

"Shhhhiiiit," Nappa Leather breathed.

He jumped out of the car, adrenaline returned. "Fuck!" Panic mixed with bile rose in his throat; he pushed both back with a deep, controlled breath.

"The bag," he said to himself. *"Get the bag and get rid of it."*

He pressed the trunk fob and it sprang open. He grabbed the bag and ran into the forest in front of him.

***

"I can't get the car out of my fucking gate!" Daryl's text arrived first thing the next morning. "I just fucking got here! I just crawled into my bed! An hour of sleep and I was woken up with pounding on my front door! Cops everywhere!

"They have strongly suggested I leave the property while they do their investigation. I complied. A cop drove me down to the Coast Hotel. I'm in a room here. I have no idea how long it will be before I can go back to my own house. Lyndsay's contacting our legal team."

"What's the big deal, Daryl? It's your house, so just go back," I replied, genuinely confused as to why he had to leave the premise.

"They're looking for a duffle bag. I don't know what's in it. I don't want to know what's in it, but they seem to think whoever crashed the car into my gate ditched a duffle bag someplace on my property."

"Okay, so let them search your property; just go back," I insisted.

I could hear the annoyed sigh of my ignorance come through the next text. "When you own casinos, mysterious duffle bags and cars crashing though your front gates look a little suspicious, Glenda."

"Ahhhhhh." And with that, the light bulb of Daryl's world clicked on once again.

"Ya, I guess it's better for you to let them have free rein of your property without you there."

"Exactly," Daryl typed.

"And the satchel? Where is that."

"Still in the safe."

"So will they let you in to get it?"

"That won't look suspicious at all, will it, Glenda? Excuse me, I need to get a satchel of cards, cheques, and keys from my safe immediately."

"Shit."

"Ya, shit. That's why Lyndsay is talking to legal."

Invisible

From: Tina Hoffmeister
To: Glenda
Subject: Computers

I have just been notified that the first shipment of computers from the Gates Foundation is on its way to Canada. XPO Logistics is in charge of the shipment. Our reference number is GF-781098.

***

"I think Jack will be joining us today," Daryl said as I threw my leather messenger bag onto the barstool beside me. "I ordered you a lager, is that okay?"

"Yes, thank you, Daryl."

"Did Tina message you about the computers?"

"Yes, this morning. When do you think they'll arrive?"

"I will not place any bets on that." He smiled, pulling his pint up for a sip. "My experience with border services has been rather unpleasant."

I laughed. "Yup, I think even Taylor is still waiting for her shoes."

"She hasn't got them yet?" Daryl's face dropped, shock mixed with anger bubbled beneath. He grabbed his phone off the table. "That's ridiculous. How long has it been?"

"Months, at least five."

Daryl leaned back in his barstool, crossing both arms over his chest. He started chewing his cheek while rocking back and forth slightly. Daryl's "tell." His body language, slightly over exaggerated, marking the moment. "There is a problem. I must fix it." It longed for a feather boa flipped over his shoulder to finish his sentence.

He unfolded his arms, scrolled through his phone, then placed it to his ear. "Taylor still doesn't have her shoes. What's going on with that?"

"Fall is coming. Taylor would love to wear the boots she picked out," I said as he hung up. "Speaking of arriving, will Tina be coming to Canada anytime soon?"

"Well, probably not until I can get back into my fucking house."

"You're still not back in it?"

"Legal said to let them be, but I'm getting angry. It shouldn't take over a week to search the fucking property; it's only nineteen acres. I think I'll tell them they need to be done by Friday, wrap it up and let me back in. We'll see what legal says."

Daryl looked up over my shoulder, and I turned my head to see what had caught his eye. Jack. He was walking slowly to our table, a hint of a smile pulled at the corner of his lip, a twinkle of amusement winked. "May I join you?"

Daryl grinned. The agitation of his life immediately fell away. As Jack sat, the banter began. Daryl uncoiled one-liners, and Jack re-rolled them in dry humour, coated them with his late-night FM DJ voice, and volleyed them back. I pulled one out of the air, wrapped it in wit, puffed it back in perfume, and it was caught by Daryl, who whipped out another under a whisper caught by Jack. Silence. His eyebrows rose. Daryl raised his head in a howl; my hands went up to my mouth, desperately trying to hold back the giggles mixed with the beer I had just swallowed.

Within ten minutes, three of us were bent over, sides aching from continuous laughter as comments from one looped into comebacks from the other. Harmonic humour. Simpatico snickers. Melodious merriment. Tables turned to see what we were laughing at. They never could. It was invisible.

Wait, Wait, Wait

"Your design is ready for review. If there are no further changes, let me know if you would like me to proceed with the building permit drawings," the email read.

Joe had finished the redesign. A garage had a guest space and a roof-top deck, just as we directed. It looked great.

"I think, Joe, I will wait until these funds clear before we proceed with the building permit drawings." And I e-transferred him over $2,000, the cost of the redesign to this point.

"I don't mind waiting," I said to Haney, "but I don't want to spend the money we've set aside now on this. I'd feel more comfortable doing it when the funds come through."

"How long do you think it will be?" Haney asked.

I started laughing. "Daryl mentioned that the two mil was being transferred from his personal account into our HSBC account. Sylvia is apparently working on the whole bundle. So? When Sylvia has it all done?"

Haney snorted.

"I know, the wait is exhausting." I agreed with him.

"Are we meeting for football season again?" Haney asked.

"Yes, I think so. Jack will be joining us too. You'll like Jack; he's quite the character."

"Are we ever going to meet Tina?" Haney continued.

I started laughing again and shrugged my shoulders. "COVID really isn't making anything easy, is it?"

Haney picked up his lunch box and his coffee cup and leaned in for a kiss. "I love you."

"I love you too. Drive carefully."

"I'm looking forward to retiring from this job, you know." He smiled as he opened the door.

It was 5:00 a.m.

The mornings once bright as the earth rotated summer in were circling the night sky into fall. Crisp air replaced the stagnant smoke and heat of July. We completed our first year in the RV.

***

From: Tina Hoffmeister
To: Glenda
Subject: 👞👞👞👞👞👞👢👢👢👢

Your daughter's shoes are at Daryl's office in Stuttgart.

That was my fault. I said to send them to that address. I misread the form. I am sorry.

I'm going to leave it to Daryl, you, and Steff to figure out how it's best to get them to your kids.

I am sorry.

***

I took a sip of my coffee. "For someone exceedingly bright, Tina, you certainly manage to do dumb shit." I laughed sardonically. A patter of rain was starting. I closed my eyes and listened. "I will miss the sound of rain on an RV roof when we build that house. I don't know why that sound soothes my soul as it does, but damn, I can listen to that all day long." I opened my eyes.

Mist hovering above the ground wove itself within the cedars. Moss hung thick off their trunks and dripped off their branches. Freddy Kruger would have been hiding beneath their bows if he wasn't in Hollywood making films. A pickup truck pulled off the road. Its lights glowed. A fisherman sat inside waiting for the break of dawn; he'd seen *The Blair Witch Project* and wasn't taking any chances. If he was going to die, he wanted to see it coming. A banjo started playing.

I knew I was safe if I didn't look under the bed. So I didn't. I picked up a book and read happy things until daylight melted away the monsters.

My phone buzzed.

"Glenda, can you meet me at Browns Social House. I have something I'd like to discuss with you," came a text from Daryl.

"Yup, let me get off my ass and shower. I'll be there by 11:00," I messaged back.

"Okay, Petey, time to get up. Let's go for a walk and get this day started."

He lifted his head at the sound of his name. Reconsidering the effort, he yawned and laid it back down again.

"Right, boy, it's just that kind of day, isn't it?"

Hummingbird Heartbeat

Blue lasers flashed. Fifty beating beams reached up to the ceiling, strobing like the heartbeat of a hummingbird. One thousand beats on the door of her iris. One thousand hands in the air dancing. One thousand seconds ago she bombed MDMA. Ecstasy entered as Swedish House Mafia sang "Don't You Worry Child." She was amused by the irony.

Her hips and her teeth started grinding at the same time. She popped in her green candy soother then threw both hands back up in the air. Neon glow-stick bracelets held them there, handcuffed by laser light. Everything was right. Everything felt good. Everything was beautiful. The snapshot of her soul in this second of her life.

It was pretend.

She stared in the mirror the next morning.

Her brilliant blue eyes were covered in a hazy hue. She blinked. Who was that yawning back at her? She started the tap, cupped cold water. Leaning over the sink, she threw it onto her face. One. Two. Three times. She reached for a towel and blotted her skin dry. Not better. Dark, muddy pools hung below her eyes. Sallow. The colour of death. Her jaw ached. A new bruise was on her left arm.

Maybe not worth it, she thought, longing to reach back into the hours before when the world was beautiful, the beat brilliant, her energy vivacious, and her face glowed. *I hate this part*, she thought. It would be at least a week before she felt herself shift into the start of normal. Six days of death traded for six hours of euphoria. *Maybe not worth it*, she thought again. She would go back to bed if she was tired, but she wasn't. She was nothing. It was as if every ounce of serotonin died. Even the memory of the night echoed empty. *What next?* she thought. *Is this the rest of my life?* She inspected the bruise on her arm and couldn't recall how she got it. She sighed. Turned. Left the bathroom. Flopped back on her bed and picked up her cell phone. A messaged from her sister: "Hey, why don't you come spend the summer with us in Germany?" it read.

Why not? she thought.

***

He was sitting at the U-shaped bar with a folded laptop in front of him and a pint of something on a coaster to the left. He was staring up. Anyone in the restaurant observing him would assume he was intently watching the TV broadcast. That's the peculiar thing about first glance—the observer sees what they expect to see. Reality, though, lies beneath, striae in time and attention. The head held at a certain angle, the steady gaze of the eye held in place by eyelids in a particular position. Hands holding a glass, a chin, a phone, each position said something. Daryl saw nothing on that TV screen. Daryl was thinking. Of what? Maybe he would say, most likely he wouldn't. He also didn't look well. I sat down beside him.

"Why are you here?" I asked. Browns, a franchise restaurant outside of town, wasn't our go-to meeting place. "You don't look so good. Are you feeling all right?"

"My ulcer's been acting up; it will be fine." He sipped his full pint gingerly, testing it out. Would it stay down? Would it come back up?

"Maybe drink water instead," I suggested, knowing full well that wouldn't happen. He smiled at me.

"The Honda is in the shop getting fixed. I had to meet the Native elders here anyway, so—"

"Have you had your meeting with them, or are they on their way?" I asked.

"They've come and gone. It was a quick introduction. The young progressive ones introducing me to the elders. I have a list for you. I'll email it. You'll be working with some of these elders and chiefs as you build their wellness centres. The Tzatziki group—"

"Tzatziki?"

"I can't pronounce their real name, so I just call them the Tzatzikis. They get a kick out of it; anyway, they're the ones who want to put in the casino. Some of the young ones figure they can just do it themselves. I've been meeting with the group of them, reminding them what casinos are really like. They have no experience. But the people I met today were connections for Bridal Falls. They don't know that the Foundation of Hope will be building them wellness centres. I was contemplating telling them, to see if that would influence them. What are your thoughts on that?"

The bartender laid a coaster in front of me. "What may I get you?"

"A pint of lager would be great."

He turned, picked up a glass, and began pulling my pint.

"I don't know, D.," I said. In a split second, the agony of waiting for things that had not transpired fell like a curtain after the final act. It was suffocating. Hope is fulfilling. Hope not met is torture. I imagined these groups living through this, and the outcome wasn't good.

"If you choose to," I said, selecting my words carefully, "I would highly recommend that you deliver what you promise in a timely fashion, or they will be pissed off, and that will do more damage than good." I sipped my beer.

He sat motionless beside me as his neurons fired. A minute later he said, "Yup."

I looked up across the bar and saw Jacquie, the nine-ounce White lady sitting quietly alone. She nodded in our direction, and I nodded back. "Is this why you asked me to come today?" I asked, turning my gaze back to Daryl.

"No. No, actually I wanted to talk to you about your daughters."

"My daughters?" My curiosity was watered.

"Yes, I've been thinking they should both be employed by Crystal Castle."

"Excuse me?"

"To take care of the do-gooder branch. They would be perfect for it. Steff is too busy. It would require some travelling. They can still do all the things they've wanted to do, like Taylor's coffee shop, the Ukraine grannies. You mentioned that Taylor was thinking of a community kitchen too?"

"Yes, the Shoe Closet was going to fund that."

Daryl nodded his head.

"Why them, Daryl?"

"It's not easy to find people to trust, and I don't know them, but I know their mother. I trust her with my life."

"Yup, you pretty much can, can't you?" I said.

Daryl smiled. "Anyway, have a conversation with them. Ask them what their salary expectations would be. They're probably conservative like their mother, so ask them what they would need to live comfortably. We'll pay all of their health care, lease them a vehicle, and give them a stipend toward living quarters."

"You're kidding!"

"No, we do this for all of our employees."

"You do realize this will change their lives, Daryl."

"I realize."

"I'll contact them and get back to you."

"I can imagine we would be looking in the area of ten thousand out a month. But let's see what they come up with."

***

"*Mama, wie schnell schlägt das herz eines kolibris?* Mama, how fast does a hummingbird's heart beat?"

"Over a thousand beats per minute."

They were sitting together outside, the table in front of them covered in papers filled with drying watercolour creations. Abbie dipped her paintbrush into pink, her favourite colour.

"I would like to be a hummingbird." She spoke thoughtfully as she dabbed the pink paint across her page. She tilted her head to the right, contemplating where she would move her brush next.

"You would, would you?" Taylor smiled.

"I would." Abbie looked up and smiled. It caught Taylor's heart.

Oh, this child, Taylor thought. *How she makes all the world glow from the inside out with a simple smile.* She smiled herself, picked up her own paintbrush, and pulled it across her own page. The start of a sunrise perhaps?

It came as soft as a whisper. The memory. It tugged her back to the moment of hummingbird beats and glow-sticks, green soothers and empty hearts filled falsely with laser light shows.

Taylor sighed. "Thank you for leading me to Germany," she breathed out gratitude to the great, good God.

"What, Mama?" Abbie asked.

"I love you," Taylor replied.

"I love you, Mama!!"

Taylor's phone buzzed beside her. She flipped it over. It was her mom.

"We need to talk! Daryl wants to put you and Dani on payroll."

MNP

"I have the cards on me. I'm at the dealership picking up the Alfa Romeo. They're just dealing with the plates and something to do with insurance. As soon as they're done, I'll swing by your place and drop the cards off," Daryl messaged.

"The car or the SUV?" I typed back.

"The car."

"Have fun with it. I'll see you when you get back to town."

***

From: Tina Hoffmeister
To: Glenda Toews
Subject: Re: Address

Good morning! Sorry to bother you, but we need your full address to have on file at MNP in Chilliwack. Daryl is meeting with the accounting firm to deliver the paperwork from HSBC. They will be dealing with the funds directly. Also, please forward both of your daughters' information so that I can forward it to Steffanie in Stuttgart: address, telephone number, and email. She will contact them directly.

Daryl has asked me to research vehicles for the foundation. Would you prefer a car or an SUV? How many do you think the foundation would need to lease right away?

***

MNP? That's new.

"What's up with MNP?" I texted Daryl.

"Fucking tired of the runaround. I went there last week, had a meeting, and they are assigning us a couple of accountants. One for your funds and the foundation, and a team for my interest in Chilliwack. Head office is sending them a file to bring them up to speed. Sorry, I forgot to mention. Tina messaged you then?

"Yes."

"As soon as they're caught up, we'll set up a meeting with you, and you can direct them on your funds. Also, they'll help you with your distribution of the funds coming from Danny."

"Oh, yes, that's a very good idea," I agreed.

"I should have done this right away. I just didn't even think about it."

"I appreciate it, actually, to have them in charge of the foundation funds is a relief."

"Did Tina mention that she has found a CFO for the foundation? At least someone she would recommend. The choice, of course, is yours."

"No, she didn't say."

"She will. We were talking about her last night. Expect an email. The car is amazing. Zoom, zoom, zoom! I'm at the Hard Rock for a meeting then I'll be on my way."

"KK"

***

From: *Tina Hoffmeister*
To: *Glenda*
Subject: *Re:Cars/CFO*

I just spoke with Daryl. Amber has worked for Danny for five years. She and her boyfriend have decided to move in together, so she's moving to Canada. He lives in Abbotsford of all places, so she'll be relocating. A CFO for the foundation is your choice, of course, but she has all of the skill and is completely trustworthy, so I highly recommend her.

Also, can you please visit the Jaguar Vancouver site and have a look at their Land Rovers and let me know if you think these would be appropriate for Chilliwack? I've also reached out to the Hyundai dealership in Chilliwack if you feel that would be a better fit. Personally, I love Audis, but BMWs are also nice. Daryl has asked me to order one for him too, as he said he will not be driving the Alfa Romeos in Chilliwack. He doesn't want to draw attention. We will get two vehicles right away, one for you and one for Daryl, and then once the foundation offices are up and running, we'll outfit your staff.

Let me know what you think.

***

"It's bumper to bumper. I'm staying here till rush hour clears. And *this* is why I chopper into the city, fucking traffic!" Daryl's afternoon text appeared on my screen. "I'll drive the cards to your place when I get into town."

"Daryl, just enjoy your new car. I'll meet up with you tomorrow. I'll get them from you then."

"Good. I have to go to the casino in Chilliwack tonight to meet with the GM anyway, so that works well. And the logistics company called me for an address to deliver the Gates' computers. I told them just to take them to the casino. Someone would be there to receive them. I hate using the casino for non-casino business, but there's nobody at the house, and it's not like you want them in your trailer!" A series of crying, winky emojis followed the words.

"The computers are here!?" I confirmed.

"Being delivered as we speak." Happy face emojis punctuated the text. "The GM called and asked why a fucking van filled with laptops was in his loading zone." Amusement bounced within Daryl's words. "Characters tomorrow? Beer Friday?" he continued.

"I'll be there at 11:00 a.m.," I replied, putting my phone down and flipping my laptop open.

My research continued. Hours of reading specific needs in the community, hours of investigating the community response. It was good. Our community had stepped into the onslaught of problems creatively. A hub set up connecting help. Good. The Foundation of Hope can concentrate on connecting the help to the schools and financing the great programs already set in place. So many people already active in Chilliwack helping. Their desire was inspiring. My imagination drew me deeper. Deeper funds, deeper possibilities, deeper impact. I closed my eyes. "Soon, God?" I whispered.

Pickled Eggs

"Go on, I bet you a wimp you can't get another in ya," Bob said, laughing.

They were sitting in front of a big glass jar of pickled eggs.

"Don't go there, Bob. You know I like a good challenge," Patrick replied, taking a swig from his mug of beer.

"One more then?" Bob teased as he stuck a fork deep into the jar to fish out another. "How many would that be? I think I'm at eight."

"One more would make ten for me. Give it here," Patrick said.

Bob handed Patrick the fork with the egg stabbed through.

"A wimp then? You better order it, because I won't have a problem getting this one down either." He grinned and chewed.

Bob flagged down the waitress. "A wimp for my friend here!"

Susan shook her head as she put the small glass of beer in front of Patrick. "Doesn't matter how old yer are, yer just a bunch of little boys."

Patrick grinned and belched as if to confirm it.

"I'm done after this one," Patrick said, lifting the wimp toward Bob in "cheers" fashion. "I have to get some rest tonight. Big day tomorrow." He gulped down the last of the beer, threw down a five for his tab, and headed home.

It was 1970; he was thirty-two. He'd been on the force long enough to be trusted with the service of securing the Queen's vehicle.

This was a big deal.

Not much big happened in Winnipeg.

This was big. The Queen of England would be here tomorrow.

Patrick buttoned up his scarlet serge, buckled the Sam Browne belt, and burped. He could taste pickled egg from the night before. He slid his feet in the long boots and stood in front of the mirror to inspect himself. RCMP full dress. He didn't get to wear it often, but when he did, he did so with pride. He was adjusting his felt hat when he felt the first rumble in his stomach. He didn't pay much attention. He had work to do.

He left the locker room and headed to the car. It was time for inspection. The Queen, Her Majesty Queen Elizabeth, would be travelling in this car. Patrick was honoured to make sure all was in perfect order for her.

His stomach groaned, like gremlins caught in a tunnel, gurgling in liquid. He caught a glimpse of the Queen. She was standing and waiting for the signal to enter the car. Patrick climbed into the back seat for one last inspection. It happened.

He couldn't stop it.

Every pickled egg he had eaten the night before had fermented into a gaseous cloud demanding to be freed.

It ripped right out of him. The sound was startling. The smell. Oh God, the smell!

He opened the door and crawled out.

The Queen was headed in the direction of the car.

He wanted to yell "Stop!"

He wanted to run and hide.

He had no other choice but to stand at attention, holding the rear door open.

She climbed in.

Oh that poor woman!

Oh God, that poor woman!

He will never forget her face for as long as he would live. He would never forget how Queen Elizabeth looked when she had to sit in a car surrounded by pickled egg fart fumes!

***

"What are you doing, Glenda?" Bart asked.

"I'm turning the channel," I replied. "News of the Queen."

"Oh, please, Glenda," Gerry chimed in, "just leave the golf on. It's a sports bar for God's sake."

They looked miserable, the two of them, but in the corner beside them, old Patrick sat, sipping his Coors Light, stifling a giggle and grinning like a goon.

"I'm Finally Here!"

From: Tina Hoffmeister
To: Glenda
Subject: Re: I'm here!

I'm here! Finally passed through border services. Eeek, I'm so excited! I can't wait to meet you and Haney and Jack! We're just sitting in Millionare waiting for the Alfa Romeo SUV to be delivered, and then we'll be on our way to Chilliwack! I can finally join you for Beer Friday! I'm so excited!!!!!

Everyone here is so nice and so respectful of Daryl. I did hear how he paid for their last Christmas party, so that might explain why they give him that extra attention. My love is just so generous with everyone! Eeeeeeeeek!

***

Finally. I read the email and let out an audible sigh. Amazing!

Quite literally, Tina and I had exchanged hundreds of emails. Today I would finally get to meet the woman who snagged Daryl's heart and my aid in the Foundation of Hope.

"What time should I go to Characters then?" I shot a message off to Daryl.

"We will be in Chilliwack by 3:00 p.m. I'll message you as we get closer."

"Okay, let me know!"

The hours ticked by, interrupted by an occasional email from Tina and a brief text from Daryl. Both were keeping me posted on their progress. Tina's messages were lively and full of excitement as Daryl toured her through the Parq and Hard Rock Casino, introducing her to the heads.

Daryl's messages followed, informative and expressive. He enjoyed watching his Tina experience their first hours in Canada together.

"We've just passed the Fraser Glen Golf Course. We're driving around, and I'm showing her all of our property. We should be pulling into Chilliwack in an hour. I'll message when we arrive."

An hour later my phone buzzed.

"Tina's having a bit of a panic attack. We've gone straight to the house," Daryl typed.

"What happened?"

"I don't really know. We were driving along, and she was chatty and excited. I drove down Evans, and all of the sudden she got pale and quiet. I asked her what was wrong and she started shaking. I'm making her some tea; she's in the shower. Maybe the whole day was overwhelming? I don't know. We're just going to have a quiet night here. Let's make plans to meet tomorrow. I'll message later"

***

From: Tina Hoffmeister
To: Glenda
Subject: I'm sorry

I'm so sorry, Glenda. I feel like such a baby. Please forgive me. I don't know what happened. We were just driving down the road, and I saw a bunch of cows. My heart started racing, and then the smell. It smells like cows. I know all of that was in my past, but it just hit me and I didn't know what to do. I really want to meet you, but I think I have to go home. I don't think I can stay here.

***

Really?

Months and months of waiting and you have to go home because of cows?

***

"We are on the boat," read Daryl's text the next day. "This morning we walked the property a little bit. Tina saw the little barn near the pond and had another panic attack. We just drove back into the city. It will take some time for her to adjust. I told her not to worry, we'll rip the barn down if that's what it takes to make her feel more comfortable. She also opened a closet and saw Denise's things. That did not go well."

***

From: *Tina Hoffmeister*
To: *Glenda*
Subject: *the boat*

Oh my God, Glenda! The boat is amazing! You should see it! We just finished lunch at Carderos. We're sitting on the deck drinking wine, and there's a little seal. He's so cute! We've named him Sammy.

I don't think I can come back to Chilliwack. I will try. I have to try to live in Daryl's world, even if that's in Chilliwack.

I didn't realize how the smells would affect me. I like the city. I can't wait for you to come and be on this boat with us! I have to go. Daryl is showing me downtown tonight!

***

And there I sat.

Staring at the cedar skyline with a beagle on my lap, balancing my emotions.

"You guys are kind of mean, you know."

"Don't be selfish, Glenda. You didn't live her history. You have no idea what she's going through."

"Do you know how many times you guys have changed plans? Or something has happened, and I'm left here waiting?"

"Glenda, you expect certain things. You have to be patient when things don't go as expected."

Back and forth, back and forth, back and forth, until the morning became the afternoon, and the afternoon became the evening, and the evening became night.

"Hello, Doug?"

"She's going to try again on the weekend." Daryl sat across from me, fiddling with his cell phone. "God, it's hard to read messages with this cracked screen."

"Who'd you throw your phone at?" I slyly grinned as I sipped the pint in front of me.

He stared at me like I had just sprouted tulips from my ears. I pulled my eyes toward my pint and wiped my own smirk off my face.

"I was standing at the top of my stairs and it slipped out of my hand. I had it caught, I thought, but *plop, plop, plop* it went down each step. Lyndsay is having more sent up."

"More? Not just one?"

"More, yes, for you and everyone who will work at the foundation," he said manner of factly. "As soon as security does their thing with them, she'll courier them up. Until then. Fuck. This!" He swiped his finger across his screen to enlarge the bottom half of the message because the top half was black. The screen didn't work.

"I have a drawer full of old cell phones, Daryl. I'll bring you one tomorrow. It should tide you over till the new ones arrive."

"I can do that?"

"I'm quite sure you can. You know, for a smart person, you're sometime not so smart." I grinned.

"I pay people to do the not so smart things in my life." He grinned. "Thanks, though. I really will appreciate not using this thing anymore. I hope we get it figured out."

"You had a nice weekend then?"

"After we left the cows, yes. Who knew a fucken cow would do that to her?" His face was animated. "She's going to try again this weekend, so we will see."

"Scents can do things like that."

"I was going to put forty Cactus Club cows on the lawn for her birthday. I guess I'll have to rethink that."

I snort laughed. "We shouldn't make fun; it's a serious issue," I said, regaining my composure.

"She was video chatting with her psychologist, and that helped," he said. "The boat helped. She did well in all areas where there were no barns, cows, and smell of farms."

"How will she ever live in Chilliwack?"

"I don't know. We may just have to stay in the city. I'm going to tear down the barn. It's almost new. Do you want barn wood? Maybe for the foundation? Maybe your house?"

"I'm sure we can make use of it. Hey, I didn't see any swanky red cars when I pulled in. How did you get here?"

"Cab."

"Cab? What the heck, Daryl?"

"I told you, I'm not driving the Alpha Romeos through Chilliwack. That is the last thing I need, drawing attention to myself like that, and the Honda is still in the shop waiting for parts. Fucking COVID has everyone waiting for everything. So I took a cab, no big deal. If they had car service here, I'd use that. We left the SUV at the hanger in Abbotsford, and the car is in my garage. It sure is fun to drive, though." He punctuated the thought with a smile.

"Where are the cards you were bringing the other day?"

He looked at me blankly.

"The HSBC cards you picked up the day you picked up your car," I reminded him.

"I put them in the safe at the casino. They're there, cheques too."

"The Chilliwack Casino?"

"Yes."

"Let's go get them."

"We can't."

"Why not?"

"I don't have the number to the safe. The GM does. He doesn't work Mondays."

"Daryl!"

"Yes?"

"Why did you leave them at the casino?"

"Simple, I didn't want them in my house. Remember? Black muscle car. Duffle bag. Smashed gate. I thought it would be better to move everything to the casino safe, and while I was there having a meeting the day I picked up your cards, it was just natural to pop those in there too. I'll pick them up tomorrow. Also, please let me know when you'll be available for a meet and greet with MNP."

"Any time, Daryl."

"Great, I'll let them know."

"Who is our contact at MNP?"

"A woman named Gloria. It was funny, I was here last week watching the Flames game, and she and another lady were sitting down over there." He nodded in the direction of the floor tables. "She came to my table and said, 'I'm surprised to see you here, but then I was surprised to see you in jeans and a hoodie when you walked into our offices last month. You're nothing what we expected. When your Cayman offices called and told us to expect your visit, we had a different image of you in mind.'" Daryl started snickering. He loved this effect he had on people. "How do you think the new vaccine passes will affect Corky's business?" The conversation shifted, as it naturally did when we were together.

"Well, day will stay the same. Generally older people are vaccinated already. Night will probably decrease. But what can we do? It's been horrible for this industry, shutting us down, re-opening, shutting down, re-open if you spend thousands for outdoor seating, half capacity, policing government protocols, listening to people police each other. People calling in because they have COVID, people calling in because they were exposed to COVID, people calling in saying they were exposed to COVID but weren't simply because they can, not show up to work and using this as an excuse every time they want to. No resumes coming in, constantly short-staffed, those who show up are doing the job of two people and still dealing with shit coming from the public or government."

"Yup." His phone was lifted to his ear.

Social etiquette pissed on by progress, chewed up by change since King Cell took the throne. I glanced out the window wondering how human beings in the presence of human beings become less important than the humans inside of a cell phone.

"She's the foundation lady." Daryl sounded surprised. He leaned back on his barstool, lifted his head, and laughter erupted from him. I glanced back in his direction. "You are, are you? Okay, yessss. All right then. Bye bye."

I raised my eyebrows.

"Doug."

"And?"

"He's been playing around, and he got into Characters' security cameras. He's watching us. He wanted to know who's that lady I'm sitting with."

"I feel like waving." I smiled. "It's a little creepy, Daryl."

"Well, I'm doing a lot of business in Chilliwack. He wants eyes everywhere."

"I understand, but it doesn't make it less creepy, though." I held up my hand, waved, and smiled.

I met Doug. Actually, Doug met me.

Jacquie

His laughter was infectious. Gargantuan giggles gushed from her six-year-old son. Everything and nothing would set this boy off.

She brushed a lock of golden-brown hair from his eyes and, resting her hands on the side of his face, leaned in to give him a great big kiss.

"Momma!" he giggled again, bouncing up and down.

How did she ever get so lucky? How is it that this beautiful, bright, lively little being was her boy? She let him go and watched him run. His feet splashed through the west coast surf. Cold, soft sand squeezed up between his toes. He saw a baby crab, leaned over, and picked it up.

The sun was getting ready to call the day night, and it glowed behind him, lighting him up in its warmth.

My boy. A wave of love curled around her heart. *God, he's such a beautiful boy.*

"Momma! A crab!" He held it up to her and started giggling again.

She opened her eyes as the memory finished. A deep sigh escaped. She ran her index finger gently across his skin, tracing the black ink of his tattoo running up his arm. It was cold.

A wave of sorrow tugged another tear out. How there could be that many tears inside her, she didn't know. They just didn't stop. This one furled with another and pulled themselves down her cheek, long and slow. She wiped them away with the tissue she'd had wadded into a hard ball in her left fist. She wanted to punch something. She wanted to disappear. She wanted to crawl into his body and take his place, that he may live and she may die. She was there anyway. Instead, she brushed her finger gently across his lips. Her chest constricted. They lay still now.

"Momma!" his deep voice bellowed from the centre of the crowd. She tapped her hand over her heart twice and then lifted it to wave at her son. He was laughing. She watched them watch him. How does he do that? They hang on to his words. They seek to be near him. God, he's funny! His gargantuan giggles grew into charismatic charm. His eye caught hers again. He grinned and winked. "Do you see that lady over there?" He leaned down to speak to someone beside him. He raised his hand that held a red solo cup and pointed his index finger directly at her. "That's my momma!"

The memory pressed against her mind and gouged its claws into her heart. She trembled.

"Take the time you need, Jacquie." The funeral director said in a hushed tone.

More tears sprang free. *How much time? When you take him away, I will never see my son again.* She thought these things as she gingerly touched a lock of his hair. "When is it time to turn away and walk out that door without my child in my life?" Grief rolled and she closed her eyes against it.

The sound of the phone call echoed in her mind.

"They found him in a hotel room. Opioids, they figure. Sorry, Jacquie, he's gone."

Gone.

Her sweet six-year-old giggling in the sand. He wanted to be a fireman when he grew up: "A fireman, Momma.

I'm going to put out fires. I want to save people's lives."
He grinned.

Instead, he became an addict.

He never dreamed he wanted that.

***

"No Mr. Beer Bottle?" There, I finally asked.

Jacquie sighed, smiled, and sipped her wine. "Cary?
God no. I sure know how to pick them." She stared at
her coaster. "A cute little something moved in next door,
younger than my son." She stopped, bit the bottom of her
lip, poured the last of her wine from the carafe into her
wine glass, and then continued. "He ran after that one."
She shook her head in disgust.

Let Me Scan 'Em

"Vaccine passes, vaccine passes, get 'em out, let me scan 'em!" Nikki commanded boisterously following the latest government requirements.

One by one we presented our phones. "Thank you, Glenda, thank you, Haney, thank you, Jack, thank you, Daryl. Now I'll get your beers." She was off.

"Still no Tina?"

Daryl fumed red. "Oh, the jet picked her up on Friday. She thought she'd bring Emily and the kids. Emily and Michael are having problems, so she figured she'd give them a fun weekend. One of Emily's kids had a fucking fever, so back they all went. I'm getting sick of it."

The Cowboys were kicking off.

"Next year, once all of the COVID restrictions lift, we're all going to SoFi Stadium." Daryl changed gears.

"Will Tina join us then? Or will there be another excuse?" I smiled.

"It's getting tiring, isn't it?" he replied.

"Ya, Daryl, it really is. Maybe she'll make it for Super Bowl."

All four of us looked at each other and erupted with laughter.

"Has peanut butter cup made it yet?" Jack asked.

"Peanut butter cup?" I was confused.

"Daryl told me your Land Rover was black on the outside, tan on the inside. Sounds like a peanut butter cup to me." Jack grinned.

"Ahhhh."

"Daryl?" Haney and I looked expectantly at him.

"The last I heard, they were to be delivered to the Toyota dealership in two weeks. Oh ya, could you send me a picture of your driver's license? They need it. I'll forward it."

"Done. Two weeks? Are you certain? My Santa Fe needs front end work and tires. Oh, the tires are super shitty. I'd rather not spend the money to fix it if I don't have to."

"That's what they tell me. Could be a month. I don't know, Glenda. You'll be fine to drive on the tires you have."

"You think?"

All three boys nodded.

"Okay then, I'll hold off on getting the work done."

Earl shuffled by, newpaper tucked under his arm, eyes on the big screen. He smiled. "Mind if I join you?" We rearranged ourselves at the Bone to make room for him. "I was watching Ted Lasso last night. Have you seen it?"

"Cheers," I whispered under my breath and pulled up my pint for a sip.

"Oh God, that Ted Lasso is so funny."

Daryl raised his eyebrows. "Cheers!" He smiled, and I raised my pint to his. Earl glanced quizzically at us, continuing. "The thing that Ted Lasso did this time …"

And Jack looked over with a smirk and a nod. "Cheers," he mouthed, as Earl continued describing the scene. "And then Ted Lasso …"

Haney kicked me under the table. I started giggling, the table erupted, and poor Earl stared at us, confused.

Here, Take My Car

"I should probably scan your pass," I said to Daryl the next day as he sat at the bar. He started laughing, pulling out his phone.

"Didn't you see Nikki scan it yesterday?"

"Oh ya, you're right. Pint?"

"Just a coffee, and may I have a bit of water please. I need something to wash the Ibuprofen down with. My knee is acting up, all this walking."

"All what walking? You don't walk." I snorted.

"They the wrote the Honda off, Big Red is still at the hanger in Abbotsford, and Alfie is in Vancouver at Millionare, so I take a cab in and walk to where I have meetings and cab to the farther ones."

"Daryl, take my Santa Fe. It's just sitting here while I'm working. It's way more convenient for you to get where you need to get."

"You sure?"

"Yes, just get it back here by five when I'm done."

"Thank you. You really have helped me out a lot, Glenda. I will never forget it. I owe you so much for your kindness."

"Ya, ya, just don't die. The tires are bad." I grinned at him.

"They've sprayed down the linoleum tiles in your foundation office with some treatment to lift the glue. I was just there before I came in."

"Did they get their demo permit then?"

"Not exactly." Daryl grinned. I shook my head. "Anyway, I have to go. Meeting with the Tzatziki band at the Miller. Thanks again for letting me use your car, Glenda. I felt a little weird showing up at meetings in a cab."

"Drier for you too. This rain!"

"And we're expecting more, they say."

"I love the rain, but this is ridiculous."

"I should go to the Caymans. I hate the rain."

"Why don't you?"

"It's always fucken something, Glenda. The pilot got COVID. Yesterday the landing gear was inspected and they need a new part. They've grounded it until it comes in. Just as well, I wouldn't want to land in it without that part. It's kind of important. Tina and I were talking this morning. We'd like to do Christmas up at the house with you and Haney and Jack and Kate. Thoughts?"

"Sounds like fun, actually."

Daryl grinned. "It will be fun. I'll see if I can get the kids there. Maybe Robbie can get some of those trailers, the movie trailers. We can park them on the property, and everyone can have their own space." He was thinking out loud. "Anyway, got to go." He sipped the last of his coffee and stood. "Thanks again, Glenda."

"See you at five, D. Pick up the cards while you're out and about, would you," I instructed.

"Can't. The GM was exposed to COVID, so he's not coming in for ten days."

I started laughing.

"Why are you laughing?"

"If I had a dollar for every excuse, I'd be richer than you right now. See ya, D."

Drowned

The sound of crashing wood. Cracking close. Fracturing farther. Shattering. Splintering. Splitting. The forest, breaking beneath the weight of water. Its roots like claws cling to the earth. The earth aches for truce. She cries to heaven for a moment to catch her breath, and heaven silences her complaint by pouring more water down her throat. She is mauled and thrashed and spate. She gives up and crumbles. The river opens wide to receive her and feasts. Churning boulders deep in its belly, picking its teeth with cedars. It gnaws and chews and devours, spewing itself over the valley.

Haney and I lay on our little bed, fully protected by four tin walls as nature moaned and pulled and pulverized.

"It was nice being married to you," I said.

"You were a good wife. Just so you know, in case we aren't here in the morning, you should know that."

"Thanks. You were a pretty great husband too. You should know that."

We squeezed each other's hands goodnight and didn't sleep a wink.

That one sounded pretty close. How will the trees on the slope hold up? Why does it sound like metal twisting? Do you really want to know that, Glenda? What's that rumbling? Rocks? Boulders? Is it that powerful?

The night groaned into day and the rain continued. We arose expecting the worst. I held my breath and opened the door. Our happy little trees stood stately. "We got this, Glenda," they said. Not a branch fell. Not a drop of water broke the creek bank.

Nature left nature alone.

We, along with our Douglas firs, stood stunned. Our souls breathed gratitude. 'Thank you, God." Short, specific, and exceedingly sincere.

The morning brought no reprieve. The rain continued to fill the earth; the earth continued to collapse. River banks broke, pulling homes from foundations, filling communities with water, threatening to drown horses, dogs, and men. Bridges broke, leaving husbands stranded on one side and wives on the other. Towns were evacuated, trucks were covered in mud. Trees continued to fall into the river, damming up their usual route, forcing the water into new veins, creating new paths, creating new problems. Highways closed. Speed boats replaced semis on the Number One. News reports came in. If you lived in northern Washington, you heard how the Canadian rivers were swelling onto American soil. If you lived in British Columbia, you heard how the America Nooksack was flooding Canadian soil. The Fraser Valley didn't care whose river it was. She couldn't, she was too busy being drowned.

"How are you?" Daryl's text arrived in the morning.

"We are good. You?"

"Safe in Chilliwack, stuck in Chilliwack."

"Stuck?"

"Freeways are closed; all choppers are being used for emergency services. My golf courses are flooded, both Fraser Glen and Chilliwack. I'll inspect the damage when the water recedes. Will Corky's be open?"

"I think so, as long as there is beer to serve."

"That might be a problem."

"Our orders might not make it."

"Gas stations have lineups. No deliveries can make it through."

"Why do people line up then? If they can't drive anywhere?"

"Good question."

"I won't be in today. Our main road is closed; hopefully it will be fixed tomorrow and I'll see you then."

"Okay, take care. Let me know if you need anything."

"Will do. Thank you, Daryl."

The next week unveiled destruction. The Fraser Valley Regional District held its breath under the water while the citizens of Chilliwack created lines. Lineups at the gas stations. Lineups at the grocery stores. Lineups at churches and community centres, all communities helping the stranded travellers. Lineups of human arms throwing sandbags to save the pump stations. Lines of complaints. The humans who helped were too tired to complain; the humans who complained were too tired to help.

Our neighbours lost the road to their house. The river ate it. Just like that. Their dream devoured. In the winter we watched kayakers bring them in propane and wine. In the spring we watched a helicopter bring out their cars. They are hikers now; feet walk in and out.

"Have you been able to get to your golf courses?" I asked Daryl as we met for a beer a few days into the flood.

"Covered. I haven't been there. I can't get close. I can't even get a helicopter to go to the city. Everything is being used for evacuations and running people back and forth for their medical treatments. It's crazy. It's like the universe is after me. COVID everywhere, volcanos erupting in Venezuela, hurricanes in the Caribbean, now fucking floods. What next?" He was frustrated and exasperated.

He asked for the tab, and his card didn't work. "What the fuck?" He picked up the phone and called Lyndsay.

"My card isn't working," he hissed into the phone. 'Yup, yup. Well, tell them to fucking figure it out fast. I'm stranded here. I can't go anywhere. You have no fucking idea!" He hung up the phone and turned his head toward the window. He started grinding his teeth.

"Daryl, I've got the tab, don't worry about it," I said, hoping to ease his angst. He turned and offered me a wan smile. "Thank you. I appreciate that." He turned his head back toward the window, staring silently, unseeing into the parking lot. Minutes later he picked up his phone "Yessss?" He listened to what Lyndsay was telling him on the other end. His breath changed as he pulled air deep into his lungs and exhaled in a long, slow respire. His eyelids closed and opened and closed in no rush. His world was standing still and his body slowed to swallow it.

His voice dropped four octaves, and three words, slow, deliberate, and demanding, emerged: "Get. It. Fixed."

He hung up his phone and resumed his gaze out the window.

I gave him a minute.

"Alexandra." I flagged down our server. "Could you grab Daryl another beer please?"

He turned his head, offering another feeble smile and a nod of thanks.

"So?" I prodded.

"There was a security issue. Tangerine shut down my cards. Something about being flagged. Seattle purchases, then Canadian purchases."

"How long until it's fixed?"

The corner of his mouth twitched. He shook his head. "They're sending new ones," he spat.

"What?"

He resumed blinking slowly.

"So use your other cards, the ones that HSBC has sent, and the Crystal Castle credit card you've arranged for the foundation," I suggested.

He smiled, close lipped.

"Well?" I waited.

"They are still in the safe."

"At the casino?"

His smile tightened.

"Where's the GM?" I asked.

"He lives in Vancouver."

"Shit."

"Exactly." He turned to stare out the window again.

Ice Ice Baby

The plug was pulled and the water drained, and Mr. Snow Mister took a deep breath and howled, long and hard and deep.

There was no break.

Nature was menopausal, and she was a bitch.

He was sitting at the tall top in Characters fiddling with his glasses when Haney and I arrived for beer Friday.

"What are you doing?" I asked Daryl as I pulled out my barstool, throwing my bag and coat over the back.

"This." Daryl held up his twisted glasses with one lens missing and put them on his face. The skin around his left eye was scratched and turning a hint of purple; a gash lay across the bridge of his nose.

"What the hell happened to you?"

"I slipped on my driveway getting out of my cab last night."

"Daryl, your driveway is heated."

"Glenda"—he shook his head at my naivety—"obviously it was on the unheated part. My knee's fucked up too."

"Daryl," I snickered in sympathy, "it really is like the universe is out to get you, isn't it?"

"I just stepped out of the cab and down I went. I hit my face on the curb, one of my lenses smashed and cut my nose and this." He pointed to his eye. "I can't fucken see." He put his skewed glasses on his skewed face. It was pathetic.

"What's your prescription, Daryl?" He looked at me blankly. "How bad are your eyes?" I continued.

"Fuck, I don't know, bad."

"Here, put on my glasses," I said while taking mine off and handing them to him.

He did as I instructed. A burst of laughter rose from his belly. "I can see! I can't believe your eyes are as bad as mine!"

"I need them now, but when we go, you can use these. Haney's driving. I can be blind for the drive home. I'll bring you another pair I never wear on Monday. You can't keep these ones, though; they're my favourite."

"Oh God. Thank you, Glenda, you have no idea."

"Well, you look like an idiot in those." I snort laughed. "Lord, it's like I have two husbands I'm taking care of. I need another beer."

"What's going on for Christmas? Are we all still headed up to your place, or has the ice changed plans?"

Daryl's countenance immediately dropped. "I told Robbie to remove all the trailers. It's just too dangerous, and my plane isn't flying anywhere in this freezing rain. Helicopters aren't either. Maybe by Christmas Eve the weather will allow us to take a chopper to Seattle. Would you want to come to Seattle for Christmas instead? I'll get Tina to rent a trailer. She can use the same outfit she used when she was renovating."

I looked at Haney, he looked at me, and we both shrugged our shoulders.

"You haven't been able to see Tina in a long time. Are you sure you want us there?"

"Absolutely."

"Okay then, if the weather is good, we'll go. If it doesn't get better, we'll just have a quiet one at home."

"I had all the lights taken down."

"What?"

"On my property. I had a company come in and decorate the house and string lights up around the trees like you did. For our Christmas. The weather has ruined everything, and it made me miserable to see it, so I had them come and take it all down."

"That's pretty pathetic," I said.

"It's how I feel. Nothing is going right. I'm stuck in fucking Chilliwack. Floods, now fucking ice. This place is hell."

"Chilliwack is nice; it's the weather that sucks."

We spent the afternoon cheering up Daryl. When it was time to go, I took off my glasses and handed them over the table and slipped him a hundred-dollar bill under the table like I'd been doing for the last three weeks. It's what you do when your friend is stuck, isn't it?

The Mark

From: *Tina Hoffmeister*
To: *Glenda*
Subject: *Re: Morning*

Good morning.

I'm glad you slept better. I definitely overdid it yesterday. I just woke up. Uggggg.

Busy day on the computer. Now it's December and it's time to finalize the final payouts for all of the accounts, except shoe closet and foundation.

This will take most of the week. Get the paperwork into the right people so funds can be distributed in the new year.

Wish me luck with my laggy brain.

I am very worried about Daryl and his health. I know he had a busy day, but his level of frustration with life is showing. We both feel so bad for him but are so happy that you, Haney, and Jack are there for him to prevent a complete meltdown. I can't even try to understand his situation.

The team just landed in Seattle and are headed to a hotel. They haven't received their Canadian paperwork yet, but Lynds is working with them.

And you are right—it is a huge blessing for her to be here. She is having relationship issues, so we have each other to cry with.

I'm going to keep the pressure on the bank, but it's not just money he needs; he needs people from work he knows and trusts around him.

I could give you a list of things Lynds has told me he is dealing with, and even my head was spinning. He keeps it all to himself. I can't imagine that, but Lynds said he doesn't like to bother people with his issues. He keeps saying, "This is the life I chose, not those around me". 🧑‍🦰♀

Anyway, thanks for being our friend and being there for him. I hope you have a good night. Hugs and kisses.

***

"Daryl."

His head was down in his phone, absorbed in something. It took a moment before he lifted his eyes in my direction. "Yes?"

The Bone was empty with the exception of himself, his coaster, and his pint that was barely touched. I wiped the top with my bleach cloth.

"Has anyone ever out-witted you, or pushed harder than you to get something you were going for so you lost out?"

"Yes."

"How did that make you feel? Mad? Angry?"

"No."

"No?"

"No. If they outwitted me to get something, I usually sit back and analyze it." He smiled "Hmmm, I didn't see that one coming kind of thing. Usually I'm amused."

"Not angry then?"

"No, if they got it, then they deserve it. Why should I be angry about that? Has Steff emailed your daughters yet?"

"No, I don't think so."

"Hmm, I'll talk to her. Her father just died. He was old, but it was still unexpected.

She's having a hard time with it."

"Tell her to take her time then. Let her grieve."

He nodded.

"You look engrossed in something."

"I am. There's rippling going on around Ukraine. Your daughter's out of there, right?"

"Yes, they left in the summer."

"Good."

"Why?"

"I think Russia will attack."

"You do?"

"Yes."

Earl walked in brushing lint off his brown sweater and laid the newspaper on top of the Bone across from Daryl. "Do you mind if I join you?" Daryl nodded toward a barstool. Earl pulled it out and took a seat. "A baby beer please, Glenda." I left to pour it.

"And I lent him $3,000 last summer and he still hasn't paid me back, and he phoned yesterday asking for more, to pay his rent." I put Earl's baby beer in front of him. He paused his conversation. "Thank you, Glenda." Then he continued. "He's a friend. I'd like to help him out, but—"

"You're his mark," Daryl said flatly.

"Excuse me?" Earl responded.

"He's using you. You gave him money; he knows you have money, and he wants more. He's not your friend; you're his mark."

Earl turned a shade of red and frowned. Daryl continued. "Anyone who keeps taking your money is using you, Earl." Earl stood up to go to the Keno machine.

"He's my friend."

"He's not your friend. He's only your friend because of your money."

Earl left to buy his tickets

"You can't trust anyone who's taking money like that," Daryl said, staring at his beer.

"Really, Daryl? Should I then be worried about you? I've given you quite a bit of money."

He tilted his head as he weighed the comment. "I guess you have, haven't you?" He went back to reading his phone. "If your daughter has friends in Kyiv, she might want to warn them, suggest they leave."

"I'll mention it to her, Daryl. Are you okay? You've barely touched your pint."

"It's my stomach. I was throwing up blood last night. They need to cauterize it again."

"Again?"

"Yes."

"The last time this happened I was with Denise in a hotel near St. Paul's. I kept throwing up blood. It had happened before, so I wasn't too worried. I expected it to pass, but it didn't. Denise wanted me to go to the hospital, but I refused. The second day I stood up and passed out. She called an ambulance to wheel me across the street to the hospital. Another hour, they said, and I'd have been dead. I had lost that much blood. But they soldered me up, and I was good as new."

"But it's happening again?"

"It's not as bad."

"Does Tina know?"

"I don't want to worry her."

"Christmas Eve is tomorrow."

"I won't be going."

"Aw, Daryl."

"The freezing rain. There's nothing I can do about it. I can't fly in it."

"We'll come and join you for a beer somewhere then, so you're not alone."

"Thank you, Glenda. I would like that."

"Okay then, Characters at 11:00 a.m.?"

He smiled and nodded.

"Those glasses suit you. I'm glad."

"I had a pair almost exactly like this a few years ago. I don't know how I can ever thank you and repay you for your kindness. I owe you so much."

"It's all good, Daryl, Just don't die. If your stomach gets too bad, please promise me you'll go to the hospital."

"I will."

"Maybe stop drinking beer?"

He smiled briefly then went back to his phone.

Enter, the Russians

I reached up and pulled the tinsel garland off the pergolas. *This is probably the last time I'm going to do this.* The thought popped in my mind. *That's okay, over ten years I've been putting up and pulling down this garland. I can retire.* I smiled.

Daryl walked in as I was reaching toward a red bulb, uncomfortably beyond my fingertips.

"Well, hello there, I guess that's the last time you'll be doing that," he said, observing my de-decorating. I caught hold of the bulb, pulled it off, and threw it in the box with the garland.

"Ha, I was just thinking the same thing myself."

"I just came from MNP."

"And?"

"They're in contact with Danny regarding your funds. Everything is ready to go. They're just navigating how to manoeuvre through the new government requirements to prove the money isn't Russian oligarchy. Once they prove there are no Russians involved, they'll submit through Fintrac and will work with you setting up cheques for all the people on your lists. It's a lot of money, Glenda."

"Good. Every single person on our lists could use it." I grinned "You have no idea how much I think about the day when we give them their cheques. Seriously, it's what keeps me going! But F the Russians! It's amazing how it's always something! Floods, ice storms, now the Russians. Do you want coffee?"

"Just one quick one. I have a meeting." He pulled out the barstool, took a seat, and opened his phone.

"Hey, did I show you this?" He flipped his phone toward me. "Robbie sent it to me. It's him and one of my grandsons over Christmas. They spent it all together in the Caymens."

"Aw, they look so happy. I'm glad at least they could change their plans and all be together there."

"Me too." He turned the phone back to himself, inspecting the photo a little longer before closing the screen and flipping the phone over.

Daryl didn't share personal information freely. This was the third time in over a year that he showed me a photo of his children. One was a posed shot of Nelson that was used for communication with NHL regarding the Calgary Flames, another of Nelson and his wife at a golf tournament, and now this one of Robbie and his grandson. Christine remained an image of a tiny dancer in my mind. On days when I was stuck at home waiting and bored, I googled the crap out of him and his family. Nothing turned up. I wasn't surprised. If I uncovered anything, I would have been very surprised. Doug wouldn't have been doing his job very well if something was left "unwiped."

"I'm finally headed to Seattle tonight."

"Oh good, I'll bet Tina is ecstatic!"

"She is, but she's been busy. Emily and Michael have split up, and Em and the kids have been living with her. They're wrecking her stuff. She had thought about them staying at her house while she's up here with me, but after the last few weeks, she's decided they should have a home of their own. She doesn't want her renovated house destroyed. They found a house just down the road from Tina's and are putting an offer on it this afternoon."

"Tina will be happy to have her space back, I'm sure."

"Yes. I have to check on a golf course I bought in Portland, and some casino business and MGM business. I should be back in time for beer Friday."

"Super, I look forward to it!"

"Oh, and the Land Rovers have arrived. Is there a time this weekend that you'll be available to pick yours up?"

"Any day that works for you, Daryl, I'll make it work for me."

"I'll let them know and I'll get back to you on that. They're in Langley, so maybe Haney can drive us in?"

"Of course!"

"Has Steff contacted the girls?" Daryl stirred a sugar into his coffee, his hand tremoring slightly. He placed the stir stick by the mug and folded the sugar packet paper into a symmetrical square. Anything he folded was deliberate and orderly. Daryl seemed at ease in disorder and with dirt around him, but if it passed through his hands, it was neat, tidy, and clean. He allowed the world to be who they were, but if it was an extension of him, it was expected to be done with precision.

Perhaps the tremor annoyed him, a part of him that wasn't perfect or precise or under his control.

"Yes, she's cc'd me in," I answered as I gazed at his trembling hand, contemplating if it was from too much booze the night before or too much booze in general. He didn't notice.

"Good, I'll have to get her to forward them to me as well. I was thinking that it could be quite fun to have her fly your daughters to our offices in Stuttgart for their first meeting, and then to make it more special, that you should be there to surprise them." He pulled the coffee mug to his lips and sipped gingerly, eyes peering over the cup, a hint of mischief flickering.

I laughed in delight. "What an amazing idea, D.! Can you imagine the look on their faces?" I broke off as the image drifted in. "They will be utterly shocked!" Daryl smiled at my glee and returned the mug to the bar. "Thanks for thinking of things like this, Daryl. To see them after all this time plus seeing where your grandmother started it all! YES! I would love to see that too."

Satisfied that my response was exactly as he had intended, he continued. "We will have to work on a good time. She'll be in the Baltics next week. We're moving our people and shutting down our casinos there, so she's going to be very busy."

"For good?"

"No. Until the Russians quit fucking with Ukraine."

"That." I was immediately pulled from my joy. "Danielle has sent messages regarding her friends there; it's not good."

Daryl opened his phone and started scrolling. "Have you heard of this group?" he asked as he spun his screen toward me. "Motopara." I scanned briefly.

"No."

"They're a branch of us. They'll be with Steff as we move out Baltics."

"It looks like an army."

"They are. Ex-military hired privately to manoeuvre in difficult areas. We can get where we need to get even in the worse circumstances. It's a branch of Doug's work. He uses them instead of his teams in more precarious situations."

I looked up from Daryl's screen. "I know you run deep, Daryl. I've lived my life not knowing that teams like this even exist. Every day you share a bit of things I have no clue about."

"You need to know about them. The foundation will need their services if your daughter is working within Ukraine, and you will need them if the foundation is working on human trafficking, as your other daughter shared."

"I like how you slowly reveal this information to me. I think if you had done it all at once, I would …"

He waited for me to finish.

"I would have not stepped foot into your world."

Daryl looked me directly in the eye. "That's exactly it. People don't have a clue how difficult my life is, or the magnitude of my responsibility. From the outside it looks fun, and don't get me wrong, I do have a lot of fun. But my life is work, all day, all night. I show you things slowly, purposely slow, so that it doesn't overwhelm you. You do-gooders"—he smiled then and took another sip of his coffee—"go into everything with rainbow-coloured glasses. You want to take aid to Colombia? How do you think that really works, Glenda, when you have to get past the Cartel? Don't think for a moment you won't be faced with that kind of thing as you bring aid to Ukraine."

"I'm beginning to see."

"Good." He seemed satisfied by my response. "I have to get going." He stood up from the barstool and tipped the last of his coffee back. I reached for my keys and unclipped my car key from its ring and tossed it across the bar to him. "I guess you won't be needing my car for very much longer, hey?"

"Nope. I thank you for letting me use it. Hopefully this weekend I'll be driving my own. See you before five. Thanks again for letting me use it."

"Just be careful. Peek down at the driver's-side tire. It's shocking how bald it is. I swear I can see cables!"

"You'll be fine, Glenda. A couple more days!"

"Thank goodness for that! Have a good day, D."

He turned one last time, almost as an afterthought. "Glenda, if your daughter's friends need help, let me know. We have our guys in Kyiv now."

"Oh."

He gave a quick nod and left.

Kyiv

"школу закінчено! School is finished!" Dmytro threw his arms in the air. The three boys had just pushed through the steel gray school door for the last time. "No more homework!"

The idea seemed almost unbelievable. Grins erupted on their faces as they came to terms with their new freedom. Dmytro gave Elijah a playful shove. Elijah deliberately fell back into Ivan, who dropped, laughing onto the grass.

"Get up, Ivan." Dmytro chuckled, reaching down with his right hand to help his friend up. Ivan grabbed hold, and Dmytro released his grip, laughing as he watched Ivan fall back to the ground.

"Ommph, you!" Ivan howled, pulled himself up, and started chasing after Dmytro, who wheeled behind Elijah.

"Oh no, I'm not your barricade!" Elijah shrieked as he wheeled himself to the right, leaving Dmytro exposed to Ivan. The boys continued to tussle until they heard a voice from a window.

"хватит, иди домой! Enough! Go home"

The boys looked at each other, shared one last shove, and then chuckling started their walk home.

"What will you do with your summer?" Ivan asked neither boy in particular but both at the same time.

"Nothing." Dmytro grinned. "I want to play video games and eat candy." Ivan smiled at the thought of that "You, Elijah?" he continued.

"We're moving back to Germany."

"Ach! No!"

"Yes."

"You won't be back next year?"

"No."

Ivan's face fell. He and Elijah had just become friends over the last months, so this news wasn't welcome. "You don't seem upset."

"We move all the time. I don't mind," Elijah responded.

"I will miss you," Ivan spoke thoughtfully.

"Ech, sissys!" Dmytro proclaimed. "Life will go on. You can message each other, and even play games online. It will hardly be like you're gone." Dmytro's voice was strong, an attempt to cover the jab of pain he felt in his chest.

They walked silently with a playful push here and there until they reached the road with the Y. Elijah took the right road, Dmytro and Ivan continued to their homes using the left road. They wave one last wave just before they lost sight of each other.

Summer in Kyiv had begun.

***

The building shook.

Dmytro pushed aside the linen curtain to get a better look of the street.

"*подалі звідти!* Away from there!" his mother instructed frantically.

He turned toward her voice. There was a pitch to it he had never heard before. He was torn. He wanted to see what all the rumbling on the street was about, but that voice coming out of his mother—its panic created a feeling inside he'd not experienced before. He didn't have time to respond. His mother was at his side, pulling his arm firmly.

"Away from there, I said! Get to your room, pack a bag. We must go!"

"Go?" Dmytro was confused. "Go where?"

"I don't know." His mother's face broke red and crumpled. Terror and tears erupted at same time. "I don't know! Just pack a bag." She cried, barely in control.

The two of them were out of their apartment in under twenty minutes and rushed down the road. They had reached the Y where Dmytro had waved goodbye to his friend Elijah eight months before. His mother stopped. He heard her mumble, "Which way, which way, which way should we go?"

"This way." Dmytro's voice was stronger than his twelve-year-old body. He took his mother's hand and led her toward the train station. She nodded and allowed her son to lead her.

Soldiers passed them, or was it they that passed the soldiers? Dmytro didn't know. His eyes darted from the soldiers to their guns to tanks he'd only seen in pictures. They were live in front of him now. Ten feet from them an explosion. A window shattered, spraying glass like a crystal rainstorm over their heads. Instinctively, their arms shot up to protect their heads. Soldiers in green khakis barley old enough to shave grabbed Dmytro's and his mother's shoulders.

"This way," they demanded.

The were led down the stairs into the metro.

Hundreds of people were already there.

"Stay in here until help arrives," the soldiers commanded.

An explosion overhead punctuated their command.

They found a place against a wall and leaned their backs to it. Adrenalin spent, their legs collapsed, and they slid. There they stayed, bags held tight to their chest, for five days.

***

"I have friends with a van. They are transporting people out of Kyiv. We're making arrangements for some to come to us in Austria, and the YWAM base in Hurlach is preparing aid both to deliver goods into Ukraine and to provide housing for the refugees. The store shelves are getting empty, and gas is low. It won't be much longer until they run out of gas. We're sending as much money in as we possibly can before that's shut down. I've been crying all morning." The message, panic weaving itself within the words, was sent by Danielle hours before but just opened by myself. I hit video chat.

"These are my friends! Maksiem has to stay behind. He put his wife and new baby on a train out of Ukraine, but all men must stay behind to fight. Mom, he doesn't know if he will ever see them again." She was crying. Hours of worry etched her face, and the tears she wiped with the back of her hand accentuated the strain. "All morning people have been sending me funds, and I've been sending them to my friends in Kyiv. Galia is waiting for some kind of transportation to get them out of the train station. Esther is staying put, but she's alone right now, just trying to help as many as she can. People have just abandoned the elderly. She can't leave them. She's making arrangements to get them their medicine and some food. The Russians are bombing hospitals now. This is just crazy."

A few hours later, in Canada, in Chilliwack, in Corky's pub, customers were complaining that the Keno machine wouldn't take their twenty-dollar bills. The contrast was stunning.

"Glenda, the pull tab machine isn't taking my ten," Mac said. "Could you please change it for toonies?"

"Oh, geeze, you poured my beer in that glass. Don't you know I don't like that glass?" Lee reminded me.

"My bill, Glenda." Randy number 2 was sitting at the Bone, waving his debit card, his pint three quarters full. It was his habit, flagging me down in an urgent need to pay his tab with no intention of leaving. Today I gritted my teeth as I watched his card demand my attention. I intentionally ignored it. I was on my way to the remote to change the TV to "something other than soccer" for Ike.

"Where would you like me to put these kegs?" the new delivery guy with rainbow hair and a silver-studded lip asked.

"Glenda, didn't you read the 86 board? We're out of fish," Curt reminded me.

The telephone rang. "Corky's pub, Glenda speaking," I said into the receiver.

"Can you tell me what time the Dollar Store is open?"

"Excuse me?"

"Well, you're right beside it. I thought you would know."

"I'm sorry, could you please just call the dollar store."

"Fine, do you have their number?"

"Uh, no." I hung up.

"Your ATM isn't working?" Tim posed his question within a statement as he pulled out his barstool.

Duane walked by. "Just so you know, Glenda, the men's room needs a bit of a cleanup."

"Hey, there's a guy, it looks like he's passed out, right in front of the door. I had to walk over him," Paul stated as I poured his pint.

The phone rang insistently. I ignored it. Whoever it was hung up and dialed back. I gritted my teeth as I picked up. "Corky's Pub, Glenda speaking."

"What's your soup today?" the voice on the other end asked.

"Glenda, that guy over there keeps walking around without his mask on," table 12 informed me.

My phone dinged. "I'm too stressed about money. I'm not coming in," read the message from our most recent hire.

Earl shuffled by the bar, head up to the Keno board, newspaper tucked under his arm. "Just a baby beer, Glenda." He turned to face me. "Crazy about Ukraine, isn't it, Glenda?"

Finally!

I felt like crying.

***

"*ми залишаємось*. We stay."

Ivan sat at the kitchen table across from his father. His mama looked concerned. "Do you think we should?" She pulled a cigarette to her lips and took a long, deep drag. Her hand trembled slightly. She exhaled a puff of smoke and closed her eyes, hoping dearly that her husband wasn't serious.

"We are Ukrainian. We will stay with Ukraine." He picked up his cigarette from the ashtray. "We stay." He sucked in the last drag and shoved the butt back into the ashtray, forcefully snuffing it out with the pressure of his fingertips. "Ivan, go to your room," he commanded.

Ivan knew better than to argue. He pushed his chair back from the table and glanced at his mama, who smiled wanly at him and gave him a wink before taking another drag from her smoke. "It will be okay, Ivan. Do as your father asks." The nicotine had done its job. Her hand no longer trembled.

Ivan moved to his mama's side and wrapped his arms around her. He could do nothing but tell her he loved her. She kissed his cheek. "You're a good boy, Ivan."

***

"Tell your daughter to tell her friends to shut off their Geo Tracking, Glenda," Daryl commanded. "The Russians are tracking those who are giving aid to the Ukrainians. If they are helping in any way, it's imperative that they shut this off."

A moment of panic swept over me. Daryl never asked for anything. Daryl never suggested I do anything. Daryl never instructed me to do anything. Today his eyes pierced through me, his voice unfaltering and firm directed me in no uncertain terms to do as he said.

"Ask your daughter for the location of her friends that are trying to get out and I'll send our team in for them. Ask your daughter for the address of the one who is staying to help and we will bring supplies to her. Do you understand, Glenda?"

I did.

And I did.

***

"No more money is needed," Danielle's message read a few days later. "The shelves are bare and the gas is gone. There is nothing more we can do for them there. Galia

484

has made it out of the train station, and Esther has sent photos of the elderly she's aided. Two hundred Ukrainian orphans are on their way to Freiburg. A family of six is on their way to our house; another family is on their way to Taylor's house. Steff messaged, and she's going to fast-track our employment with Crystal Castle Germany so that we can use our salaries to aid the refugees that are here in Austria and also with Taylor in Germany."

"Good, I hope it's soon!" I typed back.

"Me too," came her immediate response. "Elijah's had a difficult day."

"Why?" I asked, curious about my oldest grandson.

"His friend Ivan and his mamma were killed. A bomb hit their house."

Best Friend

"I've said it before, and I'll say it again. I don't know what wheels in the universe turned for us to meet. You are the best friend I've ever had." Daryl's eyes, unblinking, peered from behind his glasses. His customary lone teardrop fell down his right cheek. He removed his glasses and wiped the tear away with his fingertips. Replacing his glasses, he smiled and took another sip of his pint.

Daryl and I were sitting across from each other at a tall top in Characters pub finishing the last of our beers. Beer Friday. Haney had to work, and Jack was on his way up north to visit his son. It was just the two of us. I reached out and grabbed his hand. He nodded and looked away.

"We've been through a lot, haven't we?" I smiled and then corrected myself. "Well, *you've* been through a lot. I've just been here watching you through it, and"—I shrugged my shoulders—"I've always had a hard time making friends. I tend to be 'off putting' to a lot of people, so I find it intriguing that we are friends, and that our humour clicks and bounces off each other."

At the same time, we both said, "and with Jack!" and started laughing. It was true, the three of us together had on multiple occasions left with our sides aching because we laughed so much. We were like high school buddies, only more appreciative of this friendship that had been found in our fifties, never expecting we needed it or wanted it, but relishing the gift of it.

"We have fun, don't we?" Daryl grinned.

"We do," I agreed. "Anyway, I have to get going. Petey's been home alone long enough, I think. Can I drop you someplace?"

He sighed and then smiled. "Yes, you can drop me at Corky's. I believe I'll have your prime rib tonight. And maybe," he added as an afterthought, "we can peek in Toyota on our way. I hear our Land Rovers were delivered there, waiting for the detailing crew to clean them before we pick them up."

"Oh, did MNP send Langley the foundation paper work they were looking for to release them then?"

"It appears so."

"Well good, I'm relieved. I was going to give it one more week before I changed out that bad tire." I waved down our server and asked for the tab.

"I'm going to use the boys' room before we go," Daryl announced, standing up from our table and excusing himself.

I opened my phone to check messages as I waited for Alexandra to bring the bill. An unusual one was in my Messenger file. I glanced at it. From Cindy: "I'm not sure if you've seen this or not, but I thought I'd send it to you in case you haven't."

I hadn't spoken with Cindy for months, so I was hesitant to click on the attachment. Was it her? Was it click bait? I typed in "Thank you" and hit send just as Daryl arrived back to the table.

Alexandra arrived with the debit machine. I paid, threw my phone in my purse, put on my purple coat, and slung my entirely too big leather messenger bag over my shoulder, Daryl once again mocking its size as we walked out the door.

The drive was quick. We both glanced in Toyota's direction as we drove by, but neither of us could see anything so we just continued to Corky's. As I pulled into the parking lot, Daryl turned in my direction. "Come in for a pint. I'll buy you one."

"Shit, Daryl, you're a stinker, aren't you?"

He smiled.

"I can't have another pint, but I'll join you for one little glass, then I really have to go."

"Good!" he exclaimed victoriously.

Corky's was Friday Prime Rib busy. We squeezed ourselves into two spots at the Bone. I ordered a baby Guinness and nursed it for the next hour as Daryl and I joked around with the other regulars enjoying their Friday night.

"K, I really need to go!" I exclaimed as I tipped the last of my Guinness back.

"No, stay for one more, Glenda!" Daryl encouraged.

"Nope, I need to drive, and Petey needs dinner. I'll see you later." I grinned as I stood to gather my belongings and leave. Daryl reached over to give me a hug.

"Thank you, Glenda," he whispered.

"Aw D., you're welcome." I stepped away from him and the table and waved goodbye to everyone sitting there.

Back in the parking lot, I unlocked the Sante Fe, jumped in, and turned on JRFM to Gord Bamford's voice vibrating the airwaves asking if it's Friday yet. I smiled.

It felt really good to have a friend.

I contemplated how the future would look when COVID restrictions would become a thing of the past, when Daryl and Tina got married, when they resumed travelling to take care of business. "Bitter sweet, I think. It will change. I have to let it change and let this bit go when the time comes." I sighed. I would miss this. But

I knew my life would be filled with many other good things, and I would put myself into that. And perhaps we could manage Beer Fridays in different cities, and towns, and countries as that opened up as well. I smiled at that thought. That could be very fun. The thirty-minute drive went quickly, and before I knew it, I was pulling into the driveway. I stopped my car and quickly ran up to the RV to let a wiggly, happy to see me Petey out for a pee.

"There you go, boy. You're such a good boy. Here you go, yummy food," I said to the ecstatic pup as I put his food dish in front of him. His tail did the happy dance as he scarfed it down. He was done in under two minutes.

We left the trailer and went to the gazebo. I started the gas fire and lifted Petey onto my lap. I pulled a fuzzy blanket over the both of us, opened my phone, and started scrolling.

I opened Cindy's message again, took off my glasses, and enlarged the attachment with my thumb and forefinger. It looked more like a news article than click bait, so I double tapped it open. A picture of a younger Daryl above the newspaper headline riveted my attention. I started to read.

CALGARY ❧ HERALD

Judge refuses to release 'economic predator' on bail for fraud

Calgary Herald Blogs
Thu Dec 10 2015
Section: Crime
Byline: Daryl Slade, Calgary Herald

A Calgary man alleged to have perpetrated a $400,000 fraud while on parole from a seven-year prison sentence for committing a similar $1.5 million fraud a decade ago will remain behind bars.

In her oral decision rendered on Thursday, provincial court Judge Catherine Skene said she detained Daryl Heiligsetzer because of the risk of reoffending and because releasing him could erode the public's confidence in the administration of justice.

Heiligsetzer, 52, described by the judge as an "economic predator" when he was sentenced on July 5, 2005, to another five-and-a-half years after credit for pre-trial custody, faces two counts each of fraud over $5,000 and theft over $5,000 in the alleged scam in which he was seeking local investors to help purchase the Elbow River Casino.

"He was on parole for committing a similar fraud and he uses a different name and company to cloak his identity in this alleged fraud," said Skene.

Defence lawyer Adriano Iovinelli had sought his client's release, saying he had a place to live with family and was not a danger to the public.

Crown prosecutor Tony Bell argued the accused used a false identification, saying he was a businessman with experience in the restaurant and hospitality industry, and approached people seeking to get them involved in the purchase of the casino, which he did not own. He claimed he had a buyer but needed representation from local ownership.

Bell said Heiligsetzer told people they were guaranteed to get their money back quickly, with promised returns of 25 to 900 per cent. None of the money was ever returned, he said.

He told court the alleged offences involved 45 investors and in excess of $400,000 between January 2009 and November 2010.

Bell said the two charges relate to victims who virtually all had ties to Alberta, but were divided into two groups: One based on when Heiligsetzer was living in Calgary and the other group when he was residing in Vancouver.

The prosecutor said "there was never any serious attempt to negotiate a casino purchase.

"In the previous fraud, Heiligsetzer bilked dozens of people - most of them trusting city cops - out of more than half of their $2.87 million in investments in a hockey equipment company.

"Daryl Heiligsetzer, for 31 months from January 2001 until July 2003, concocted and perpetuated a massive, fraudulent scheme through lies, deceit and false pretences," provincial court Judge Brian Stevenson said at the time.

"He was able to establish credibility to the scheme in two ways: Using well-known trade names of products... and (Staff Sgt.) Kirk McCallum, a longtime friend and associate."

Stevenson said the so-called "Ponzi" scheme involved the offender paying initial investors their profits from subsequent investors' money.

The fraudster used $1,226,967 of the fraudulent profits for himself ($261,897), his wife ($154,655), his girlfriend ($196,557) and the business expenses of his company, Flarrow Hockey Sticks ($613,858).

An agreed statement of facts indicated Heiligsetzer approached friends and acquaintances and told the potential investors that his sporting goods business could purchase outdated hockey equipment from Bauer or Easton at reduced prices and sell it to small retailers in Canada, the United States and Europe.

He said he needed money to pay the suppliers in advance and guaranteed investors between 15 and 35 per cent return on their money within 90 days of the investment. Heiligsetzer will be back in court on Jan. 13.

dslade@calgaryherald.com(mailto:dslade@calgaryherald.com)
Twitter.com/heraldcourt((www.twitter.com»))

My heart started throbbing. My mouth went dry. My chest constricted.

***

I typed "Daryl Heiligsetzer" into google search and another newspaper article popped up.

CALGARY ⟨image⟩ HERALD

Con man jailed for second scam

Calgarian was on parole when he duped investors of more than $400K

The accused ... at all material times was on parole or in custody due to a previous conviction related to a Ponzi scheme.

KEVIN MARTIN

A convicted Calgary con man who ran a second scam while on parole for the first will serve the equivalent of a 4 1/2-year penitentiary sentence.

Provincial court Judge John Bascom on Tuesday accepted a joint Crown and defence sentencing submission for Daryl Heiligsetzer on a charge of fraud.

Crown prosecutor Tony Bell told Bascom that Heiligsetzer was on parole when he duped approximately 45 investors of more than $400,000.

The scheme involved the purported purchase of a casino, Bell said. "No money was spent on a casino and investors never saw any profit or return on their capital," Bell said. He was reading from a statement of agreed facts.

"The accused utilized two aliases during the scheme and at all material times was on parole or in custody due to a previous conviction related to a Ponzi scheme," he said.

Bell said at one point during the scam, Heiligsetzer had his parole revoked for eight months but continued to run his con using aliases.

"Investors were promised a return of between 25 and 900 per cent, and received documents purporting to confirm their investment," he said.

The scheme was run between January 2009 and October 2010.

In July 2005, Heiligsetzer was sentenced to 5 1/2 years on top of time already served for a Ponzi scheme that mostly targeted Calgary Police Service members.

Defence counsel Adriano Iovinelli said Heiligsetzer, 53, is a native Calgarian whose brother is on the police force.

The father of three adult children was arrested in White Rock, B.C., in October 2015, Iovinelli said.

Heiligsetzer has been in custody since, Iovinelli added.

Credit for that time will be deducted from the 4 1/2 years.

KMartin@postmedia.com twitter.com/KmartinCourts Material republished with the express permission of: Calgary Herald, a division of Postmedia Network Inc.

* * *

I closed the article, shut my eyes, and listened to the tinkling of thirty pieces of silver as they hit the floor.

Navigate That

I stood at the edge of the gravel road and looked down.
What once led feet, and fisherman, cars and campers had
been chewed away by the river. A chasm of nature. It left
man stranded on one side or the other. The road was gone.
Devoured in the November storm.

Magnificent and terrifying. Man makes plans, builds
houses and roads, and nature chews them up. "Here you
go, a new path, navigate that."

Navigate that.

I closed my eyes and took a deep breath, a sigh. "Will
the heaviness ever go away?"

I ached.

I had ached for months.

I did all the things I needed to do to prevent myself
from being sucked into the vortex of darkness, but I
could feel it slithering around my feet. The constrictor,
manoeuvring its body around mine. Its intent? Destroy.

I ached under it.

I ached in it.

I turned my head up and a sob escaped, drawing a
moan out of the deep. The tears started again.

For months I pulled back the tentacles one by one.
Thousands of them had threaded themselves through my
mind. Piece by piece I peeled, analyzed, and cut.

Each one held an emotion.

Each one held a question.

Voices from my childhood demanding to brand me 'stupid', had.

"You are stupid."

The words jeered and mocked in a team taunt.

"I'm so stupid, how did I let that happen?"

And guilt echoed, "Look at how foolish you were. You brought all this false hope to the teachers, to your family, your husband, your sister, your daughters, your friends. You should be ashamed. Look at what you've done to them." Tisk tisk, it hissed.

When the voices of the day finished spitting, the murmurs mocked the night:

"Here is a cheque for you. Buy that house! Pay off that debt! Go to school!"

Every single face of every single person that we had invested for flamed.

"Oh God!"

That hope we had for them!

The sorrow seared.

The students in the school, the plans we had planned, the big community help, the grannies in Ukraine, the community kitchens in Germany and here in Chilliwack.

Like a coffin lid sliding closed.

Light snuffed out.

I lay there gasping for air as the weight of dirt threatened to crush.

And the house.

The very thing that started it all. The desire to push a prayer to fulfillment.

"To have the mortgage I have now or, better yet, no mortgage at all."

The prayer taunted me.

My desire flashed in me.

Selfishness screamed.

Maybe if I didn't have that in my sight. Maybe I wouldn't have been sucked in.

The cost of desire.

Thousands of dollars?

The cost of desire.

A crushed soul?

The cost of desire.

Was anything real?

How could it have felt so real when everything was untrue?

Every conversation I rewound and replayed, looking for all the things I missed.

Re-reading the book.

Looking with new eyes.

Trying to make sense of it.

Who was Tina Hoffmeister? It was him?

Hundreds and hundreds of emails from me to her from her to me. Him?

Steff from Germany, building a future with my daughters. Him?

He kept the stories straight. How?

How cruel! How bizarre! How weirdly amazing!

A psychopath? Truly delusional?

Brilliant?

I thought he was my friend. Best friend, he had said. How?

How could he sit there and weave and wind?

Creating hope, and dreams, and desire.

How could he sit and laugh with me, knowing not a thing was true?

What was the purpose of that?

Some money?

Really? He traded that for money? All that work for some money?

It didn't make sense.
Certainly it must have been something more.
And the serpent slithered.
How perfect.
He used all of my hopes and dreams.
My own desire.
He used it to crush me.
I shivered and gagged.
How easily it was done.

"The woman you created for me gave me the fruit and I ate," Adam whispered.
"The serpent deceived me and I ate," whispered Eve.
"How simply the serpent used desire and beauty to get me to bite," whispers I.

I stepped toward the edge of that gravel road. If I stepped where I had stepped a hundred times before, I would drop twenty feet into a churning river.
It could be easy enough to do.
"Oh God—help."

You Can Tell Your Story

"Where would you go if you ran away?" He was sitting at the head of the table on a kitchen chair with steel legs sitting on felt feet meant to protect the floor that didn't need protecting. It was cut deeply already in the battle of life, so flimsy felt did nothing. One chair leg sat on a corner of a tile holding it down. At least that was useful.

I dipped my toast finger into the soft-boiled egg till the yolk bubbled over the top and ran down the sides of the egg cup, covering the picture of Peter Cottontail with yellow goo.

"The mountain." I licked yolk off my finger. "I'd go up to the mountain and live by the creek and sneak down at night to steal food from you." I smiled. I was eleven.

My dad lit a cigarette, inhaled deeply, and breathed out a band of smoke before taking a sip from his coffee cup. "The mountain?"

"Yes, I would love to live in the mountains by a creek. I would run away there."

"What would you do?"

"I would sit by the creek and read my books."

"You would run away up to a mountain by a creek to read?"

"Yes. Or I'd go find a convent to live in."

He choked on his coffee.

I licked butter running down my wrist.

"Why a convent?"

"It would be quiet there, no fighting. I could read my books."

"Still read?"

"People in books are nicer than people in real life."

***

"So is there anything I can do?" I asked the still-a-lil'-wet-behind-the-ears cop. He shrugged his shoulders. A drip of water from the awning landed on his shaved head. He took a step back to be entirely covered by it. It was raining; it was cold. There were no free conference rooms, so he'd brought me outside, under the entrance to the RCMP station, staring into the parking lot.

"You acknowledge it was your choice to give him money. You might try to sue him civilly, but there's not much we can charge him with. Yes, you gave him money trusting what he was saying was true, so"—he kind of scrunched up his face and waved his head side to side— "but it would be very difficult to charge him with fraud."

"That's not actually what I meant. I know our money is gone. He didn't ask me for any. I just gave it to him, and I did give it to him based on believing what he was telling me was the truth, so yes, it is fraud, but that's not what I meant." I was speaking quickly, my eyes darting up and down the street. *Oh God, what if Daryl walks by and sees me standing here talking with the cop?* I apologized to Constable Jr. "Sorry, I'm watching over your head to make sure I don't see him walking down the street." I slung my messenger bag over my other shoulder, turned my eyes to his, and continued. "What I do mean is there anything I can do so that he doesn't do this to someone else? He was talking about our Native bands, and casinos with them, and our friend Jack! How do I warn Jack? Do I just say "If Daryl brings up investments, don't invest?"

"Well, no, you can't really say that."

"So I just have to let them figure it out themselves? Can't you go to them? Warn them?"

"No, they have to come to us."

"So what can I do? I can't let Jack and all the people in restaurants and pubs in Chilliwack get taken advantage of. What *am* I allowed to say?"

Constable Jr. looked me straight in the eye. "You can simply tell them your own experience."

"I can tell them my story," I reiterated what I heard Jr. say.

"Yes, you can tell your story."

One Lousy Paragraph

Crocuses I had planted two years ago were peeking their little purple heads up through the moss. I leaned over them and cleared dead needles that had fallen from the cedar above. A couple of dry branches were leaning a little too close to a new bud, so I pulled them away. The creek babbled a little louder today. When it rains, it does that. The clouds were gone, lifted off the majestic mountain that stole my heart the minute I saw it over two years ago. It still had snow on it. It would until August. I knew that now. I knew a lot of things now.

I turned to walk back to the trailer and looked in the pit that once was filled with fire. One day there will be a house there, I hope.

It's been hard.

"Don't be afraid of doing the difficult thing." Jordan Peterson's voice echoed in my mind.

"Oh, fuck off, Jordan." I giggled as I wiped snot off my face with the back of my hand.

But I know he's right. I know that once we come out of this, we will feel incredibly accomplished, and there will be great joy in that.

"Come on, Petey, let's go inside." He happily scampered up the steps.

I sat down in my leather armchair in front of the window and pulled my heated blanket over my knees and stared outside.

"God, I love those trees. Thank you for letting me live here," I whisper. "Help the hurt go away. God, it hurts. Help me through this hurt." I looked at the pit. "What do we do now?"

You could write a book. The thought danced in my mind. *It's kind of an amazing story.*

"I don't know how to write a book," I answered myself. "How would I write a book?"

And Jordan Peterson replied, "If you want to write a book, then write a book. Write one paragraph a day. It doesn't even have to be a good paragraph; one lousy paragraph is better than no paragraph."

"One lousy paragraph, huh?"

I sighed, picked up my laptop, and opened a document program. I stared at the blank page and then closed my eyes. "One lousy paragraph?"

"Yes, one lousy paragraph."

I opened my eyes. My fingertips rested on the keyboard. I sighed again and then typed:

"I met the owner of SoFi Stadium …

Her Tiny Hand

"Damn you, Daryl." Taylor laughed.

We were lying on a blanket on the grass under the trees. Zeke and Abbie were playing in the creek; three-year-old Ellie bopped her head of ringlets from side to side as she flicked on and off her pink flashlight. The baby was in Taylor's trailer, sleeping.

"Houses aren't cheap here in Canada or in Germany, hey?"

"No, they aren't," I said.

Taylor took a sip of her wine. "Oh, if only he had been telling the truth." She smiled and sighed at the same time. "Oh well."

They had arrived in Canada three weeks before. We had two weeks left before they flew back to Germany. A friend lent them a trailer, and they were camping with us on our property.

"What about this for the basement?" I turned my laptop toward her for her to inspect. "That would work." I was designing a new house: smaller, more affordable, with no windows on the east side to save the expense of sprinkler systems.

"Maybe add a wall there, and a banquette. They're great for big families when they visit," she suggested. "When do you think you'll start building?"

"I don't know. I really don't know. Everything is so astronomical in price right now, and, well, our bank account is much smaller." I shrugged at the reality.

"It's too bad you couldn't have that first house; it was beautiful!"

"It really was, wasn't it?"

"Damn you, Daryl!" We clinked our glasses and laughed again. There wasn't much else we could do. "I shouldn't feel so bad, should I? I mean, thirty-two cops, right? If he was able to outwit thirty-two cops, then perhaps he's just so much greater than my gullibility. Oh God." I shook my head at the magnitude of it all.

"Raphie would love to meet him. Are you still in contact?"

"Yes, I talk to him occasionally."

"Have you seen him."

"No, not since the day after I read those news articles. I met with him, and he wanted to explain."

"Did he deny it?"

"Oh no, he admitted he is Heiligsetzer, said he was in prison for a short time but took a different name because of the stigma attached to people who've been to prison. He's upset with Chilliwack for using the newpaper articles to ruin our friendship. I straightened his thought and told him I wouldn't have cared if he was an ex-con. I wouldn't have invested with him for sure, but our humour would still click, in that we'd be friends. Jack and I talk about that a lot. He didn't need to be Daryl the Trillionare for us to like him. He could have just been himself. But Daryl keeps going back, blaming the articles for severing our friendship."

"What do you say to that?"

"I direct his eyes back to the truth and say, 'The fact that not one thing you promised me or anyone else came to pass is what gives the newspaper articles credibility, and it's *that* that severed our friendship, not what's in the newspaper, but what you haven't done."

"What did he say to that?"

"He agreed."

"Wow! Incredible!" Tay sipped on her wine and continued. "Has anything happened at all, even one little thing?"

"Well, I did call MNP right away. They'd never heard of him. And the rest? The foundation, the Shoe Closet? Crystal Castle? The cards and cheques and wire transfers? The Land Rover, the jet, the helicopters? Your employment, meeting Tina, Lyndsay, Steff, Jane, his kids? The computers, the manual, the help for the school? The investments we made for all of our friends and family? Not one thing. But he absolutely insists he is who he says he is, he still insists the funds are coming, he still insists everything is true. "You will see, Glenda," he says.

"That's so weird."

"I know. I don't know if he needs to believe it or what. It's very strange. I hear he's been seen walking around town still. Once I heard he was seen on the Island. He's told me he's sold all of his interests in Chilliwack. If he's moved or not, I have no idea."

Taylor smiled and sipped. "Who found them? The newspaper articles?"

"I heard a server. His real name was on his vax pass. I should have scanned it, but I didn't. His name was googled, and the newspaper clippings came up. They were shared around Chilliwack and landed in Cindy's lap. I'm so very thankful to her for sharing them with me."

"Are you mad at him?"

I sighed and ran a finger down one of Ellie's ringlets. She turned, gave me the evil eye, and pulled away. It had been almost three weeks that she'd been watching me from the sidelines, trying to determine if Granny was safe, repelling any advance I made to enter her space, cringing away from me and glaring. Taylor had warned me. "Give her space, Mom. This one needs to come to you." I thought I'd been doing pretty good, but damn those ringlets. Who wouldn't want to play with them?

I smiled at her. *Damn you're a spunky one, Ellie, just like your momma.* I turned back to Tay. "It's so weird. I should be so angry with him, but I'm not. I'm just super super sad. It's like there's no room inside me to be angry because the sadness fills it up."

I sighed deeply; the heaviness lingered still. "It's hard."

It was hard talking about it. I caught my breath as sorrow tried to squeeze out again. I gritted my teeth and took a sip of wine to push it back down so we could continue the conversation without me oozing tears and snot. It worked. I continued. "The only time I felt a little bit of anger was when he took your money. He could have said, 'No, Glenda, I can't do that for her,' but he took your money. I told him that too. 'You took my daughter's money, my daughter with small children, who needs that money more than you or I.' I'm so sorry, Taylor." Involuntary tears welled up yet again.

"It's okay, Mom." She smiled gently. "We did that in faith, and even though it didn't turn out as we expected, we let it go so it can do what it was intended."

"That's a great way of looking at it, isn't it?"

Let it go. Let it do what it was intended. It's like I've heard those words before.

"I really don't want him to hurt others. I've considered myself a very strong human, but this, wow, this really did a number on me. I can't imagine what it could do to someone who doesn't have the mind or the support or faith in God. It's been hard."

"Grief?" Taylor acknowledged.

"Yes, it's absolutely like a death." I wiped the tears away with my hand, gave a tight-lipped grin in Taylor's direction, and took another sip of wine.

"It must be so hard on his kids," Taylor continued

"I know, and his ex-wife! I can't even imagine what it was like for her. The responsibility of raising children with someone who would tell you everything you wanted to hear yet crumble your foundation with lies? It's amazing she survived! And those kids! I feel like I know them so well. He's so proud of them. All of those stories he shared about them, were they true? Were they made up? I don't know! If one thing truthful came out of him, I would hope it was that, the absolute pride he has for his children and the deep respect for Jane."

I sighed again. I had been doing a lot of that, sighing, as if it alone had the possibility of answering the questions. "I don't know that they have any kind of relationship, and how sad is that? What a lonely life he lives. Such a strange way to want to live your life. I don't understand it at all."

"Message him, see if he'll meet with Raphie."

"You sure?"

"Yes, Raphie is intrigued with him."

"I know, he's so intriguing," I agreed as I grabbed my phone to text Daryl the invite.

"Well, hello there," he responded almost immediately. "I would love to meet your family, but I won't be in the Fraser Valley until the beginning of September."

"That could work; they don't leave until mid-September," I typed back.

"If it works, I will be happy to. I hope you are well. I miss you."

"I miss you too, D."

It was true. I missed my friend Daryl Schmidtt. I still do. I wish he was real.

"Time to start dinner, I think." I stood up, brushed some moss off my leg, shook the sorrow from my mind, and started walking back to the trailer.

I felt a little hand slip into mine.

I looked down.

Little Ellie had slipped her wee hand inside mine like she'd done it a hundred times before. Her ringlets bounced as she silently walked with me, hand tucked in mine.

Wow.

I closed my eyes.

"This."

In that moment, a veil of hurt was lifted and all that was good and right was back.

This little three-year-old drew near and grasped my hand because she wanted too.

It's shocking what humans can do too each other.

But it's utterly amazing how the perfect timing of placing a hand inside another can righten the world in an instant.

Afterword

The stories within this book are true as I experienced them. The stories shared with me by others are as true as they were in their telling. Only they can validate the truthfulness of their own stories.

Not being an eyewitness for the stories told to me by others, I did use my imagination to paint a picture of how it could have looked. The intent was to deliver an imaginative word picture for the reader as I imagined it when the story was being told to me. While they were built on facts, the stories weren't forced into 100 per cent accuracy, and scenes and dialogue were recreated.

Carl's story was built off of his injury, his time in Vietnam, his smokey, crusty, quirky, humourous character. I imagined what could have possibly happened to him in Vietnam. Vets in the pub don't share the terrible things they've witnessed.

Some names, characteristics, and places have been changed, and some events have been compressed.

Conclusion

Do not be overcome by evil, but overcome evil with good

Those words whispered to me as a I walked over branches, waded through puddles, crunched leaves underfoot, and stomped through snow.

It was evil.

Not the hideous, dripping blood, jump out of a dark basement corner, grab your feet from under the bed kind of evil.

More sinister than that.

To dig out desires and weave and plot and manoeuvre and play.

"Let's see what happens if I do this, dangle that. Pull these strings of pathos. Tell stories to erect ethos and weave in golden threads of logos."

To play with another simply because you could.

That is evil.

I was overcome by evil.

I was sucked deep into it and drowning.

I walked hundreds of miles trying to shake it.

The words were always present, always there, with every step whispering, *Do not be overcome by evil, but overcome evil with good.*

A hundred miles later I understood it.

Respond by stepping into doing what is good.

And then a thought grew:

What if I published the book? What if I took the profits of the book and funneled those profits to those areas we wanted the Foundation of Hope to help with? What if these stories within the book actually paved the way for that help? What if people reading this book were frustrated by the whole story and could do something about it, and that something was geared to help people?

So.

The profits of this book will be split 30/70. Thirty per cent will be retained by the author to help recoup her bad investments, to repay those she personally knows who invested with Daryl, and to build that dang house. Seventy per cent will be directed as follows:

1) into the Chilliwack community with the intention of the funds to be used for the prevention of homelessness (managed by Glenda)

2) into Germany with the intention of responding to human care, homeless or not (managed by Taylor and Raphie)

3) into Ukraine with the intention of aiding the abandoned elderly (managed by Danielle and Simon).

Know that when you buy this book and share it with others, it will be you who will be doing the helping. Let the spirit of the Foundation of Hope live, not on the back of some rich dude, but by each of us, the ordinary, slipping our hands into the hands of others.

If the story made you angry, then buy another copy, because it will help someone.

If the justice system frustrates you, then get justice. Buy another copy, because it will help someone.

Share the story with your friends and your neighbours. Buy them a copy, because it will help someone.

And if you happen to be reading this book in a pub or a restaurant, consider purchasing another copy. Leave my story on your barstool for the next person. If they are sitting beside Daryl, it will defiantly help someone very quickly.

As Daryl would say, "Win, win."

***

For more information about
Hope's Projects, please visit
glendatoews.com

***

"What do we do with customers who are making out in the booths?" TJ texted Tina late on a Thursday night.

"Usually we ask them to stop," Tina responded. "Why, who's making out?"

"It's Daryl. You know, Glenda's friend. He's in booth 5 making out with someone. I think it's that Jacquie lady"

Sitting at the bar holding a keno ticket and a beer,
he watch my face scrunch back 'Daryl' tears.
"You know I'll be your friend for free?" he grinned
I snort laughed through my snot.
"God, I love you Doug!"

———

In Memory of
Doug Corley
'Little Doug'
April 1959-May 2023

———

We wave good-bye to your whiskers and
your wit wondering why the one never
grew and how the other always did.

CPSIA information can be obtained
at www.ICGtesting.com
Printed in the USA
JSHW021050020723
44093JS00002B/19